Praise for
Joe Posnanski
and
The Machine

"One of the best sportswriters in America offers a definitive account of the 1975 Cincinnati Reds. [His] conversational style brings to life a great season."
— *Washington Times*

"The best book ever written about the Big Red Machine.... [A] fast-paced narrative that takes the reader not only into the clubhouse but inside the players' heads as well.... Rose is at once the pursued and the pursuer, unloosed on his teammates as a force of nature, consumed not only by his desire for money and women and hits, but for team success as well. Yes, the book belongs to Sparky and Pete, but it is Posnanski's book first and foremost. He calls the shots as the writer.... And it all rings true.... It's quite a ride.... The book that will be the one fans read 100 years from now to figure out what made the greatest assemblage of 1–8 position talent tick.... You'll see Bench, Morgan, and Sparky in different lights than you've ever seen them before.... It's nothing short of beautiful.... More than anything, though, I think the reason I liked the book so much is that it made me care again."
— *Cincinnati Enquirer*

"Posnanski offers an eloquent reminder that the great Cincinnati Reds teams—especially the '75 Reds—deserve a place of prominence in our memory, same as this book demands a place of prominence on your shelf."
— *New York Post*

"The best sports book I've read in recent months is *The Machine*. . . . A fun, engaging, and fascinating look at one of baseball's all-time great teams." —*St. Louis Post-Dispatch*

"I didn't put it down until I had read straight through. . . . The best baseball writer around, Joe transports the reader back to 1975 for a detailed look at arguably the greatest team ever. No Reds fan will want to miss this book. No baseball fan should either." —Jim Callis, *Baseball America*

"Posnanski brings the 1975 Big Red Machine to life. . . . He imparts an insider's feel for the clubhouse dynamics among the players and for the thinking of their sneaky-smart manager, Sparky Anderson. . . . [A] winner of a baseball book." —*Booklist*

"If you like baseball you will love this book. If you don't like baseball you will wonder how you could not like baseball when a book about the game is so entertaining. This is Joe Posnanski's second baseball book, and both are masterpieces. . . . Even though I knew how it all came out, I couldn't stop reading. . . . The writing in this book is inviting, the storytelling magical, and the detail fanatical." —*Augusta Chronicle* (Georgia)

"Need something to lift your spirits as a sports fan? Then you need to turn to the Cincinnati Reds. . . . I'm talking about *The Machine*, [a] book . . . about arguably the greatest team of all time, and written by arguably the finest sportswriter plying his craft these days, Joe Posnanski." —*Oxford Press* (Ohio)

"A scintillating read, with some newsworthy nuggets."

—*News Tribune* (Tacoma, Washington)

"An up close and in-depth treatment of the Big Red Machine [and] the 1975 World Series. . . . Delightful reading. . . . If you don't have the time for the book now, buy it, and keep it for hot stove reading—you are going to love it."   —Harvey Frommer, harveyfrommersports.com

Praise for
The Soul of Baseball

"You won't read a better baseball book this year."   —*Newsday*

"I cherish every moment I ever spent with Buck O'Neil. I'm sure readers will cherish *The Soul of Baseball* because Buck was every bit of that, and because Joe Posnanski is a very talented and lucky man. Imagine, a year spent with Buck O'Neil . . . you don't have to imagine it, it's all here."   —Bob Costas

"Engaging and spirit-lifting. . . . Like Mitch Albom's Morrie, O'Neil possesses a relentless, infectious optimism. . . . Posnanski's writing strikes a lovely overall tone, avoiding a descent into mawkishness. While the dark side of the Negro leagues inevitably emerges—players being shut out of restaurants and absorbing ugly epithets—O'Neil's positive nature always endures. . . . Coming from an indefatigably sunny 94-year-old, it seems an instruction for how to live."

—*Sports Illustrated*

"If you're like me, then many of your favorite books got that way because the author and subject are a perfect match-up for each other. I've read only a handful of books like this. They include Richard Ben Cramer on presidential candidates and campaigning (*What It Takes*), David Halberstam on the media (*The Powers That Be*) and William Manchester on Winston Churchill (*The Last Lion*). Now I have a new addition for this rarefied group: Joe Posnanski on Buck O'Neil, in a new book called *The Soul of Baseball*."

—John Lowe, *Detroit Free Press*

"The games and the players and the hijinks on and off the field that O'Neil enjoyed are presented by Mr. Posnanski with grace and style. . . . Mr. Posnanski has twice been selected as the best sports columnist in America by the Associated Press Sports Editors. Reading *Soul*, it's easy to see why." —*Washington Times*

"In *The Soul of Baseball*, Joe Posnanski presents the most energetic and delightful ambassador baseball has ever had." —*Boston Sunday Globe*

"I don't care what your troubles are: This book WILL make you smile. Joe Posnanski, a brilliant observer and gifted writer, has found a wonderful subject in Buck O'Neil, Negro League baseball legend and world-class philosopher—a man who always found a way, no matter what life threw at him, to have happiness in his heart. I never had the honor of meeting Buck O'Neil, but I feel as if I know him well, thanks to this poignant, very funny, and ultimately inspiring book." —Dave Barry

John Sleezer

About the Author

JOE POSNANSKI is a senior writer at *Sports Illustrated*. From 1996 to 2009, he was a sports columnist at the *Kansas City Star*. He has twice been named the best sports columnist in America by the Associated Press Sports Editors. His previous book, *The Soul of Baseball*, was the winner of the prestigious 2007 Casey Award for the best baseball book of the year. He has also won the nation's top honors as a feature writer and project writer, and he has been nominated for awards by the Associated Press Sports Editors twenty-one times. In 2009, he won the National Headliners Award for sportswriting. Joe and his wife, Margo, live in Kansas City with their two daughters, Elizabeth and Katie.

www.joeposnanski.com

THE MACHINE

Also by Joe Posnanski

The Soul of Baseball: A Road Trip Through Buck O'Neil's America

THE
MACHINE

A Hot Team, a Legendary Season, and
a Heart-stopping World Series:
The Story of the 1975 Cincinnati Reds

Joe Posnanski

HARPER

NEW YORK · LONDON · TORONTO · SYDNEY

HARPER

A hardcover edition of this book was published in 2009 by William Morrow, an imprint of HarperCollins Publishers.

THE MACHINE. Copyright © 2009 by Joe Posnanski. All rights reserved. Printed in the United States of America. No part of this book may be used or reproduced in any manner whatsoever without written permission except in the case of brief quotations embodied in critical articles and reviews. For information address HarperCollins Publishers, 10 East 53rd Street, New York, NY 10022.

HarperCollins books may be purchased for educational, business, or sales promotional use. For information please write: Special Markets Department, HarperCollins Publishers, 10 East 53rd Street, New York, NY 10022.

FIRST HARPER PAPERBACK PUBLISHED 2010.

Designed by Lisa Stokes

The Library of Congress has catalogued the hardcover edition as follows:

Posnanski, Joe.
    The Machine : a hot team, a legendary season, and a heart-stopping World Series: the story of the 1975 Cincinnati Reds / Joe Posnanski.
        p. cm.
    Includes bibliographical references.
    ISBN 978-0-06-158256-1
    1. Cincinnati Reds (Baseball team)—History. 2. Baseball—History. I. Title.
    GV875.C65P67 2009
    796.357'640977178—dc22   2009023154

ISBN 978-0-06-158255-4 (pbk.)

10 11 12 13 14 OV/RRD 10 9 8 7 6 5 4 3 2 1

For Elizabeth and Katie

CONTENTS

THE MACHINE

October 22, 1975

World Series Game 7

Losers. Pete Rose stomped the dirt off his cleats and marched through the dugout, a crazed look on his face. He stopped in front of each man, glared, his face a mask of rage, an angry drill sergeant, a harsh father, an unforgiving judge. In the moment, Rose hated every last one of these sons of bitches. He knew that, in the moment, they hated him too. But they did not hate him enough. They could not hate him enough. They could not hate him with the white-hot disgust that burned inside him right now. The Cincinnati Reds were going to lose. He could not believe it. Impossible. The Machine was going to lose. He already could feel the acid of defeat seething in his guts. He wanted to take a baseball bat to their heads. Yes, it was a problem. Nobody could hate quite as hard as Pete Rose.

"Bunch of losers," Rose shouted. "We can't lose this game! We will not lose this game!" His words echoed through the dugout, bounced out into Fenway Park, drowned in the roar. In the stands of Fenway Park, the fans shrieked and begged and hollered. In the Boston chill, their breath came out like smoke. But it wasn't only these fans here cheering, no, it was all of Boston, all of Massachusetts, hell, it was the whole eastern seaboard—and it was more piercing than shrieking, louder than hollering, something closer to wailing. The Red Sox were about to win the World Series. This was Game 7, the sixth inning. The Red Sox led the Cincinnati Reds by three runs.

Two hundred years had gone by since Paul Revere rode from Boston to Lexington to warn John Hancock and Sam Adams that the British were coming. Fifty-seven years had gone by since the Boston Red Sox had won the World Series. Now fathers and mothers from Boston to Lexington, from Bangor to Providence, shook their sons and daughters awake—The Red Sox are coming! The Red Sox are coming!—and New England families stood together in front of televisions, bleary-eyed, tears welling, and they screamed too.

Pete Rose could see them all in his mind. This was his curse. Even in the midst of the biggest game of his life. Rose could see the big, stinking Boston tea party they would throw when the Red Sox won. He could float over the scene in his mind, a Goodyear blimp, and see a hundred thousand people crowding into Copley Square or Harvard Square or Kenmore Square or some damned square, all those Boston Red Sox fans, make it two hundred thousand of them, men and women and children topped by red and blue baseball caps, all of them screeching with the inflection of John Kennedy, all of them raising a pint to the Cincinnati Reds, the Big Red Machine, the Big Dead Machine, the team that blew it again.

Rose could see it all so clearly. He might have been an ignorant son of a gun from the West Side of Cincinnati. "I've written more books than I've read," he blustered to those reporters who circled around his naked body after every game. But he could see.

This had been a World Series for the ages. Each of the first six games had something to mesmerize the nation—a hero, a goat, a moment of controversy, a dramatic and unexpected turn. The crescendo had crashed the night before, in Game 6. The improbable kept happening. Brilliant catches. Perfect throws. Far-fetched home runs. Comebacks. The air was heavy with tension. The Red Sox loaded the bases in the ninth, nobody out, and Boston's phenom Fred Lynn lifted a shallow fly ball to left field. Pete's lifelong Cincinnati friend Don Zimmer, Boston's third-base coach, screamed, "No! No! No!" Denny Doyle, the runner at third base, heard "Go! Go! Go!" George Foster's throw beat him to the plate, and Cincinnati catcher Johnny Bench slapped Doyle with the ball. The fans were spent. In the eleventh inning, Cincinnati's second baseman Joe Morgan crushed a fly ball to right field, a home run for sure, but the ball died in the thick Boston air, and Boston's Dwight Evans ran back, leaped, desperately stabbed his glove in the air. The ball hit his glove and stuck there. Exhaustion. Nobody could see straight. Rose saw. He babbled like a child hours past his bedtime.

"Isn't this great?" he kept asking teammates, opponents, umpires, anyone. "Isn't this great? This is the best game I've ever played in. Isn't this great? People will remember this game forever. Isn't this great?"

The Red Sox won the game in the twelfth inning. Carlton Fisk cracked a home run that bounced off the left-field foul pole. He elbowed his way around the bases through the frenzied and drunken crowd. They rang church bells in small New England towns. Sparky Anderson, the Cincinnati Reds manager, woke up in the middle of the night again and again in a cold sweat. Rose still felt good. He knew the Reds would damn well win the seventh and final game. He knew it with all the arrogance he had in his chest. The Reds would win Game 7. They were too good to lose it.

"That was their World Series victory," he told teammates before the game. "Now it's time to get ours."

Everyone nodded, pumped their fists, smiled. But did they see it the way that Pete did? Well . . . no, apparently they did not. Here it was, the sixth inning of the game they could not lose, and the Reds were losing badly. They were playing dead. The offense had not scored a single run. They were about to blow the World Series.

"How could we come all this way to play like a bunch of losers?" Rose shouted. There were two outs in the inning. There should have been three. Pete kept the inning going. He was on first base, and his teammate, friend, business partner, nemesis Johnny Bench hit a routine ground ball—a double play, for sure. Only Rose would not allow a double play, he could not allow it, he barreled into second base with all the fury and violence he had been raised to unfurl. His beloved father, Big Pete, a savage sandlot football player well into his forties, taught Little Pete one lesson about fighting: hit first. Pete raced in with everything he had; he was ready to knock Denny Doyle into left field. Doyle managed to jump out of the way, but his throw soared too high to finish off the double play. Pete was out, but the inning was still alive.

"What the hell is wrong with this team?" Rose shouted, dusting off the dirt from his kamikaze slide. "What the hell is wrong with you?" He paced back and forth, choking in the dust of the dugout, a lion in his cage. He slapped the knees of players. He pumped his right fist. The din outside grew louder, the howls of those desperate and bundled-up Boston Red Sox fans. Fenway Park seemed to be dressed in black wool. And the noise sounded like a wave crashing over a junkyard—all roar and rattle and squeak.

"We're not going to lose this game," Rose shouted. "No way. You hear me? We are not losing tonight. You know what people are going to say about us? We're nothing. They'll say we're losers."

Pete walked up and down the bench and looked hard at each player's face.

"We're not fucking losers," he shouted.

Joe Morgan played second base. He was Pete's best friend. Every day, Pete and Joe would go at each other, mocking, testing, pushing the limits of that friendship. Joe would taunt Pete about his lack of power—"Why don't you just wear a dress to the plate, Rose?" Pete would mock Joe's five-foot-seven height—"Don't stand too close to the bat rack, Morgan, someone will pick you up by mistake." And it would go from there, back and forth, every day, nastier and uglier, gathering pent-up rage about race and strength and what it is to be a man. Of course, they didn't mean any of it. And of course, they meant it all. Joe Morgan became the best baseball player in the world in 1975. Pete was on his ass every step of the way.

Dave Concepcion played shortstop, and he played it brilliantly. His father back in Venezuela had wanted him to be a doctor; Davey could not stand the sight of blood. But he did have those surgeon's hands. He picked up ground balls to his left or his right with precision; on the field, he never bobbled the ball, never looked off-balance. Off the field, though, balance was harder. "I am a *superstar*," he would tell his teammates, challenging anyone to disagree.

"Shut up, Bozo," Pete would say.

"Yeah, shut up," Joe would say. "There are four superstars on this team, and you're not one of them."

The next day, Davey would again remind them all that he was a star.

George Foster, the left fielder, rarely spoke. It was easy to forget he was in the room; then, every now and again, he would offer up a surprisingly droll line, and he would deliver it in his high-pitched voice, and everyone would laugh. He hit long home runs. George said he got his massive power from the Lord, and he did not drink or smoke; he could be seen by his locker reading the Bible almost every day. The religion made Pete and the others a bit uncomfortable. But he hit long home runs.

At least George talked sometimes. Center fielder Cesar Geronimo was almost mute. His parents had sent him to the seminary in the Dominican Republic, and he had every intention of becoming a priest. But at night he would listen through the static to New York Yankees games on the radio. And during the day, he played softball and hoped that a miracle would happen. A miracle did. The New York Yankees thought he might make a good pitcher and signed him at a tryout camp. The Reds scouts watched him play and thought he could be a beautiful defensive outfielder. The players called him Chief. He played center field like a dream.

Right fielder Ken Griffey might have been the fastest player in the National League. The Reds' first-base coach, George Scherger, used to say that when Griffey ran, you could not hear his feet touch the dirt. Griffey was always smiling, but he was not always happy. He had a lot on his mind, but he didn't think that was anybody else's business.

Johnny Bench, of course, stood at first base. They were the two icons of this team—Johnny and Pete. Johnny was probably the most famous baseball player in America in 1975. He hung out with comedian Bob Hope. He performed on television. Pete, being from Cincinnati, was the most beloved player on the Reds, the player everyone cheered. (In Cincinnati they often booed Bench.) Writers often flew into Cincinnati to do stories contrasting Johnny and Pete, and they usually came away with something about opposites. Bench was an Oklahoma farm boy, Rose a hard-edged city kid, Bench a round-faced power hitter, Rose an angular man who slashed singles, Bench a graceful and confident catcher, Rose a street hustler with no true defensive position. They managed to sound like friends in the papers, though teammates suspected they despised each other. They had gone into business together for a while—they owned a bowling alley together, they owned a car dealership, they shared the same agent—but they did not talk much. And when they did talk, when they joked around, their exchanges lacked the light touch of ballplayers mocking each other.

"You look tired," Bench would say. "Poor guy. Maybe you should try catching for a while. That's real work."

"Maybe you should try hitting," Rose would say. "You can save your energy because when you hit .250 you don't have to run the bases."

"Look at you, Rose. Breathing heavy. You don't know what hard work is like."

"Well, Bench, I'll tell you this. I probably would have gotten tired doing what you did last night."

The sportswriter Tom Callahan probably hit closest when he said that Pete owned Cincinnati and Johnny owned the country . . . and they each wanted what the other guy had. They had feuds. They turned on each other. They nearly came to blows. When Joe Morgan joined the team, he was told that he had to pick Rose or Bench—he could not be friends with both.

But it wasn't simple. They were connected too. Pete was one of two players who showed up at Johnny's wedding. And Johnny protected Pete. In 1973, during the last inning of a playoff game between the Reds and the New York Mets, all hell broke loose. The Shea Stadium crowd—fueled by alcohol, adrenaline, and leftover anger after Pete Rose had brawled with the Mets' beloved shortstop Bud Harrelson—amassed around the field as if arranging a siege. Rose stood on first base, an open target. The fans wanted Rose. Bench saw blood in their eyes, and he pleaded with manager Sparky Anderson to get Rose the hell out of the game. Anderson refused. So Bench stood on the top of the dugout steps, bat over his shoulder, ready to rush the field and take them all on to save Pete Rose.

Then, finally, there was Tony Perez. He was standing at home plate, ready to hit. They called him "the Big Dog," or "Doggie" for short. Doggie had grown up in Cuba, before Castro's men came rushing down from the mountains. He had been raised to spend his life lugging bags of sugar at the refinery near his home. That's what his father did, that's what his brothers did, and when he turned fourteen that's what he did too. He would never forget the way his body felt at the end of those days. He had always told his mother that he wanted something more: he wanted to play baseball in the United States under the bright lights. She told him to grow up and stop dreaming about nonsense.

"You will work in the factory just like everyone else in this family," she told him. He signed with the Reds for $2.50, the price of a visa. While he played ball in America, Cuba fell to Castro. Doggie had not seen his mother in more than a decade.

What made Doggie different was hard to explain . . . it was a kind of peace. He never made anything too complicated. See the ball, hit the ball. That's what he said. He knew when to joke with a teammate, and he knew when to lay down the law. He knew how to break tension. The sportswriters around, they liked Tony fine, for what that was worth, but they did not know him. The sportswriters were on deadlines, and they needed quick quotes and witty one-liners, and that was the realm of Pete and Johnny and Joe. Inside the clubhouse, though, everyone looked to Doggie. He seemed to have the answers.

"Why you so worried about, Skip?" Doggie had said to the manager, Sparky Anderson, just a moment before he went to hit. Anderson looked lost. He had indeed jolted awake in the middle of night, sweating, an unremembered dream still haunting him. He could not remember falling asleep, but he remembered waking up another dozen times with the uneasy feeling that the Reds had already lost this game. Anderson relied on hunches and premonitions. He had dropped out of high school and was so self-conscious about his lack of education that he would not write letters. "I don't spell too good," he used to say. The man had an almost infallible instinct about baseball and men.

"What do you mean, Doggie?" Anderson said. "We're losing three to nothing."

"Ah," Perez said. "Don't worry. I hit a home run."

He pronounced "hit" like "heat"—*I heat a home run*—and Anderson, even in his state of panic, smiled. Doggie went to the bat rack, grabbed a bat. He watched Rose break up the double play and then heard him cursing and insulting and rousing players in the dugout. He stepped in to face Boston's pitcher, Bill Lee.

"Throw me that slow one," Perez muttered to himself. Earlier in the game, Lee had thrown his slow curve, a lollipop of a pitch that peaked at about ten feet off the ground and then dropped gently into the strike zone. Batters wait for fastballs—it is in their nature—and slow pitches shock the nervous system. Doggie was mesmerized, and he could not unleash his swing. "Throw it again," he muttered now.

Pete turned from his yelling to watch Tony Perez hit. Bill Lee began his windup, and then he unleashed it one more time, his slow curveball, and Perez saw it, his eyes widened, and he did something funny in his swing. He buckled, like a car trying to jump into second gear.

Up in the Fenway Park press box, the dean of Cincinnati sportswriters, Si Burick, watched the pitch come in. Burick had been writing for the *Dayton Daily News* for fifty years. He was the son of a rabbi, and he started writing about sports in the paper when he was sixteen—four years before the stock market crashed in 1929. Burick saw the pitch floating in, and he watched Perez double-clutch. Before Doggie even swung the bat, Burick uttered two words he thought nobody else could hear.

He whispered: "Home run."

A SHOW LIKE THEY NEVER SEEN BEFORE

February 1 to April 6

> *You're no good, You're no good,*
> *You're no good,*
> *Baby, you're no good.*

—LINDA RONSTADT, "YOU'RE NO GOOD"

Nobody knew for certain where the name came from. Rose claimed to have invented it, of course. Well, that's Pete for you. He had come up with this whole convoluted story, one about a 1934 Ford coupe he owned, an antique from those Depression days when you could get your Ford painted any color you wanted so long as it was black. Rose's coupe was cherry red. Rose said he called his coupe the Little Red Machine. So naturally he called the team the Big Red Machine. Pete said that's how the name came about, that's how the Big Red Machine was born. No one believed the story. No one ever believed Pete.

Bob Howsam believed he inspired the name. Howsam ran the Cincinnati Reds, and he thought of himself as something of an innovator. Back in the 1950s, he owned a minor league baseball team, the Denver Bears, and he came up with so many gimmicks and promotions that some years the Bears drew more fans than teams in the major leagues. He would try anything. Once, he approached a chemist and asked if it was possible to concoct a spray that could make the ballpark smell like a bakery. He explained: everyone loves the smell of bakeries. The chemist explained: no, it is not possible.

When Howsam became general manager of the Cincinnati Reds

in 1967, he wanted his team to have an image based on an identity that separated them from the times—something altogether separate from the hippies, long-hairs, and bra-burners who danced to that sitar music in the Summer of Love. He wanted a baseball team that would not terrify the good and decent family folk of Cincinnati. He decreed that every Reds player would wear his hair short, his uniform would be wedding gown white, and his shoes tuxedo black. No one would wear a beard, of course. On the field, the pant legs of their uniforms would end just below the knee, and everyone would see the red of their socks. Off the field, they would wear ties and jackets. He wanted them to be, yes, a machine, a Big Red Machine, as powerful and inoffensive and coldly efficient as the big red Zamboni machine that polished the artificial turf field at Riverfront Stadium between innings. Howsam would believe until the end of his life that it was his Zamboni machine that inspired the name. It did not. The team was routinely called the Big Red Machine by 1970, when his Zamboni first swept the field.

A sportswriter in Los Angeles named Bob Hunter claimed to have coined the name back in August of '69, just after the Reds scored nineteen runs in a game against Philadelphia. Hunter had quit law school to become a baseball writer, and he became somewhat known for his witty nicknames—his favorite being the time he called Bill Singer, a pitcher known for his endurance, "the Singer Throwing Machine." Hunter always claimed that after the Reds scored all those runs in Philadelphia, they went to Los Angeles, and he felt like they deserved a nickname that fit their offensive majesty. He carefully considered the color of the uniform and their relentless run-scoring power and dubbed them the Big Red Machine. The trouble with his story is that the Reds did not go to Los Angeles for a month and a half after the Philadelphia stampede. And by then the name had been in papers all over the country.

The best bet is that Dave Bristol, the old Reds manager, came up with the name himself. Bristol was one of those men held in bondage by the game; he never quite received as much as he gave. Bristol was a good baseball player, but not quite good enough to play even a single game in the major leagues. He was a faithful manager, but baseball owners rarely felt the same faithfulness to him. Bristol would be hired and fired repeatedly in his life. As he said, in his Georgia drawl, he never took it personal. He had to be around baseball. He needed the game. And this is what happens when you need them more than they need you. Bristol's destiny was to spend a lifetime managing losing baseball teams for vain millionaires like tycoon Ted Turner, who once fired Bristol so he could manage the Atlanta Braves himself. Turner's experiment in self-reverence lasted one day—plenty of time to make Turner into a national laughingstock—and then the beleaguered Turner mercifully fired himself and rehired Bristol. At the end of the year, Turner fired Bristol again.

In 1968, though, Bristol was young and blissfully unaware of his tortured baseball destiny. That year, Bristol's Reds suddenly and rather unexpectedly started hitting baseballs very hard. Bristol seemed as shocked by this turn as anyone—the two previous seasons his Reds had hardly scored any runs at all. The Reds scored more runs in 1968 than any other team. They scored more runs still in 1969. And some-time during that year—maybe it really was after that nineteen-run sonic boom in Philadelphia—a giddy Bristol began calling his team the Big Red Machine.

Bristol never claimed to have come up with the nickname on his own. Maybe someone mentioned it to him. He could not remember. And he did not care. His Reds were marvelous. Pete Rose banged 218 hits that summer when Neil Armstrong walked on the moon. Two sluggers, Tony Perez and Lee May, cracked long home runs. A twenty-one-year-old catcher named Johnny Bench burst into star-dom. The Reds scored runs at will, and after happy games, Bristol would wander into his clubhouse and see his players sitting on stools, still in uniform, drenched in sweat, raising beer cans to each other. They toasted: "How about the Machine? How about us? Nobody can stop the Big Red Machine!" It was, Bristol would say, the best time of his life. Then it ended. The Reds scored many runs, but they finished third. Bristol was fired. Howsam decided Bristol had taken the Machine as far as he could.

Bob Howsam hired Sparky Anderson to manage the Reds in 1970. That shocked everybody. "Sparky Who?" was a headline in the next day's paper. Sparky was like the other woman who shows up at the reading of the will and walks out with the house and the Rolls. He was thirty-five years old when he was hired—he was younger than any other manager in the game—but his hair was shock white. He kept a can of black hair dye with him, and he smeared that stuff through his hair constantly, but he could never quite paint over the white, and he could never quite convince people he was as young as his years.

He had one of the odder playing careers in baseball history. He played one full season in the big leagues. And that was all. That doesn't happen much. Baseball seasons bleed into each other, players get called up and down, they get second chances. Not Sparky. He was George Anderson when he first began playing ball, Georgie to his friends. They began to call him Sparky because of his violent temper. He got thrown out of dozens of games. During one of his many umpire spats in the minor leagues, a local radio announcer shouted, "Look at the sparks fly! That's one sparky fella!" Sparky became known throughout baseball for his uncontrollable rage, which was better than being known for his other flaw: he could not hit a lick. The Philadelphia Phillies liked his spirit and traded three players for him in late 1958, and they named him the starting second baseman for the 1959 season. On opening day, eighth inning, Sparky lined an RBI single off of an aging star, Don Newcombe. He played almost every day that summer when *Explorer 6* sent back photographs of Earth and Hawaii became a state. And at the end of the season, the Phillies' management still liked Sparky's spirit, but they did not like his .218 batting average or his home run total. (He hit zero—"Never even hit one off the wall," Sparky would say.) They sent him down, and Sparky would never play another game in the major leagues.

He did play in the minor leagues for a while longer, and he became a manager, but his temper still raged. One day, Sparky found that nobody in baseball wanted him around. He sold cars for a while, Ramblers, and he was pretty lousy at that too. He only made a living because his boss, Milt Blish, would throw some extra business his way. Yes, Milt Blish saved his life. He was quite a man. And whenever Sparky tried to thank him, Milt would wave him off and say: "Real friendship means you don't ever have to say thank you."

Yes, Milt told Sparky that he had to put away those unhelpful feelings. He put it bluntly: feelings are for chumps. When Sparky would try to sell cars, he would get angry when people tried to cheat him. He fell for sob stories. If a customer talked about how little money he had, Sparky would say: "Look, I really don't think you can afford this car." He kept doing that until he realized that he was going broke, and the wise Milt Blish said, "George, don't you realize those people are just going to another car dealership to buy a car they can't afford?"

So Sparky put away those feelings. When he got another chance to manage a minor league team, he was transformed. Sure, he still got angry with the umpires. Sure, he still raged against his players. But now he cut the rage with funny stories, scraps of wisdom he had run across . . . he became a character, a baseball manager right out of central casting. When he became the Reds manager, people said that Bob Howsam must have lost his mind. People wrote letters to the editor and called Sparky a small-time nobody. Everybody made fun of the way he talked, his mangling of grammar, his lack of education, the clothes he wore, the lingering gray in his hair. On a bus ride in that first year, Lee May, a massive first baseman from Alabama, grew tired of Anderson's constant chirping. May said, "Aw, what do you know? You're just a minor league motherfucker." And that's what the Reds called him.

Well, so what? Feelings? Nothing more than feelings? Who needed them? All Georgie Anderson wanted his whole life—all he ever wanted since he was a boy living in a two-room house in the heart of the neighborhood that became Watts—was to be around baseball. Then, against odds, against hope, he became manager of the Big Red Machine. Feelings? Forget it. He told friends, "There ain't no way I can lose." First year, he took those players of the Big Red Machine and he flattered them, whipped them, inspired them, insulted them, and guided them to the World Series. Yeah. First year. How did they like their minor league motherfucker now?

The Reds lost that World Series to Baltimore—the Orioles' third baseman, Brooks Robinson, the human vacuum cleaner, made a series of superhuman defensive plays. "Guy busted us up single-handed," Sparky muttered. Well, it was okay. "I've still got the best team in baseball," he said. "I guarantee ya we'll win it all in '71."

The team collapsed instead. The Reds stopped scoring runs. They lost more games than they won. Rumors swirled that Sparky would be fired. How about that? They were thinking about firing him one year after he took the Reds to the World Series. Well, so what? "We'll win it in '72, I guarantee it," he told reporters. That spring, he worked his players to exhaustion—Sparky's favorite, Johnny Bench, called that spring training camp "Stalag 13," the concentration camp from the television show *Hogan's Heroes*. Pete Rose called Sparky "the Exorcist."

"Why's that?" Sparky asked.

" 'Cause you work the devil out of us," Rose said, big goofy grin on his face.

Who cares? When the season began, Sparky mercilessly yanked his pitchers out of games the instant they showed weakness. They hated his guts for it . . . who cares? Sparky never liked pitchers anyway. He bullied and charmed his team back to the World Series, and this time they played the roughneck Oakland Athletics, a team made up of players with long hair and mustaches, every kind of hippy-dippy ne'er-do-well. Sparky knew a team like that could not beat his disciplined, controlled, pristine Big Red Machine. Only, the A's won the World Series in seven games. Sparky said the loss felt like dying.

And so it went. In 1973, Sparky guaranteed his team would win. The Machine got beat in the playoffs by an unimpressive New York Mets team and an angry New York crowd that constantly seemed on the brink of rioting. "New York ought to be the next atomic bomb testing site," Anderson said after that loss, and then he apologized, and he felt dead inside. Then came 1974 and the worst season of all. The Reds won 98 games, more than every team but one. But that one team was the Los Angeles Dodgers, and they won 102 games and went to the playoffs instead. This was beyond heartbreak. Sparky Anderson lived in Los Angeles. He hated, just hated, the Dodgers.

"You know how you judge yourself?" Sparky would tell his players. "You judge yourself by what's on the back of your baseball card." The back of Sparky's baseball card stated that in five years his Reds had won three division championships and two pennants, but they had never won it all. That seemed good. But Sparky did not see it quite that way. Sparky figured that for five years he had the best team in baseball, the very best, and they had never won it all. Whom could he blame? Johnny Bench? Hell, no, Johnny Bench was the greatest catcher Sparky ever saw. Pete Rose? Hell, no, nobody ever played the game with more guts and energy than Pete. Joe Morgan? Hell, no, that little man could beat you every which way you could be beaten. The team? Hell, no. The Machine was the best goddamned baseball team Sparky ever saw.

He blamed himself. "I'm not good enough," he told friends. "It's me. I'm costing this team. I'm the weak link." Then he would snap out of it and shout, "But I'll show them! Nobody in the world could manage this team better than ol' Sparky." Feelings. Who cares?

Things were unhappy at his home in Thousand Oaks. He wanted

baseball to begin so he could get away. Sparky had not spoken to his oldest son, Lee, for more than a year. They were having the same fight that fathers and sons were having all over America.

"You're going to cut your hair," he said as he watched Lee working on his motorbike in the garage. Lee's hair was down to his shoulders. He looked, well, cliché or not, he looked like a girl. "Come with me right now, I'm taking you to the barber."

Lee did not even look up. Quietly, he said, "No."

No. Just like that. For a moment, Sparky thought about settling things like he had always settled things, with fists and rage and sparks. But he could not fight his own son. Instead, he cut him off. He stopped talking to Lee. Every now and again, he felt like breaking through the silence, only he would see Lee, and he would see that his hair had grown a little bit longer, and he would seethe again and turn his back. He was Sparky Anderson, baseball manager of the Machine, the cleanest-cut team, the team that represented the America he believed in. If a player grew his hair too long, Sparky had relief pitcher Pedro Borbon cut it. If the player refused to cut his hair, Bob Howsam traded him. This was how it had to be: Sparky would talk to reporters for hours about how this country was going to hell, what with the drugs and sex and atheism and, especially, the long hair. Think about this, he would say. If a man can't be counted on to cut his hair, how can you count on him to pitch the eighth inning? How can you count on him to be a good neighbor or keep our communities safe or help heal our sick? How can you count on him to be a good son and do all the right things? Sparky could not even stand to look at his own son.

Instead, he sat in his favorite chair at home, and he read stories about how the Dodgers—with their star Steve Garvey, who was being called "Captain America"—were the best team around. He read how his Reds were through. He read those stories over and over; he wanted to memorize every word. He wanted every slight, every insult, to pierce through him.

"The Dodgers are no dynasty," he suddenly yelled toward his wife, Carol. "They're a onetime deal! You hear me!"

Carol heard him. The phone rang—a sportswriter from Cincinnati calling to talk baseball.

"Don't write this," Sparky said, "but the Dodgers are done. You mark my words: you're going to see something, boy. We're going to give people a show like they never seen before."

February 3, 1975

CINCINNATI
Dick Wagner's office

Pete Rose heard himself bragging about all his walks, and it made him sick. It had come to this. Pete Rose hated taking walks. Everyone knew that. He would sometimes swing the bat at bad pitches on purpose to avoid taking a walk. This cut to the heart of Pete Rose the ballplayer. Harry Rose did not raise his son to walk. The Roses did not accept charity. Pete would by God take first base, conquer it. There was a game in 1974, the Reds trailed the St. Louis Cardinals by seven runs in the late innings. Bob Gibson was pitching for the Cardinals, "Bullet Bob," the scariest pitcher in the game. Batters hit a measly .228 against Gibson over his seventeen-year career, and he took every hit personally. Gibson threw a pitch inside, Pete tried to pull out of the way, and the pitch ticked Pete's uniform.

"Ball hit him," the umpire, Bill Williams, shouted, and he pointed toward first. "Take your base."

"The ball didn't hit me, Bill," Rose shouted back, and he stepped back into the batter's box.

"Yes, it did, Pete, I heard it hit you, take your base."

"No. You heard wrong. I'm telling you the ball didn't hit me."

"You're taking the base, Pete. The ball hit you, quit being silly. . . ."

"I'm not taking the base, Bill. Didn't hit me. Let me back in the box."

Pete kept arguing during a lost game that the baseball did not hit him, he did not want the free base, he wanted to get one more swing at the most intimidating pitcher of the time. In the end, the umpire made him take first base, but Pete did not take it well. For the rest of the inning, he yelled, "The ball didn't hit me!" That's how much Pete hated walks. He wanted to swing away. Always.

Now, though, Pete Rose talked about walks. It was humiliating. In 1974, Pete had 106 walks, the most of his career, and through gritted teeth he said that old Little League line: "Hey, a walk is as good as a hit, right?" Pete explained that all those walks helped him score the most runs in the National League. That was worth something, right? Rose looked across the desk at the Reds' vice president of administration, Dick Wagner, to see if his words were having an effect. Wagner glared back blankly. Dick Wagner was a hard man. For years, he managed the Ice Capades. He knew how to intimidate athletes and squeeze dimes out of small-town promoters.

"Pete," Wagner said quietly, "this is not about your walks. This is about your batting average. I believe you hit [here Wagner lifted a paper close to his face], yes, you hit .284, which is, of course, well below your usual standard. I know you were as disappointed as we were. As you know, we pay you to hit .300. Also, we noticed that you are not in quite the same shape you once were. You seem heavier this year. And with your age . . ."

Wagner went on like this for a while. Rose stopped listening. He never should have brought up those walks. He was Pete Rose, "Charlie Hustle," a surefire Hall of Famer, a hitting machine. Still, what choice did he have? The Reds wanted blood. They wanted to cut his pay. Rose led the whole National League in runs scored, and they wanted to slash his salary by more than $30,000. Every year it was like this—Rose had to fight for every dime. He had to threaten to show up late to spring training. He had to threaten to sit out the season. He had to go to these agonizing sessions (and without his agent, Reuven Katz—the Reds would not let Katz in the door) and defend himself like it was Nuremberg. This is how it was for baseball players in 1975. Teams owned players for perpetuity. Most players had second jobs in the off-season. The game was about to change, and players were about to make more money than they had ever dreamed. But it had not changed yet. And Pete Rose, with his .284 batting average in 1974, felt naked and alone.

"Just do what I did," Johnny Bench had said in that cutting, know-everything voice he had perfected. A year earlier, Johnny had gone into his salary meeting with the Reds, and that son of a gun handed them a blank contract. Pete had to admit that was a ballsy move. Johnny said: "Pay me what you think is fair," and he smiled and walked out of the room, like John Wayne. Yes, Pete could not deny it: John had style. But he was also coming off a great year. And the Reds loved him, they worshipped him, they paid him $150,000 just to see the smile on his face. If Pete ever did something like that, ever just gave the Reds a blank contract, they would not pay him enough to cover his car payments. Pete felt the Reds had it in for him. Of course, he felt that way about everybody.

"Pete, we feel like we are being more than fair here," Wagner said, and his voice was beginning to boom now. Bad sign. Wagner had a nasty temper. A year before, the guy had cursed out the team chaplain. Bob Howsam had negotiated salaries himself, but that was in a gentler time. Now players were getting brassier, getting advice from agents, working more closely with their union boss, Marvin Miller. So Howsam had Wagner, his hit man, do the negotiating. "He would sit in his ivory tower and pretend that he was above it all," Reuven Katz would say many years later. "And he would have Wagner fight his bloody battles."

Wagner told Rose that the Reds—because they valued him, because they knew how much he had meant to them over the years, because he was named the league's Most Valuable Player in 1973—

would not cut his salary by $30,000. They would only cut it by $10,000.

"I'm not taking a pay cut," Pete said.

"I understand your emotions, Pete, but when you did well, the club was always willing to cater to your needs, and now . . ."

"I'm not taking a pay cut," Pete said, and with that he got up and said, "And I am not some fat boy." He stormed out of the room. On his way out to his car, he would remember, he muttered to himself, "Damn it, I cannot believe I brought up those walks." Three days later, Rose signed a contract with the Reds. The salary numbers were not released, which suited Pete just fine. That way he did not have to explain why he had taken a $5,000 pay cut from those sons of bitches.

February 21, 1975

CINCINNATI

The Netherland Hilton

Johnny Bench felt good about the numbers in the paper. There were 650 pounds of roast beef here, 100 pounds of roast ham, 1,200 egg rolls, and 4,000 mixed drinks. There was a five-tiered, five-foot-high chocolate cake—5 being the number Johnny Bench wore as catcher of the Cincinnati Reds. The newspaper said the food alone cost $8,000, which was about right, give or take a couple hundred. People would have to be impressed. The median income in America was barely more than $12,000. Johnny Bench spent $8,000 for the food at his wedding.

Vickie Chesser wondered again how this had happened. Everything had moved so fast—too fast, her friends kept telling her. But they could not see it. Johnny was perfect. They did not know him. They had not seen the way he acted around little Phillip Buckingham.

Phillip was five, all kinds of curly hair, his body ravaged by leukemia. Sick children are drawn to ballplayers, and ballplayers are drawn to sick children, and Vickie would watch as the two of them talked, soul to soul. Sometimes, when they talked, it seemed like Phillip was the adult and Johnny the child. She saw the way Phillip looked at Johnny, so full of love, so full of life. No, her friends could never understand. For the first time in her life, she was in love, really in love.

Johnny had hoped that Bob Hope would make it in for the wedding. He knew that President Gerald Ford would not make it, not with Vietnam smoldering to its inevitable conclusion. And Johnny was not surprised when Joe DiMaggio sent his regrets. The talk show host Dinah Shore wanted to come, but she could not get away. But the singer Bobby Goldsboro was there, and John had hoped Bob Hope would make it too. They had traveled together to Vietnam to entertain the troops. There was this one time, funny story, this one time when Johnny was in the back of the plane sleeping on a bed of blankets with Tara Leigh, she was one of the Ding-A-Ling sisters, she was one of the Golddiggers, the girls who would add a little sex appeal to *The Dean Martin Show* on television. Beautiful girl. Anyway, they were huddled together, just trying to get some sleep, nothing untoward going on, and Bob Hope wandered back and ended up stepping on Johnny's head. Bob told that story all the time. Got big laughs. Johnny had really hoped that Bob Hope would make the wedding, but his schedule would not allow it.

Vickie knew that Johnny had only called her in December because he heard from a buddy that she was "one swinging lady." Well, he had been given bad information. She didn't swing, you know. He called her up cold, no introduction, and invited her to come with him to Las Vegas. Her first reaction was to hang up the phone, but there was something strong in his voice, something solid. He offered to send her a plane ticket and buy her a separate room. "What do you have to lose?" he asked, and there was something about that voice, something so sure, something different from all the other guys she had dated.

Then he invited her to join him at a wedding. What could go wrong at a wedding?

Johnny had told teammates after the 1974 season ended that it was time for him to get married. He was almost twenty-seven. He'd had his fun. Johnny had always lived an orderly and planned life. Before his first full season in the major leagues—that was 1968—he announced that he would win the Rookie of the Year Award. He won that. He then told reporters that he would become the best player in baseball. That happened in 1970, when he hit 45 home runs and drove in 148 runs, numbers no catcher had ever reached. And Johnny Bench wasn't a normal catcher; he revolutionized the position. He snagged pitches one-handed. He pounced on bunts with the quickness of a snake striking. His arm was a marvel—he threw out so many base runners that by 1972 players had more or less stopped trying to steal against him. *Time* magazine put him on the cover that year, with the understated headline: "Baseball's Best Catcher." He told reporters that baseball was not big enough to hold him, that he needed to stretch out, and he did that too. He sang in nightclubs. He played a guard on the television show *Mission Impossible* and a waiter on *The Partridge Family*. He hosted his own television show and opened his own restaurant in Cincinnati. Now, he said, it was time to get married. All he needed was the perfect wife. He saw Vickie Chesser in an Ultra Brite toothpaste commercial on television. She had a nice smile.

Vickie liked the way he looked. Johnny had a round-faced handsomeness; there was something vulnerable in the way he looked. And yet, at the same time, he seemed bulletproof. He seemed so sure all the time—sure of where he was going, sure of what would happen when he arrived, sure of their future together. Their courtship happened in a rush; within days of their meeting, he was talking marriage. He overwhelmed her. Vickie did not care for baseball, but her father back in South Carolina explained that Johnny Bench played with such vividness and authority that you could not take your eyes off him. Vickie understood that. He had power. When he proposed to her three weeks after they met, she could not think of anything to say except yes.

Johnny liked that she knew nothing about baseball. It made him feel like something deep in them connected. He also liked the way they looked together. At first, Vickie had talked about having the wedding in her hometown, in Mount Pleasant, South Carolina, but they both knew that could not happen. Well, he knew it for sure. Johnny was a Cincinnati star. He had a Cincinnati wedding in mind, one that would stop the town cold. He did it all—wedding planner, press agent, groom. A friend offered to buy the liquor. A thousand invitations were sent out. Thirty cooks were hired to prepare the food. "It's a chance to show my artistry," Stuart Johnsen told the Associated Press; Johnsen was in charge of decorating the eighteen-pound baked salmon. Story after story appeared in the newspapers about the happy couple. When Johnny was asked how he would describe his future wife, he said: "Shapely."

Vickie marveled at Johnny's certainty; it was like he had been planning for this wedding his whole life. He wanted a big, gaudy, celebrity-filled wedding; well, that's what she wanted too. She chose a china pattern but happily switched to Lennox Laurent because she saw how much Johnny liked it. She chose a crystal pattern and changed that too when Johnny showed a preference for Genova by Baccarat. Well, the Genova was nicer. She let him open their wedding presents. "He gets such a kick out of it," she told a reporter. "I just like to watch him."

While the reverend spoke at Christ Episcopal Church that day, Johnny leaned over to Vickie and whispered: "Hey, you clean up pretty nice." And she said: "You look pretty good yourself with your hair combed." It was like something out of a movie. At the reception, Pete Rose kidded Johnny about a quote in the paper where he talked about being a fan of bigamist Brigham Young. Pete and Merv Rettenmund were the only players from the Machine at the wedding; the others already were down in Florida getting ready for the season.

"You know what they say about married guys?" Pete said.

"What's that?" Johnny asked.

"They can't pull the ball no more," Pete said. Johnny laughed. He would always pull the ball. Across the crowded room, Vickie was getting tossed and twisted and hugged from every direction. She had a nice smile.

Johnny and Vickie cut the cake, shoved pieces in each other's mouths, kissed for the cameras. The day after the wedding, Johnny and Vickie headed for Florida and the start of a new baseball season. Before leaving, though, they got a phone call. Little Phillip Buckingham had died.

February 28, 1975

TAMPA

Spring training

The players would each remember Sparky Anderson's spring training speech a little bit differently in later years, but everyone recalled his main point. He announced that the Machine was made up of two different kinds of players. First, there were the superstars. To be more specific, Sparky said, there were four superstars—Pete Rose, Johnny Bench, Joe Morgan, and Tony Perez. Those four made their own rules. Those four had no curfew. Those four had special privileges. If Johnny wanted to go golfing every so often during spring training, he could go. If Pete wanted to blow off some steam at the dog track, well, Sparky might give him a few extra bucks. If Joe needed to come in late so he could finish school, that was all right by Sparky. If Tony needed a little rest, then Sparky would fluff the pillow. Those four were royalty.

"The rest of you," Sparky said, "are turds."

This was the law of the Machine. Sparky never hid it. He knew some managers tried to treat everyone equally. Well, Sparky was not one of those men. He had learned another of the great rules of doing business from the car salesman Milt Blish: you scratch my back. . . .

"If you want to be treated like one of them," Sparky said to the turds as he pointed toward Bench and Rose, "you have to *play* like one of them. You have to *work* like one of them. I don't treat everyone the same. I don't believe in it. I'll give you as much as you give me."

Then Sparky looked out over the players who made up the Machine, the team that had to win, and he very clearly said the words that so many of them would remember for the rest of their lives. He said: "Boys, this team is like my television set. Nobody messes with it."

"I'll be honest with you," the kid relief pitcher and turd Will McEnaney would say more than thirty years later. "None of us ever knew what the fuck Sparky was talking about."

Sparky picked his least favorite turd on the first day of camp: a kid name John Vukovich. Sparky had seen bad hitters all his life. Hell, he had been a bad hitter all his life. But this new guy, Vukovich, well, he was a whole other level of bad. First time he saw Vukovich go through batting practice, he already had a nickname in mind: "Balsa." That was because whenever Vukovich hit, the ball seemed to just dribble off the bat like milk off a baby's chin, and the dead sound Sparky heard made him wonder if the kid's bat was made out of balsa wood.

"Can't you do anything with him?" he asked his hitting coach, Ted Kluszewski, whom everyone called Big Klu.

"What do you want me to do, shoot him?" Big Klu asked back.

Sparky considered the offer. A couple of months earlier, Bob Howsam had told Sparky that the team was going to trade Tony Perez to get a third baseman. Sparky had mixed emotions about it. He loved

Perez—everybody loved Doggie—and the guy was still one helluva tough hitter. But a trade made some sense. The Reds needed someone to play third base—it was the one overwhelming flaw of the team. Six different men had played third base the year before, and not one of them was worth a damn out there. Danny Driessen had been Sparky's great hope; he was young and determined, and like Sparky told the reporters, he was one helluva hitter. Trouble was, Danny Driessen looked scared out of his mind when he played third base. They call third base "the hot corner"—baseballs rush at you like angry wasps— and Danny couldn't handle that. One time he simply forgot to step on the base to force out a runner. Kid was terrorized out there. No, Danny couldn't play third base. But he could play first base, a much safer defensive position, and Sparky found himself daydreaming about a trade and a new infield, with Danny at first base and a young star like New York's Graig Nettles or Kansas City's George Brett playing third.

In the end, though, Howsam did not trade Tony Perez. Instead, he went out and traded for Balsa, a part-time player from Milwaukee who was a magician with the glove. His hands, Sparky thought, were like boxers', but he could not hit his own weight. Hell, he could not hit Sparky's weight. Through four mostly bleak seasons, Balsa's batting average was .157.

"With our lineup, you won't need his hitting," Howsam had told Sparky. "We'll still score plenty of runs. Just put him at third base and let him make all the plays—every hit he gets will be a bonus."

Before spring training started, Sparky could admit that Howsam made some sense. Even after spring training started, he could admit it when he was away from the ballpark, at the hotel, by the pool, lounging in the sun. Howsam's words rang true on lawn chairs. Sparky would put Vukovich at third base and let him save all those runs with his brilliant defense. And sure, the Machine would still score plenty of runs. Sparky had Tony Perez back, he had his guys Bench and Morgan and Rose, he had a few turds who showed promise—yes, in the lazy humidity of midafternoon, Sparky had himself convinced. But early the next morning, he would come back to the ballpark in Tampa, and he would feel that moist Florida chill on his arms, and he would watch Balsa hit slow, useless ground balls during batting practice, he would watch Balsa hit candy bloops to the shortstop. Then the rage would bubble all over again—there was no way on God's green earth that he could have that turd playing every day for the Big Red Machine. Not this year.

"Fix him, damn it," he screamed at Big Klu.

"You mean that literally?" Big Klu asked.

"I don't know what I mean," Sparky said, and he kicked the dirt.

"The Nautilus machine" became the punch line for Tony Perez's favorite spring training joke. Baseball players—most of them anyway—did not lift weights in 1975. The compelling wisdom of the time was that baseball players who lifted weights would lose their flexibility, though the compelling wisdom of the day may have been written by baseball players who did not want to lift weights. Let the football players do that stuff.

Still, the Reds had one of the very first Nautilus pullover machines. It was a gift from Arthur Jones, the inventor. Jones had this idea that he could create a machine that would help everyday people build up their muscles without going to a dark gym and lifting enormous barbells for hours. Who had the time to be Charles Atlas? Jones hoped to spread the word of his miraculous machine by giving one to the Cincinnati Reds. He wanted to say that his machine pumped up the Big Red Machine.

Of course, none of the players used the thing except to hang jockstraps on it. Nobody even knew *how* to use it. That was why Tony Perez invented the "Nautilus machine list." It was a simple gag: He would walk around the clubhouse and suddenly notice a player. And he would say, "What are you doing here? You are supposed to be working on the Nautilus."

The player would laugh. But Tony would look at him seriously.

"You gonna be in big trouble with Sparky," he would say. He pronounced "big" like "beeg." "He put you on the list. Didn't you see the list?"

Some players fell for it. Most didn't. But it tickled Doggie either way.

"Hey, fatty," Doggie said to Joe Morgan. "How much you eat this off-season? It's a good thing your name on list to work out on Nautilus today. We can't have a fat second baseman. I cannot go and field all your ground balls."

Morgan smiled. He always thought that this was what made the Machine different. This was their power. Nobody had feelings. Nobody showed weakness. Nobody took offense. When you played for the Machine, you never worried about the other team heckling you—the cruelest taunts always came from your own dugout. They called Morgan shrimp, midget, piss-ant, and much crueler and cruder stuff. But it was okay. Joe knew how to fight.

"Doggie, what are you even doing here?" Joe asked. "Weren't we supposed to trade you? I guess we couldn't find even an American League club that would take your sorry ass."

Yes, Joe had a way of stabbing for the heart. Tony Perez had spent an agonizing winter in Puerto Rico worrying about being traded. Howsam called Perez into his office on the last day of the season, and he asked for permission to trade Perez. That's how it worked in 1975. Only a few years earlier, players were traded freely, like baseball cards, and it didn't really matter what they thought about it. They had no right to stop any trades, no control of their own destinies. But times were changing. The Major League Baseball Players Association had hired a tough old labor economist named Marvin Miller, who had negotiated for the steelworkers' union. And Miller scared the hell out of the baseball owners. They rushed to offer concessions in the desperate and ultimately doomed hope that they could hold off the inevitable pain of player free agency. Perez had been with the Reds for more than ten years, and because of that he had the right to veto a trade if he wanted.

"I just want you to sign this waiver," Howsam said, and he slid a paper in front of Doggie.

Perez would not sign the waiver. He could not sign it. He was an original member of the Machine—a founding member, to tell the truth. He signed with the Reds in 1960, just as the United States broke off relations with his native Cuba. He had given up his life for baseball; Tony had seen his mother and father once in a dozen years. The Reds were his family. He could not imagine himself playing for any other team.

Doggie also could not imagine why the Reds wanted to trade him. They called him "Big Dog" (and variations of that canine theme— "Doggie," "Pup") because, as the Reds' old manager Dave Bristol said countless times: "If the game lasts long enough, the Big Dog will win it." Doggie had driven in ninety or more runs for eight straight seasons; nobody else in either league had done that. The brilliant *Los Angeles Times* columnist Jim Murray did not even know how close he was to the mark when he wrote: "Perez runs more to Gary Cooper than Carmen Miranda." Murray was writing a gag, making the point that Perez was not hot-blooded like people might expect a Cuban player to be. But Gary Cooper was about right. Perez was the marshal, the calming force of the Machine, the star who did not act like a star, the surest bet to drive in that runner from second base at high noon.

Reporters in general, though, did not get Doggie. They liked him fine, and they respected him. But they had trouble summing him up. Reporters on deadline needed droll quotes and pithy lines or cutting (and brief) analysis. Pete Rose would sit in the clubhouse and think up clever lines for the reporters. Joe Morgan, even then, sounded like he belonged on television.

"How'd you do it, Doggie?" the reporters would ask after he smacked another game-winning hit.

"See the ball, hit the ball," Perez would say every time—every time—and after a while everyone around him, including those reporters, would say the words with him. Then they would go to Pete or Johnny or Joe to get the quote they needed for the paper.

In the clubhouse, Tony Perez may have been Gary Cooper, but outside it he remained in the shadows—so much so that even his general manager, Bob Howsam, and his manager, Sparky Anderson, did not fully appreciate how much Doggie meant to the team.

"If we do trade you, we will try to trade you to a contender," Howsam said. "But I cannot make you any promises."

Perez did not speak. There was nothing to say. He did not sign the waiver. He went home to Puerto Rico, and he ran every day on the beach, and he let the realities consume him. If the Reds wanted to trade him, there still was not much he could do about it. Yes, technically, he could refuse the trade. He could embarrass the Reds. But where would that leave him? It would leave him stuck on a team that did not want him. He could not live like that. He waited every day for the news that he had been traded, and he prayed every day that the news would not come.

A miracle happened. Every time the Reds tried to trade Perez, something fouled up. The Reds were close to trading Doggie to Kansas City for George Brett, only the Royals chickened out. The Reds were close to trading Doggie to Boston for a rookie third baseman, Butch Hobson, and a tall beanpole of a pitcher named Roger Moret, but that fell through. There was even some talk about Doggie going to three-time World Champion Oakland for third baseman Sal Bando, but Oakland's owner, Charlie Finley, was dependably undependable and that deal died in committee.

That left only one trade on the table, and it looked all but certain: Perez would go to the New York Yankees for their All-Star third baseman, Graig Nettles. The trade made too much sense not to happen. The Yankees needed a quiet leader, someone who could help lift the team from a ten-year World Series drought, their longest since World War I. And Nettles would give Sparky Anderson that third baseman who could play breathtaking defense and hit long home runs. Back home in Puerto Rico, Doggie imagined himself in Yankee pinstripes.

But that trade disintegrated too. The Reds wanted a pitcher thrown in. The Yankees wanted someone they could plug in at third base. Talks stalled. Then talks broke off. Negotiations began again. Then broke off again. Middle East talks. Then one day, Howsam became frustrated with it all and announced that there would be no trade. A miracle. "Who knows?" Howsam told reporters. "This spring I may look at our ball club and say I'm the luckiest son of a gun for *not* making a deal."

The rest of the winter, Tony Perez wondered how it would feel to come back to the club. Everyone knew the Reds almost traded him. Would everyone look at him differently? Would they lose a little respect for him? Would they worry about him? Would they treat him like a sick patient?

"Hey, Doggy," Morgan said. "They can still trade your ass anytime, you know. I can just picture you after one year in that American League as a designated hitter. You'd balloon up to 280 pounds."

"Fatty," Perez said, flexing his arm, "it all muscle. And your biggest muscle is your mouth. You better get to that Nautilus, they waiting for you. You on the list."

Perez grinned. It was just the same.

March 13, 1975

TAMPA
REDS VS. TWINS

Gary Nolan did not understand what was rumbling around in his stomach. He had never felt the butterflies before. They fluttered and flapped in his stomach, gnawed at his esophagus, kicked at his small intestine. This was spring training. The game did not even count. He thought, *So that's how nerves feel.* Gary Nolan was back pitching for the Cincinnati Reds. He was not quite twenty-seven years old.

Gary noticed how Carol, his wife, was looking at him through the netting as she sat behind home plate. How many times had he seen that haunted look the last couple of years? She was scared for him. Well, hell, it figured. He was scared too. This was their last shot. There was no point in making it sound any prettier than that. Gary had not won a major league baseball game in more than two years. He had not even pitched in a real big league game since August 1973, back before Watergate blew up. Gary stood on the mound, threw the last of his warm-up pitches, and then reached around with his left hand and massaged his right shoulder; the shoulder did not hurt exactly, but it did not feel right either.

All around the field, newspaper reporters watched him closely; their spiral reporter's pads were out and pointed at him. He was the story of camp: the Amazing Comeback of Gary Nolan. He was what everyone was talking about. Sparky, too, was staring at him, piercing him with his eyes, and teammates in the field leaned forward toward him. Gary could not shake the feeling that on his first pitch of the game, the stitches holding his shoulder together would rip apart and his arm, quite literally, would detach and fly toward home plate.

How did he get here? Gary remembered so vividly that warm summer evening in Oroville, an old gold rush town in California that—like most gold rush towns—had dwindled and deteriorated through the years. Gary was ten years old, of course—that's the most magical age to be a baseball fan—and he sat on the living room couch next to his old man, Ray. They listened on the radio to the San Francisco Giants ball game. The announcers were Russ Hodges and Lon Simmons. "Tell it bye-bye, baby," Russ used to say when one of the Giants—like Willie Mays or Hank Sauer or Orlando Cepeda— hit a home run. Gary had started injecting "Tell it bye-bye, baby" into his daily talk.

"So, this is what you want to do, huh?" Ray asked Gary. Ray did not care for baseball. He worked as a switchman for the Union Pacific. He worked hard, of course, and like so many men of his generation, Ray did not make time in his life for fantasies and childhood dreams.

"Baseball, huh?" Ray continued. "So you think that's what you want to do with your life?"

Gary looked up at his dad, and then he said the funniest thing. He said: "Yeah. But is it real?"

Ray didn't know what to make of that. Is it real? Is what real? "The baseball," Gary said. "Is it real? Are they really playing? Is this really happening, or is it . . . just . . . is it real?" The next day, Ray loaded Gary into the car, and they drove 150 miles along bumpy two-lane roads and managed to get to Seals Stadium on Sixteenth and Bryant. They watched the Giants play the Dodgers. Other baseball-playing men, when looking back at their first baseball game, remember sentimental things. They recall holding hands with their fathers, the hugeness of the players, the vivid crayon green of the grass, that singular ballpark smell of popcorn and sweat and cotton candy and beer. Gary remembered that it was all so real, so tangible; he had seen his own future up close. Gary did not dream about playing big league baseball like other boys he knew. He planned for it. He had been born for it.

Gary was such a good pitcher in high school that baseball scouts scalded the asphalt on California 70 to Oroville. Sometimes there would be twenty-five scouts sitting in the stands—he was like a second gold rush. Gary threw a dazzling fastball. He had impeccable control. He had that certain poise that young pitchers (and young men) rarely have: he seemed to know precisely what he was doing. The Reds drafted Gary in the first round of the amateur draft just days after he turned eighteen years old. The Reds sent their top negotiator, Jim McLaughlin, to Oroville to cut a deal. Jim wanted to work with the father; that's how these things normally went. "Naw, talk to Gary," Ray said. "He's a grown man."

Gary negotiated his own deal, and he signed for $40,000. The number was so large that the Reds refused to release it; the newspaper reporters duly called it "a gigantic deal." Gary thought he could have gotten even more money, but he did not want to waste time fighting for pennies. He rushed toward his destiny. Gary pitched his first major league game when he was still eighteen years old. The first batter he faced was Sonny Jackson, known as a tough out. Gary struck him out on three pitches. The second batter he faced was Jim Landis, an eleven-year veteran who had played in an All-Star Game. Gary struck him out too.

"Were you nervous?" the reporters asked after that first big league game. Nervous? He shrugged. He told them: "I don't get nervous; I was hit harder in high school."

A little later that year—this was 1967, two days after the start of the Six-Day War—Gary struck out Willie Mays four times in a game. Willie Mays! His hero! Nobody had ever struck out the "Say Hey Kid" four times in a single major league game. The next afternoon, Gary jogged happily in the outfield, and he heard a loud, piercing whistle. He turned around, and there was Willie Mays motioning Gary to come over.

"Son," Willie said, "I was overmatched."

Well, there it was: destiny. Where do you go from there? He had overmatched Willie Mays, his hero, maybe the greatest player who ever lived, and he had just turned nineteen. Dave Bristol, the Reds manager, told the press, "He ain't got no ceiling," and the double negative did not restrain his emotions. Gary struck out 206 batters that first year, more than any nineteen-year-old since the great Bob Feller back in 1938. "Don't be scared," Feller told him, man to man, when the season ended. "Make them scared of you."

Gary knew exactly what Feller meant. They both knew what it was like, to be nineteen and commanding and bulletproof. The next spring, Gary felt a twinge in his arm. He kept on pitching. He felt other twinges. Then he started to notice that his arm hurt more often than it felt right. Then, one day in '72, he felt like there was a spear sticking out of his arm.

How did Gary get from there to here, from nineteen-year-old phenomenon who overmatched Willie Mays to twenty-six-year-old long shot trying to impress a crowd of cynics on a dusty spring training field in Tampa? His stomach tumbled and twisted, and again he saw his Carol behind home plate, looking at him with the worried face, like they were about to walk into the doctor's office and find out the results of a cancer test. He tried to give her a knowing smile, a wink, but he could not pull it off. She could see through him. Carol had lived four houses down in Oroville. They married at seventeen and had their first son before the Reds signed him. She did not know baseball, but she knew everything about him. She knew he was scared.

Gary winced as he threw the last of his warm-up pitches, though his arm did not hurt. He winced out of habit. His arm had hurt so much, for so long, that pain had become a part of him. Now there was a numbness where the pain had been. The pain was gone, but so was the electricity that had buzzed in his arm in 1967. Gary could not throw particularly hard anymore. He could not snap off a curve that dived to the ground. He no longer could look at batters with his childlike disdain and think, *Buddy, you have no chance.* He had to be a different pitcher now, a magician, an illusionist, he had to bend the ball crooked when they expected it straight, throw it slow when they anticipated fast, pitch it up when they were looking down. Gary missed his old arm. In a strange way, he even missed the pain.

People had doubted him. That was what hurt most. He remembered that when he first felt the pain in his arm, Sparky Anderson had told him: "Pitchers have to throw with pain. Bob Gibson says every pitch he's ever thrown cut him like a knife. You gotta pitch with pain, kid."

"What the hell is that supposed to mean?" Gary wondered. He knew about pain. He had pitched with pain. He tried to explain that this was a different pain, agonizing pain that shot through his body when he released the ball. This was not pain you pitch with. Sparky sighed, sent the kid to the doctor, but the X-rays came up negative. And Sparky told him again about Bob Gibson pitching through pain. "You've got to be tough. You've got to keep on pitching through the pain."

And the cycle was formed. Gary pitched . . . and when he pitched, he pitched well. But the pain was overwhelming. He had to stop. He went to Sparky. The X-rays came up negative. Sparky would tell him to pitch again.

In 1972, Gary Nolan might have been the best pitcher in baseball. By mid-July, he had won thirteen games, his ERA was a remarkable 1.81—all of his promise and all of his talent were finally coming together. And he was miserable. His arm throbbed constantly—even when he slept. Then, midway through the year, the pain jumped even higher, to a whole new level, and he had to stop, he could not pitch even as Sparky implored him to go on. The pain roared through him. "Enough to make you cry," he told reporters, which didn't make it sound any better.

"Trade Nolan, sell Nolan, release Nolan. In short, get rid of him," a reader from Dayton wrote in a letter to the *Cincinnati Enquirer.* "I am tired of hearing the stories about his potential. Every winter Nolan 'guarantees' twenty wins for the coming summer, and every summer Nolan spends half the time on the disabled list. He hardly ever pitches."

Nolan pleaded with Sparky to believe him. "Don't you think I would be out there pitching if I could?" he asked. Sparky seemed unconvinced. His teammates wondered too. There was another unspoken rule when you were on the Machine: you did not complain about pain. Johnny Bench played catcher for 150 games every year—who hurt more than he? He never talked about it. Pete Rose never missed a game, ever, and he played baseball like a stunt man—he crashed into second basemen, shrugged off beanballs, dove into bases headfirst. Little Joe Morgan had been spiked, cut, slashed, knocked into the outfield, and slapped with tags that felt like Joe Frazier left hooks. He did not talk about it. If you wanted to play for the Machine, you did not show weakness, you did not back down, and you did not get hurt. Nolan tried again to pitch, but each delivery felt like surgery without anesthetics.

"When's Nolan going to pitch again?" reporters asked Sparky.

"Hell, I don't know," Sparky said, and he could not mask the disdain. "Ask him."

The Reds' doubts hurt as much as the arm. One day, the Reds executive Dick Wagner called Gary and said that the club had set up an appointment for him with a dentist. A dentist! "We think this will cure you," Wagner said. Well, Gary went to the office, and the dentist fished around in his mouth for a few minutes and finally said, "I have found your problem. You have an abscessed tooth." Gary shook his head; he had never felt any pain in his tooth. The dentist explained that such pain often transfers to another part of the body—maybe the right shoulder. The dentist pulled the tooth, and he promised Gary relief.

There was no relief, of course; his shoulder hurt more than ever. Dentists from around the country wrote in to say that there was no way an abscessed tooth could cause a man's arm to shoot with pain. Gary understood. The Reds had sent him to a witch doctor. They thought the pain was all in his head. He winced and grimaced through the playoffs and World Series, then moved his family out of Cincinnati, back to Oroville, where he would not have to hear whispers about gutlessness or see any more dentists. He pitched two games in 1973. He did not pitch at all in '74. He would sit at home watching television—*Mannix* was his favorite show—and he knew that his career was over. The pain felt unbearable and permanent.

"I've been dead for two years," Gary said to Pete Rose. "And no one has even thrown me a funeral."

Many years later, Gary Nolan would look back and say he had two overwhelming thrills in the game of baseball. The first was something universal, something they all treasured. He loved putting on a major league baseball uniform. He loved being in the clubhouse, loved to hear the cheers and boos, loved striking out Willie Mays, loved the way the beer tasted after victories. Simply, Gary loved being a big league baseball player.

The second thrill was more specific and more personal. It happened one day in 1974, when he went to see Dr. Frank Jobe, the Los Angeles Dodgers' orthopedic surgeon. Jobe, in his own way, transformed baseball as much as Babe Ruth, Jackie Robinson, and Roberto Clemente. When Gary went to see him in 1974, Jobe was also seeing a Dodgers pitcher named Tommy John, who had badly injured his elbow. John's career was over—pitchers did not come back from damaged elbows—but Jobe had this long-shot idea. Jobe thought that he might fix the elbow by replacing the damaged ligament with a ligament taken from another part of the body, like the wrist or the knee. Nobody had ever tried anything like it. Jobe placed John's odds of pitching again at one hundred to one. But Tommy John did pitch again; he pitched as well as he had before, sometimes better. The procedure became known as "Tommy John surgery." And it saved countless pitchers' lives.

Jobe took X-rays of Gary's shoulder from a different angle, and sure enough, he found a one-inch bone spur swimming in there. Jobe thought that if he removed the bone spur, Gary had a chance to pitch again—certainly he had a better chance than Tommy John. The Reds management—even after hearing about the bone spur—did not want Jobe to perform surgery. They still thought that Gary just needed to get tougher. But Gary knew the surgery was his only chance. Jobe removed the spur, and Gary did the rehabilitation quietly and away from the ball club.

And that was how he ended up on the mound here in Tampa, pitching both without pain and without the arm-explosion of his youth. He pitched three innings against the Minnesota Twins. He did not give up a run. The baseball scouts who had come to see Gary Nolan shrugged . . . he did not look bad, but he was not the same. His fastball was gone. But Gary knew that. The fastball *was* gone. Yesterday was gone. The only question in his mind was: could he still get hitters out? Gary thought that maybe he could.

And the second thrill of his life? No, it was not pitching well that day in spring training while his wife watched from behind the net. It was not striking out Willie Mays four times. It was not even the day he made it to the big leagues. No, the second thrill in baseball happened when Frank Jobe found that sharp bone spur and said very softly: "I have no idea how you pitched in that sort of pain. You must have been in agony." Someone believed him. And Gary felt like a man again.

March 25, 1975
TAMPA

In the Cincinnati clubhouse, players were still talking about the fight. Pete, of course, kept talking about the white guy. Did you see him? The white guy showed all kinds of heart. Chuck Wepner. But nobody gave him a chance. They called Wepner "the Bayonne Bleeder," which is not an especially intimidating name for a boxer. What chance would a boxer called the Bayonne Bleeder have against Muhammad Ali, the greatest, "the Black Superman," the heavyweight champeen of the world? This wasn't a fight; it was a blood-letting. The only thing bookies took bets on was what round the Bayonne Bleeder would drown. Jim Murray of the *Los Angeles Times* wrote that to entertain a crowd that would pay to watch a fight like this, they should follow up by gassing butterflies and setting fire to baby carriages.

Then the fight began. And the white guy wouldn't go down. He took every blow, walked through every punch, he made it all the way to the fifteenth round with Ali. Wepner even knocked the champ down. The white guy! Of course, Ali later said it was no knockdown, he had slipped. And yeah, Ali's trunks flushed red with Wepner's blood. And sure, the whole thing was a joke . . . the champ taunted and mocked and played around most of the fight. He kept the tomato can upright just to entertain the booing crowd. Still, you had to admit it, Wepner stood for fifteen rounds. The white guy!

"He got knocked *out!*" Joe Morgan shouted at Pete. They were always shouting at each other, Pete and Joe. "You are like an old married couple," Tony Perez would say, and they were, like an old married couple you might see on television, like Archie and Edith on *All in the Family*, or Sonny and Cher before they called it splits.

"He got knocked out with nineteen seconds left," Rose yelled back. "Did anybody think this guy could last until there were nineteen seconds left in the fight? Everybody thought he would get knocked out in the first round. . . . Hell, the white guy even knocked Ali down."

"Would you two shut up?" Johnny Bench yelled across the clubhouse.

"It was a slip," Morgan said.

"Yeah, like you slipped when you swung at that pitch in the dirt yesterday," Perez shouted.

Pete and Joe. Those two could get everybody in the locker room going. Funny thing, that's exactly what Sparky had hoped for when he put Joe's locker next to Pete's. That was in 1972, when the Reds traded for Joe. Nobody in Cincinnati liked the trade, not even Sparky.

The Reds traded Lee May, a team leader and powerful hitter, and Tommy Helms, a Cincinnati boy, for a pack of players, headlined by Joe Morgan.

And who was Joe Morgan? He was no headliner, that's for sure. About the only thing most Cincinnati fans knew about Joe was that he hit .256 the year before. About the only thing that Sparky knew about Joe was that he was supposed to be selfish, moody, and a general pain in the ass. Anyway, that's what the Houston manager said about him. Of course, the Houston manager was Harry Walker—"Harry the Hat" everyone called him—from Pascagoula, Mississippi. Harry the Hat won a batting title in 1947, which coincidentally was the same year that he and his brother Dixie and the St. Louis Cardinals tried to form a league-wide boycott to protest the arrival of Jackie Robinson, the first black man to play in the major leagues in the twentieth century. The boycott was crushed, and Harry the Hat was traded to Philadelphia that May. Walker would say that he mended his ways and opened his heart. But Joe noticed that when he was around, Harry the Hat would say something like, "It will be a black day before I . . . whoops, didn't mean to say that, Joe, you know, figure of speech."

No, Sparky did not like the trade much. But it wasn't his job to like trades . . . it was his job to make do. "I just want you to know that whatever happened in Houston is over," Sparky told Joe when they met. "You get a fresh start here." And he had the clubhouse kids put Joe's stuff in the locker right next to Pete's. Sparky hoped that whatever the hell it was that drove Pete Rose to the baseball edge might rub off on Joe Morgan.

It worked. It worked better than Sparky could have ever dreamed. "Damn, I'm a genius," Sparky would tell friends. Joe Morgan, almost overnight, became best friends with Pete. And Joe Morgan, almost overnight, became one of the best players in baseball. He hit more homers, stole more bases, scored more runs than he had ever done before. "That little man can do everything," Sparky said, and he had real wonder in his voice. The next year, 1973, Joe was even better. Year after that, 1974, Joe was even better than that.

He really could do everything. Joe could beat teams more ways than anyone else around. Take 1974. Joe had a .427 on-base percentage, which led the league. On-base percentage is probably the most important single baseball statistic because it tells you how often a player gets on base (and conversely, perhaps more importantly, how rarely he makes an out). While Joe had never batted .300—which was what the fans and reporters mostly cared about—he had reached base more than 40 percent of the time each of his years with the Reds. He drew 120 walks in 1974, second in the league. He stole 58 bases, third in the league. He hit 22 home runs—one of those to beat the Dodgers late in the year when the Reds were still fighting for the championship. He won the Gold Glove for his superior defense at second base. And his attitude? "Smartest player I ever coached," Sparky gushed endlessly to reporters about the greatness of Joe Morgan. Sparky overflowed with the faith of the converted.

How much of Joe's transformation was inspired by his pal Pete Rose? Well, Pete did have a way of getting inside people. "You had to be around Pete every day to understand," Joe would say. "We all loved baseball. Doggie, Johnny, me—we all loved the game. But I think any of us would tell you that Pete loved it a little bit more. It changed me to be around that."

Something black and primal drove Pete Rose. Take the All-Star thing. In 1970, they played the All-Star Game in Cincinnati, and the game stretched into extra innings. In the twelfth, Pete led off second, and his teammate Jim Hickman cracked a single to center. Pete never hesitated—that was something he always told his teammates, never pause, never doubt, never hesitate, never slow down—and he rounded third and raced home. Sportswriters in the morning editions around the country were split in their descriptions between "snorting bull" and "rolling train." Amos Otis, the American League center fielder, scooped up the ball and made a strong throw home. The ball and Pete reached home plate about the same time. But Pete was bigger. He smashed into catcher Ray Fosse, busted the poor kid's shoulder, sent the baseball flying, and defiantly scored the game-winning run. The crash would take on more meaning because Ray Fosse was only twenty-three and the most promising young catcher in the game; he was never quite the same after. More than thirty years later, he would still wake up with the echoing pain of that collision ringing in his shoulder. To add a little irony to it all, Pete had had Fosse to his house the night before for dinner, though Pete never saw any irony at all in it. Pete was the kind of guy who would invite you to dinner at night and run right through you the next day to win a ball game. It was all part of the deal.

People often asked Pete if he regretted smashing into Fosse—hell, it was just an All-Star Game. It didn't count in the standings. Pete's response was telling. He did not even understand the question. They were playing baseball. His was the winning run. Fosse was blocking the plate. Pete had no choice.

That was the thing Joe picked up from Pete Rose. Everybody wanted to win. Some players needed to win. But Pete really had no choice. He had to hit .300 or he felt like less than a man. He had to get two hundred hits every year or he felt time slipping away. He had to win because his old man, Harry Rose, told him so. Rookie pitcher Pat Darcy would always remember playing Ping-Pong with Pete in the basement of the Rose home. Pat won game after game. And after each game, Rose would shout, "Again!" and then, "Again!" game after game, hour after hour, until sweat soaked through his shirt, and Darcy realized that no matter how many times he beat Pete Rose, there would be another game and another for all eternity. And that's when Pete Rose beat him. Yes, Sparky was smart to put Joe's locker next to Pete's.

"You do know that Ali let the bum hang around," Morgan was saying. "You are smart enough to realize that, right?"

Rose smiled. "All I know," he said, "is the white guy went fifteen rounds with the champ. We're athletes too, Joe! We're athletes too!"

Sparky Anderson sat behind the desk in his spring training office, and he opened his Bible. He read from the book of Matthew. "Drive out those demons," Matthew said. Sparky had George Foster on his mind. George was a young outfielder, and he had talent. Baseballs jumped off his bat, but Sparky thought there was something soft about him, something that held him back. Baseball was a game to be played hard and rough. When Sparky was young, he worked as batboy for a local team for only one reason: so he could steal equipment for games in the neighborhood. That's what baseball meant to Sparky. He wanted players who wanted to play ball so badly, they would steal the bats off the rack and balls right out of the burlap bag.

Did George love baseball that much? It was hard to tell. He hardly ever even talked. He didn't drink, didn't smoke, didn't womanize, as far as Sparky could tell about those things. George didn't do much of anything that ballplayers do. George read his Bible all the time (*all the time*), and it made Sparky nervous. He was, as the saying went, searching for himself. George even went to see a hypnotist. The guy put George under and then asked him all kinds of crazy questions, and you know what he found? He found that George had this latent fear of getting hit in the head with a pitch. Good information. Ninety-eight percent of all baseball players had a latent fear of getting hit in the head with a pitch. Sparky thought it was about damned time George found himself.

"Hey," Sparky called out. "Chaplain. Can you come in here?"

Wendell Deyo walked into the office. Wendell became team chaplain in 1974—he was the first team chaplain the Cincinnati Reds ever had. It was his idea. Wendell had been an athlete in college—baseball, football, whatever he could play—and he found his faith when his best friend died in Vietnam. He found that in his own life, faith and sports blended together; he wanted to help athletes bridge the physical and the spiritual. He lived near Cincinnati, so he reached out to the Reds. It was, as they say, a mixed blessing.

"Hey, what the hell is this?" Joe Morgan shouted out when Wendell held his first chapel service in the Cincinnati clubhouse. Pete joined in the shouting, and it did not do much for the atmosphere. Wendell moved the chapel into the weight room, since none of the players ever went in there anyway. That did not calm things down much. After a few weeks, Dick Wagner—the man Cincinnati columnist Tom Callahan called "Howsam's Halderman"—called Wendell to his office. Wagner started yelling before Wendell could sit down.

"What the fuck are you doing to my team?" he said by way of introduction. And then: "Listen, I come from a business where I once walked into my boss's office, and he was screwing his secretary on his desk. You know what I did? I quietly backed away and walked out and never said another word about it. That's my background. And that's the kind of company we run here. And I don't need you messing up my players with your talk about God. Am I being clear?"

Well, Wendell had to admit: Wagner was being clear. The Reds wanted an environment where bosses could diddle secretaries on desks without being sermonized. Still, Wendell stuck around—he had his mission. And he found that some players were beginning to seek him out. The player who reached out to him most was George Foster. The kid longed for peace. He longed for reason. And he also longed for playing time; Sparky would not let him off the bench.

"I can't help you get playing time," Wendell said. "But I can help you be closer to God and help you deal with what he has given you." George understood. They became friends. Sparky knew it.

"Chaplain," Sparky said as Wendell sat down, "can I ask you something?"

"Of course, Sparky."

"I'm reading this here Bible, and they're talking about all these demons. Matthew's talking about demons. Are these like real demons, or are they like, you know, symbols for something?"

Wendell smiled. He had not expected a biblical question.

"Well, Sparky, I think they're real. You know, there's a war going on, good and evil, and the demons are evil, the evil that must be cast out."

"Oh, sure," Sparky said softly. "I see. You know, I try to read this Bible here, and I sometimes have questions. I'm hoping, if it's okay, I can ask you some of those questions from time to time."

"Of course, Sparky," Wendell said, as he stood to leave. "Of course. Anytime."

"Oh, Chaplain, one more thing," Sparky said. Wendell turned. And Sparky said: "Don't turn George Foster into a fucking religious freak. He's fucking soft enough now."

April 6, 1975
SHARONVILLE, OHIO

Sparky's coaches hated the Sharonville Holiday Inn. Well, it just did not make any sense. Why in the hell were they living in a hotel in some bedroom community that was a pain-in-the-ass thirty-minute drive from Riverfront Stadium in downtown Cincinnati? There were perfectly good hotels right across the street from the ballpark. They were baseball men; it just didn't make sense. Of course, the coaches did know why they were living out in Sharonville.

"Jeff's there," Sparky said. "And we go where Jeff goes."

"But," they said to him, "we're talking an hour of driving back and forth on Interstate 75."

"Jeff's there," Sparky said. "And we go where Jeff goes."

Jeff was Jeff Ruby, the Holiday Inn manager. Sparky loved that kid. It didn't take a psychologist to figure it out: Jeff was the son he had wanted Lee to be. Sparky would never forget having lunch at the old

Holiday Inn, one that was near the ballpark, and he saw one of the hotel employees leaning on his mop, not doing a thing, the sort of laziness that always set off Sparky. He thought America was sinking because of shiftlessness—"How long will thou sleep, O sluggard? When wilt thou arise out of thy sleep?"—and he was just about to say something to this sluggard when he heard that voice, dripping with New Jersey: "Hey, pally! If you can lean, you can clean! Get moving!"

That was Jeff Ruby, a mouthy Jewish kid who had gone to Cornell. Sparky called him "bubula"—Yiddish for "babe"—and when Jeff transferred out to Sharonville so he could be manager of his own Holiday Inn, well, Sparky transferred out there with him. It would not be a baseball season without Jeff. And he didn't give a damn if his coaches had to drive a few extra minutes.

"Bubula," Sparky whispered to Jeff over dinner that night. (That was another thing: Sparky often whispered when he talked to Jeff, like they were sharing a secret.) "People don't know, bubula. They think they know this team, they think they know the Big Red Machine, but they don't know anything. Bubula, we're going to be good. We're going to be really good."

Jeff smiled. He'd heard versions of this speech before. Every year, the day before the opener, they would have dinner, and every year, the day before the opener, Sparky would predict that the Reds would win the World Series. So far it had not happened. So far, the Machine had finished every season in disappointment. But there was an edge to Sparky's voice this time.

"Remember, bubula," Sparky was saying, "in life you don't treat people the same. You don't treat Humpty Dumpty like you treat King Tut. Don't fool yourself about people. Some people will let you down in life. And you can't let them let you down. Do you understand? You have to get those people out of the way. You have to follow your stars.

"I'm telling you," he continued, "the stars will win it for us this time."

MARSHALL

April 7 to April 19

> *Some people choose the city.*
> *Some others choose the good old family home.*

—ELTON JOHN, "PHILADELPHIA FREEDOM"

Opening Day, April 7, 1975

CINCINNATI
REDS VS. DODGERS

Baseball has always been a game of myth and fables. One of the most powerful of these is that a career military man named Abner Doubleday, the man who aimed the cannon that fired the first shot in defense of Fort Sumter in the Civil War, invented the game. Doubleday, it was said, sketched out the game's rules and played the first games on Elihu Phinney's farm in a picturesque New York town called Cooperstown. It was a sweet fable, no less so for being entirely untrue. The real origins of baseball are murky and serpentine. Baseball probably derives from games like cricket and rounders and perhaps a game called oina played in Romania during the fourteenth century. Baseball surely gained its shape and rhythms in the small towns across the young American nation, where people played their own version of bat-and-ball games. Civil War soldiers played base ball—two words, back then—all over the nation.

There are no mysteries, though, about where baseball—the professional game, the one we know, the American pastime, peanuts and Cracker Jack—was invented. That game sprang to life in Cincinnati in 1869, and it sprang to life for the most American of reasons: a group of Cincinnati business leaders grew tired of watching the local baseball team get their heads kicked in game after game. They had to get better players. And so they decided to pay the players money. Of course, teams had been paying players for years, but always covertly; there seemed to be something unseemly, especially in the years after the war, about paying men to play a gentlemen's sport. The Cincinnati businessmen decided there was something quite a bit more unseemly about losing. They paid a New York jeweler named Harry Wright $1,200 to play outfield, and they asked him to put together a baseball team that could stick it to the elitists from New York and other eastern cities.

Harry Wright traveled to New York and other eastern cities and hired a few of those elitists (including his brother George, widely viewed as the best player in the world). Years later, Harry Ellard, a Cincinnati journalist, published the list of players on that first professional team, their jobs, and their salaries.

Harry Wright	center fielder	jeweler	$1,200
Asa Brainard	pitcher	insurance	$1,100
Douglas Allison	catcher	marble cutter	$800
Charles H. Gould	first baseman	bookkeeper	$800
Charles J. Sweasy	second baseman	hatter	$800
Fred A. Waterman	third baseman	insurance	$1,000
Andrew J. Leonard	left fielder	hatter	$800
George Wright	shortstop	engraver	$1,400
Calvin A. McVey	right fielder	piano maker	$800
Richard Hurley	substitute	unknown	$600

It was $9,300 well spent. They called themselves the Cincinnati Red Stockings, named after the gaudy red stockings they wore. They traveled the country to play the best teams (charging 50¢ per ticket), and they were unbeatable. They won all 57 games they played in 1869. The games were not close. The Red Stockings beat the Atlantic Baseball Club 76–5, and they beat the Pacific Baseball Club 66–5. Rough statistics were kept—George Wright hit .633 with 49 home runs. The Red Stockings' most daunting player may have been their pitcher, Asa Brainard. In those days, pitchers were supposed to pitch the ball underhanded—this is where the term "pitcher" came from—and they were supposed to let batters hit the ball. Of course, from the start, pitchers always looked for an edge. Brainard figured a way to sneak in a little extra wrist snap, which put spin on the ball and made it significantly harder to hit. Many people believe the term "ace" for outstanding pitcher began with Asa Brainard's first name.

For a moment, in that year when Ulysses Grant became president and Susan B. Anthony formed the National Women's Suffrage Association, Cincinnati was the hub of baseball. The moment did not last. By the end of the year, there were more than a dozen professional baseball teams, and after that, two dozen, and soon Cincinnati found itself priced out of the high-stakes game it created. The Reds, as they became known, joined the National League in 1876, but they won just nine of their sixty-five games. And soon after, they were thrown out of the National League because beer was sold in the stadium on Sundays.

Baseball years were trying after that. The Reds did get back into the National League, and they won the World Series in 1919 against the famed Chicago Black Sox, the team that got paid by gamblers to throw the Series. The Reds won the championship again in 1940, the year before America went to war. It didn't satisfy anyone. Toward the end of the "Red Scare" of the McCarthy years and thereafter, from 1956 to 1960, the Reds changed their name to the more patriotic "Redlegs," but the Redlegs drew so poorly that there was talk about moving them to another city. The Reds were good in the 1960s—they won a pennant in 1961 and almost won another in 1964—and the

Machine won more games than any other team in the early 1970s, but those Reds were never the best. The only time they were first was on opening day—the first baseball game of every season was played in Cincinnati, a tip of the cap to the first professional baseball team.

"I don't want to just start first," Sparky Anderson said to reporters. "I want to finish first."

Sparky Anderson stopped on the way to the ballpark to buy three hibachi grills. It was always cold on opening day in Cincinnati. As he drove, Sparky reminded himself again not to make any guarantees. He had to control himself.

It was never easy for him. The trouble was that Sparky was two men at heart. He was Georgie Anderson, son of a housepainter, a hardscrabble kid who would read the Bible now and then and lie out at the pool every day and daydream back to the happiest days of his life, his young days in South Dakota, in a little town called Bridgewater, where the jail was never locked and his father would spend Halloween sitting inside the family outhouse with a shotgun to be sure nobody stole it. Georgie Anderson had a heart of gold and a quiet nature. Georgie could not send a steak back if it was overcooked; he didn't want to hurt anybody's feelings. Georgie would let the phone ring because he did not feel like talking. Georgie would drink milk to soothe the ulcer that burned inside. Georgie spent every day of the off-season walking through his yard in California, pulling any weeds that dared to appear. Georgie sometimes felt like he could be happy for the rest of his life pulling weeds.

Few people knew Georgie Anderson. They knew Sparky Anderson, manager of the Big Red Machine, purveyor of wit, guardian of baseball's tradition, soother of ill feelings, botcher of the English language, defender of an America gone by. And as Sparky Anderson, he could not stop talking. He could not stop entertaining. He could not stop making bold predictions. Because if there was one thing that

Sparky knew completely, it was that he had the best damned baseball team that had ever been put forth on God's green earth. He would get going on Johnny Bench or Pete Rose or Joe Morgan, especially Joe. He loved that little man, and well, he would sometimes start crying in the middle of a sentence, that's how much he loved those guys. They could play baseball better than he ever dreamed, better than anyone else, and still they listened to Sparky, they played hard for Sparky, they kept their hair trimmed and their uniforms clean and their minds on the game, all for Sparky. He wanted to tell the whole world about them. He wanted to shout out their names. He needed to guarantee victory because that's what they deserved. Victory.

Trouble was, year after year, he predicted the Reds would win the World Series, and then the Reds did not win the World Series and he felt terrible. He had made his stars look like losers, like chumps. Every year, he told himself to shut up, let the season play out, let everyone see for themselves the wonders of the Big Red Machine. But then some loudmouth sportswriter would talk about the Dodgers, and Sparky would say, "The Dodgers? Hell, the Dodgers ain't even in our league." And it would start all over again. Sparky could not help himself.

"I'm not going to guarantee anything this time," he had told the press. Of course, a couple of days later he had said, "If the Dodgers are going to beat us, they're going to have to win a hundred games." And then for the column in the *Cincinnati Post* he wrote (through his ghostwriter Earl Lawson), "We've got a good ball club, a real good one, and I think if we stay injury free we'll still be playing in October." It was another guarantee.

Now it was opening day, and his Reds were playing those Dodgers, and Sparky knew that they would give him a microphone and have him address the sellout crowd. It was a bad place to put Sparky Anderson, and he knew it.

President Gerald Ford could not make it to Cincinnati for opening day, just like he could not make it to Cincinnati for Johnny Bench's wedding. Vietnam was collapsing. The king of Saudi Arabia had been shot. The world would not stop. Ford liked baseball all right, though he had gotten some grief for supposedly saying that he watched a lot of baseball on the radio. Ford felt certain he did not say that. He tried to make up for it when he was given a season pass from Major League Baseball and had his key speechwriter, Robert Orben, write a few "ad-libs" for the occasion.

"I played football in college, but I also had a great interest in baseball," Orben wrote for Ford. "There's something about a sport where you don't have to wear a helmet that appeals to me." Ford, noting that baseball players do wear helmets, crossed out the line. He did not want to be mocked again.

"There are a lot of similarities between baseball and politics," Orben wrote and President Ford said. "One of the worst things you can hear in baseball is: 'You're out.' Same thing in politics."

With Ford back in Washington, the designated politician of the day was Robert Taft, the Ohio senator and grandson of former president and baseball pioneer William Howard Taft. In his younger days, William Howard Taft had played baseball in Cincinnati—it was said that he could hit with power—but his real contribution to the game was that he became the first president to throw out the first pitch at a game. That was 1910. A legend was built that day: The story went that Taft—the heaviest American president—grew uncomfortable in his small seat and stood up after the top half of the seventh inning. When he stood, everyone in the stadium stood, and that was the first seventh-inning stretch. That story, like most great baseball stories, is probably not true.

Robert Taft rolled into the ballpark in a horse-drawn carriage. He looked good, everyone thought, considering that a biting wind blew through the stadium and Taft had suffered a heart attack only two months earlier. The senator wore a giant button that read, Go REDS, BEAT THE BUMS. He threw out the first pitch to Johnny Bench. Everyone cheered. Jim Lovell, the astronaut who brought *Apollo 13* home after an explosion, stood to be recognized. Everyone cheered again. The largest crowd ever to see a baseball game in Cincinnati—52,526 people—crammed into their seats at Riverfront Stadium. Sparky was handed a microphone.

"I can honestly say this is the finest baseball team we have ever brought north," he said. "We're going to make you proud."

Across the way, in the other dugout, the Dodgers relief pitcher Mike Marshall shook his head. "Well," he muttered, "it's good to see that Sparky's as full of shit as ever."

Here was the lineup that Sparky Anderson sent out to face the Los Angeles Dodgers that opening day, along with the ages and approximate salaries of those players.

Pete Rose	left fielder	33 years old	$150,000
Joe Morgan	second baseman	31 years old	$120,000
Johnny Bench	catcher	27 years old	$175,000
Tony Perez	first baseman	32 years old	$110,000
Dave Concepcion	shortstop	26 years old	$75,000
Cesar Geronimo	center fielder	27 years old	$26,000
Ken Griffey	right fielder	24 years old	$18,000
John Vukovich	third baseman	27 years old	$16,000
Don Gullett	pitcher	24 years old	$31,000

It was a good lineup, a great lineup even, though it had holes. Concepcion was not a powerful enough hitter to be batting fifth.

Griffey was too good a hitter and too fast a base runner to be batting seventh. And Vukovich . . . Sparky did not want him in the lineup at all.

The Reds were playing in what everyone expected to be the toughest division in baseball, the National League West. Most sportswriters thought the Dodgers would win the division and, after that, the World Series. The Reds were picked second, but many people expected the Atlanta Braves to contend too; the Braves had great pitching led by the knuckleballer Phil Niekro and a young pitcher named Buzz Capra. The Houston Astros had been a pretty good team in 1974, though tragedy struck in January when star pitcher Don Wilson was found dead in his Ford Thunderbird, which had been running inside the garage. The San Francisco Giants, after years of success, were on the downturn, and the San Diego Padres were expected to be routinely awful. Most people were convinced that it would come down to Los Angeles and Cincinnati, and the teams were playing each other seven times in the first eleven days.

"Good," Sparky said. "We might as well find out right away which team is best."

George Foster stared out at the field. It was the fourteenth inning, and he was still on the bench. "I've seen more baseball games than any player alive," he had told reporters. "Why, I even know some of the players personally." George squeezed a rubber ball again and again. He was twenty-six years old, and he had been beaten up by baseball. Lately he had come to believe he would never get his chance. Foster knew that admitting defeat was the first step on the road to perdition, but what else could he do? He had been with the Reds for four years, and nothing changed. They hardly noticed him. Sparky never even looked his way. Foster read his Bible every day in search of answers. "Be patient therefore, brethren, unto the coming of the Lord." Yes. The Lord was coming. But how patient could a brother be?

Sparky thought Foster was weak. Foster knew that. It was funny, really, if you thought about it. Sparky was five-foot-nine, maybe, white hair, wrinkled, tired under the eyes—the guy looked like somebody's grandfather even though he was just forty-one years old. And Foster was a physical marvel, the very picture of strength. He stood six-foot-one, had a twenty-eight-inch waist, arms roughly as big around as Sparky's legs. During batting practice, he crushed the longest home runs on the team. Nobody on the team was stronger than George Foster. But Sparky meant something else.

Sparky, at that moment, was looking up and down the bench but avoiding Foster's eyes. Foster could not help but feel a bit amused. The April wind chilled the dugout. Charcoal burned on Sparky's new hibachi grills, and players gathered around to warm their hands. Gray smoke blew out of the dugout; the place smelled like a barbecue pit. Sparky was stuck. It was the fourteenth inning, two outs, the score was tied, and the Reds outfielder Cesar Geronimo was on third base. Sparky wanted to win this game badly, wanted to send his message to the Dodgers. The Reds pitcher was due up, so Sparky had to choose a pinch hitter. He had only two choices. He could send up Doug Flynn, a rookie who had never played in a major league game before. Or he could send up Foster. George studied Sparky's face; he could see how badly Sparky wanted to go with someone else.

"Foster," Sparky finally yelled. "Grab a bat."

It was done. George felt his insides shake. George figured that at his age he was not supposed to feel nerves. He had been in the big leagues, on and off, since he was twenty years old, and these jittery moments were for kids. Still, he felt as nervous as he had felt on his first school day in California when he walked into Roosevelt Elementary School and saw that he was the only African American in the class. His family had moved to Hawthorne from Alabama—in Alabama, George did not know any white people. Except, he said, policemen.

Now those childhood nerves gripped him again. It is just one at-bat, he told himself. It is just one game. He tried to tell himself that. Only, his mind would not let go. This was not just one at-bat. This was not just one game. This was his career. This was his life. If he could come through here, crack a single up the middle, crush the baseball off the wall, drive home the winning run, give Sparky Anderson the win he so desperately wanted and needed, well, his life might change. He might get to play more. He might convince Sparky that he was not weak, that he could be a star in this game if given the chance.

And if he failed? Well, he could not fail. Sparky *was* wrong about him. George was not weak. He was not soft. No, he did not drink or smoke or screw every groupie who loitered around the team hotel. But, George was sure, those were not things that made a man. A man was . . . well, all George Foster really knew was that he could not fail. He would drive Geronimo in. He would win the game. He would not fail.

The Dodgers pitcher was Charlie Hough, a twenty-seven-year-old man from Honolulu whose career had ground to a halt in the minor leagues until he learned how to throw a knuckleball. There is something mystical about the knuckleball. Baseball is a game of speed. To a fan in the stands, everything moves fast: the pitches, the crack of the bat, the runners, the fielders, the umpires' calls. The knuckleball moves slowly. It doesn't fit the eye, doesn't keep up with the pace of the game. The knuckleball pitcher hardly seems to be trying. But the knuckleballer isn't going for speed. He is trying to throw the baseball so that it does not rotate—when thrown well, the ball dances and quivers to the whims of air resistance, bouncing like a balloon in the wind. When thrown well, a knuckleball is not only impossible to hit with a baseball bat, it's darned near impossible to catch with a padded mitt. Bob Uecker, the old Braves catcher, used to say that the secret to catching a knuckleball was to wait until it stopped rolling and then pick it up.

George Foster stepped into the batter's box and watched a couple of knuckleballs float by. Nerves were supposed to go away once the action began, that's what everyone said, but Foster only felt his hands shake. He saw a knuckleball coming, and he swung hard. He topped the ball. No! He saw the ball rolling slowly down the third-base line, fair territory. No! Foster started to run to first base, and he felt like he was stomping grapes, he was barely moving at all. He had been exercising in the dugout all game long to stay warm, to prepare for this moment, and now his legs felt cramped. It was like that dream, the one where you run and run but you stay in place, you gain no ground. Still, he ran.

Foster could not see what was happening behind him. Geronimo raced for home; he would score only if Foster could make it safely to first. The Dodgers' third baseman, Ron Cey, rushed forward—well, he sort of rushed; Cey's wobbly running style had earned him the nickname "the Penguin"—and scooped up the ball and threw hard to first base. The baseball and George Foster reached first base at the same time. First-base umpire Paul Pryor had been a minor league baseball player for a few years, and he had been an umpire in the big leagues since 1961. He had made calls like these too many times to even think about them. It was all instinct.

"Safe," Pryor shouted.

The Reds won the game. The largest crowd ever to see a baseball game in Cincinnati stood and stomped in the chill. Reds players rushed out to jump on Geronimo and Foster. A couple of the Dodgers players rushed Paul Pryor for a moment, then angrily slipped away. "I know in my heart we had the man," the Dodgers' first baseman, Steve Garvey, said, but nobody around cared much about Garvey's sour grapes.

"George beat the throw by that far," Sparky Anderson said in the clubhouse, and he held out his shaky hands for everyone to see. "My hands, they always shake," he said happily.

Foster cheerfully talked to reporters. Pat Darcy, the Reds' rookie pitcher who held the Dodgers scoreless in the thirteenth and fourteenth innings, looked over the bottle of champagne that Joe Morgan gave him as a gift. "From my own personal stock," Morgan said. Pete Rose told reporter after reporter how this was a big win, huge, enormous.

And Joe Morgan, the Reds' star second baseman, leaned back contentedly on his stool and pulled out a cigar. "The Dodgers," he said, "can't possibly believe they are better than us."

April 9, 1975

CINCINNATI
REDS VS. DODGERS
Team record: 1–0

They were called Reds, yes, but they were the most conservative outfit in sports. Bob Howsam and Sparky Anderson created this seemingly endless list of rules. Everyone had to keep his hair short—the reliever Pedro Borbon had been charged with the role of team barber. Everyone had to wear black shoes, all black; clubhouse boys were responsible for blacking out any white logos with shoe polish. Everyone had to wear his pant legs at the knees so the red socks would be seen. No one could wear a beard. No one could be seen in public without a jacket and tie. No one could drink any alcohol on the team plane. And so on. And so on.

The thing that separated the Reds, though, was not the rules themselves. It was the way the players took the rules. "What the hell would Bob Howsam or Sparky have said if I decided to wear my hair long?" Pete Rose would ask. "What would they have done if Johnny Bench decided to wear his pants low? What if Joe Morgan had wanted to wear a mustache? What do you think they would have done? They would not have done shit."

Perhaps. But the men of the Machine did not break the rules.

They did not bend the rules. No, it was the opposite: they embraced the rules, and in a strange way, they even loved the rules. The Reds players saw themselves as defenders of another time, a better time, a time when the great St. Louis Cardinals player Stan Musial would smoke under stairwells so that no kid would see him. The Reds players like Johnny and Joe and even Pete saw themselves as baseball players from that time before America lost wars, before the college kids burned draft cards, before *Sports Illustrated* ran a cover photograph of Chicago White Sox first baseman Dick Allen with a cigarette dangling out of his mouth.

"We need more heroes, especially for our young people," Johnny Bench told the *St. Petersburg Times* sports editor Hubert Mizell. "Even if we have to keep 'em a little naive, it's worth it. . . . I was seventeen years old before I knew that any major league ballplayer smoked or drank. It didn't hurt [me] either."

Yes, those Reds players had a pretty good idea what a ballplayer was supposed to be like: he was supposed to drink milk and say "gosh" and hit home runs for sick children in hospitals. And while none of the Reds players did those things, well, they came close enough. Anyway, they kept their hair short. They acted the way a ballplayer was supposed to act.

Mike Marshall, on the other hand, did not. Marshall was the Dodgers' relief pitcher, and he was the one guy who scared the living hell out of the Reds. He was just so . . . odd. There was nothing at all physically intimidating about the man. Marshall was thirty-two years old, balding, no taller than five-foot-ten. His muttonchop sideburns curved toward the corner of his mouth, and he wore a bushy mustache, and he seemed to be trying to look like Alexander II of Russia. Marshall did not throw hard at all; it was his tepid fastball that inspired Jim Bouton, in his classic book *Ball Four*, to invent "Doubleday's First Law": "If you throw a fastball with insufficient speed, someone will smack it out of the park with a stick."

So why did Marshall terrify the Reds? For one thing, he was a doctor; anyway, that's what people called him. He wasn't the sort of doctor the Reds players could appreciate; he did not set casts or pull tonsils. He had earned his doctorate in kinesiology. When games ended, he shunned groupies of all ages and shapes and spent his free time with researchers. During the off-season, he taught classes at Michigan State. The topic of his dissertation was "Classifying Adolescent Males for Motor Proficiency Norms." It made Marshall angry when reporters got that wrong.

Dr. Mike Marshall was less a baseball player and more like, say, Bobby Fischer, the American chess genius who that same week abdicated his place as world chess champion rather than face off against the Soviet Union's Anatoly Karpov. Fischer seemed to be standing on some sort of principle, though nobody quite knew what principle or where he stood on it.

Marshall, too, seemed to stand on baffling principles. For instance, he refused to sign autographs, even for kids. Especially for kids. "As an athlete I am no one to be idolized," he told *Sports Illustrated*. "I will not perpetuate that hoax."

The Reds thought: What kind of Communist would not sign an autograph for a kid? It was un-American. The Reds players believed wholeheartedly that baseball players not only deserved to be idolized by kids, but *should* be idolized by kids. That's how it was when America was strong. Kids looked up to the pitcher Walter Johnson, and then they went off to fight World War I. Kids looked up to Babe Ruth, and then they endured the Depression. Kids looked up to Lou Gehrig and Bob Feller and Joe DiMaggio, and then they went to fight again in World War II.

"With Watergate, and with politicians under attack and all kinds of investigations, it's important that the young people have somebody to look up to," Bench told *New York Daily News* columnist Dick Young, and he was speaking for the whole Reds team. "Maybe it sounds corny to a few people, but that's what made this country."

Still, none of that quite gets to the heart of why Marshall so paralyzed the Reds. They could deal with his quirkiness, his scholarship, his subversive attitude toward autographs, even his bizarre notion of baseball being insignificant in the grand scheme of things. But there was one other thing about Marshall that spooked them.

That son of a gun could pitch every . . . single . . . day.

"He can't keep it up," Pete Rose said again and again during the 1974 season. The Dodgers were a good baseball team that year, but the Reds felt sure they were better. Even as the Dodgers pulled ahead in the race, the Reds felt sure that they would win in the end. General manager Bob Howsam would sit in his office and compare his Reds players to Dodgers players, man to man, and it was like they said on the Snickers commercial of the time: no matter how you sliced it, it came up peanuts. The Reds had better players. The difference was Marshall. He seemed inescapable. The Dodgers beat the Reds in back-to-back games in April—Marshall pitched in both games. In three nasty games in Los Angeles (the fans threw garbage and batteries at Rose), the Dodgers swept the Reds—Marshall pitched in all three games. The Dodgers beat the Reds three out of four back in Cincinnati in early July, and Marshall pitched in the three victories.

It was crazy. It was unprecedented. Marshall pitched in 66 of 97 games before the All-Star break. He pitched two out of every three days. And his arm never seemed to tire. His body never seemed to break down. There was something wrong about it, something unnatural—a pitcher was supposed to throw his pitches, then grab a beer, dump his elbow in a bucket of ice, and deal with pain until his next time out. Marshall did not seem to feel pain. He seemed invulnerable. He announced that he had discovered secrets about pitching. He claimed that he had conducted experiments that proved a pitcher using the correct form could throw every day. But he did not need to show his experiments; he was a living example. In late June, early July, Marshall pitched in 13 straight games, a record. In September, Marshall pitched in 18 games as the Dodgers held off the Reds. Marshall pitched in 106 games in 1974, which beat the old record by an amazing 14 games. And Marshall held the old record too.

"They didn't beat us," Rose told reporters after the season ended and the Reds had lost. "They can't beat us. We beat ourselves." Only it wasn't true. The Dodgers did beat them. Marshall beat them. He won the Cy Young Award. He finished third in the Most Valuable Player voting, behind his teammate Steve Garvey (though every Reds player knew Marshall was more valuable). Then, during the off-season, Marshall announced that he had made some more discoveries and that in 1975 he would no longer pitch two out of three days—he would pitch three out of four instead. When asked about beating the Reds, he smiled and reportedly said: "They're like facing a high school team." He later claimed to be misquoted, though he did not disagree with the sentiment.

"We've got to get that son of a bitch," Pete Rose shouted on opening day when Marshall came into the game. Only they could not get him. Marshall pitched five scoreless innings, and he looked over to the Reds dugout and smiled.

Now it was the second game, and Marshall came in again. The Reds loaded the bases against him, but could not score. In the eighth inning, the Reds again loaded the bases, and again they could not score. What was this Marshall voodoo? The Dodgers led 3–2 going into the ninth inning. Marshall was still pitching.

Then it happened. Ken Griffey led off the inning with a long triple to right-center field. Darrel Chaney, everybody's favorite turd on the team (Chaney actually had "Turd" T-shirts made for his teammates, and everybody loved him; Chaney's problem was that he could not hit), punched a single to center field and Griffey scored. The turds had tied the game! After a bunt moved Chaney to second, Sparky Anderson needed a pinch hitter again, and he called on his shortstop, Davey Concepcion, who was trying to overcome a lingering groin injury. It was an odd choice. Marshall had gotten Davey out nine straight times—Davey could not even hit the ball out of the infield against the guy. Concepcion was entirely spooked.

As soon as Davey realized that he was going to face Marshall, he became agitated. He got up and started moving around, trying to get his blood going. It was forty degrees, his body felt chilled. He could not get loose. He finally ran downstairs to the team sauna. He stepped into what the papers called the "100-degree swelter" and he maniacally exercised until his body felt loose. Then he raced back upstairs, and when he stepped into the batter's box to face Marshall, sweat poured off of him. Marshall threw his fastball inside, and it jammed Concepcion, but Davey was loose enough and strong enough to bloop it to center field for a single. Chaney scored. The Reds beat Mike Marshall.

"We finally beat that son of a bitch," Pete shouted in the clubhouse after the game.

"Luck," Marshall said with conviction.

In San Diego, Gary Nolan felt the nerves again. Damn, these butterflies were becoming a habit. He made it through spring training, he won his old pitching job back, he even began to feel a bit like his old self. That beautiful pitching arrogance—that little voice that told him that nobody could hit him—had begun to sing again. Only now he was pitching in his first real game in almost two years, facing his first real batter since 1973, and he could not hear that little voice. He reminded himself that he was still a young man—he would not turn twenty-seven for another month. His arm, though, felt biblical.

"I feel relaxed," he had lied to the *Cincinnati Enquirer* baseball beat writer Bob Hertzel before the game. "It's almost like I haven't been away." That's how he wanted to feel. That's what he wanted people to think. But it wasn't true; he had been away, and he was a different pitcher now. He could not throw pitches by hitters. He had to trick them, befuddle them, make them feel uneasy somehow. He thought about what the great old pitcher Warren Spahn said: "Hitting is timing. Pitching is upsetting timing." Yes, that's what Gary had to do now. He had developed this new changeup, one that seemed to hesitate before reaching the plate. That changeup was now Gary Nolan's best pitch. He had to upset timing.

The first San Diego batter he faced was Enzo Hernandez, a quick little Venezuelan shortstop. Hernandez played a good shortstop, but he was probably the worst hitter in the National League. He hit .232 in 1974 with zero home runs—that was probably his best offensive season. Gary officially had faced Hernandez twenty-six times and allowed just two cheap singles. Hernandez could not hit the old Gary Nolan with a tennis racket and a book of hints.

But Gary was not his old self. There was a part of him, a small part, that wanted to dream that one day his fastball would just show up again, like a high school friend. He stared down Enzo Hernandez, and he threw his best fastball, and Hernandez jumped all over it, crushed it, a double. And Gary stood on the mound and shook his head. There were no dreams left, and there was no going back. This was going to be a whole new life.

April 14, 1975

LOS ANGELES
REDS VS. DODGERS
Team record: 4–2

Pete Rose hated playing baseball in Los Angeles. That was what he thought as he stood at the base of the left-field wall and watched Ron Cey's home run float over his head. The fans taunted him. They threw stuff at him. They insulted him. They called his mother names. Pete usually loved this stuff. But there was something different about Los Angeles. He could not stand these people. They got into his head.

It drove him mad. Pete took great pride in his toughness; nobody got into his head, nobody, not ever. He learned that from his old man, Harry Rose—Big Pete, they called him—who spent his days working at Fifth Third Bank in Cincinnati and spent his weekends cracking heads with the kids on football fields. Big Pete was still playing semi-pro football when he was forty-two. Everyone told the story of the time Big Pete played a game with a broken leg. If you asked people on the West Side of Cincinnati to name the toughest man in town, two out of three would name you Big Pete Rose.

And Little Pete idolized his old man. During the 1973 playoffs, Pete Rose toppled New York Mets shortstop Bud Harrelson on a double play, and that set off a major fight, turned the whole city of New York against him. Pete shrugged: "My dad didn't raise me to play like a little girl," he told the New York reporters. The next day he hit a game-winning home run in the tenth inning, all while the Mets fans booed ominously.

"How'd you do it, Pete?" those reporters asked.

"I'm better when they boo," Pete said. "I have been my whole life. Fans better get used to it. The more you hate me, the more I'll beat you."

That was his mantra, his core baseball philosophy: "The more you hate me, the more I'll beat you." When they booed him in Chicago, in Philadelphia, in Houston, in New York, he would have fun with the fans. He would toss a baseball to the fan who booed him loudest. He cracked jokes: "Hey, you don't even *know* my mother." It was fun. But in Los Angeles, the boos felt threatening. He would give baseballs to fans in Los Angeles, and they would throw those balls back at him when he wasn't looking. He would try to talk to the fans, and they would shout him down, throw bottles at him, pour beer on him. Pete hit .077 at Dodger Stadium in 1974.

"What the hell did I ever do to these people?" he asked Steve

Garvey, the Dodgers' first baseman and the most beloved baseball player in Los Angeles. Rose and Garvey played baseball in similar ways—they both hit .300, they both cracked two hundred hits, they both cared about their teams but also about their own statistics. Garvey worked out a complicated program in 1974 designed to get him his two hundred hits. The system involved bunting every so often, punching the ball to right field every so often, and staying in games until the very end even if the scores were lopsided. The system was so precise that Garvey finished with exactly two hundred hits; he got the two hundredth hit on his last at-bat of the season. Rose also had a detailed knowledge of his own statistics; he could tell you off the top of his head his batting average against left-handed pitchers and right-handed pitchers, during the day and at night, on grass fields and on artificial turf. He and Steve Garvey spoke the same language.

"These people hate me like I killed their mothers," Pete said.

"You play for the wrong team," Garvey told him.

"No, there's something more," Pete said. "It isn't normal."

Garvey shrugged. The Los Angeles fans loved him. They called him "Captain America." *Sports Illustrated* that week featured him on the cover next to the headline "Proud to Be a Hero." Garvey was a hero: he traveled around the city, spoke to every Optimist Club and in every VFW hall. He told the story of visiting a kid name Ricky in the hospital, a kid who doctors said had an 18 percent chance of living. When Ricky was told that Steve Garvey was there to see him, though, he squeezed Garvey's hand. Not long after that, he walked again. "I knew then," Garvey would tell the teary-eyed people in the crowd, "that Steve Garvey had a place." Yes, he was one of those old-fashioned ballplayers who could heal sick kids.

So maybe that was it: maybe out in Los Angeles people saw the world through the Hollywood prism, maybe they could only see the world as good guys (Clint Eastwood, James Bond, Hawkeye Pierce, Steve Garvey) and bad guys (politicians, Dr. Goldfinger, Frank Burns, Pete Rose). Pete went hitless again, and he watched helplessly as Marshall easily shut down the Reds in the ninth. The Dodgers won the game and moved into a tie for first place.

"You know," Rose mumbled to Sparky Anderson, "maybe I should sit the next one out. I don't feel like I'm helping the team."

Nobody could believe Big Pete's kid was saying that.

The next day was tax day, and Sparky finally had it out with his son Lee. He could not stand it anymore. They had not spoken for more than a year, not since that day in the garage when he told Lee to cut his hair and Lee quietly said, "No."

"Someday you will respect me as your father," Sparky shouted.

"I already do respect you," Lee shouted back.

Well, Sparky could not make any sense out of that. If the boy respected him, he would cut his hair. Right was right. Sparky Anderson would sooner trade away a talented pitcher like Ross Grimsley than allow him to grow his hair long. He would quit managing baseball before he would manage a bunch of long-haired hippies who did not respect the game and the best damned country in the world. A couple of years earlier, Oakland A's owner Charlie O. Finley called Sparky and offered him the manager's job for the two-time World Series champs. Sparky said no, of course. He was too loyal to leave Cincinnati. But even more than that, he could not manage all those wild players in Oakland with their long hair and their mustaches. To Sparky, to many men of his generation, long hair was two steps away from atheism and three steps from anarchy.

He had to break the silence with Lee. The tension was eating him up inside. The team was playing lousy, the media was crowning the Dodgers, his third baseman could not hit, and the toughest goddamned baseball player he ever saw, Pete Rose, was asking to sit out the games in Los Angeles. The season had only just begun, and already it was going down the toilet. Sparky went home to Thousand Oaks to see his family, to confront Lee. He looked at his oldest son, saw the way his hair fell to his shoulders. And the fight began fresh. It was a fight about hair, but, as Sparky would realize years later, it was also a fight about something deeper.

"You're going to be a bum," Sparky yelled at Lee, and the fight went on from there—Sparky would later call it a knockdown, drag-out fight, the worst of his life. When it ended, Lee had retreated to his room, and Sparky had to go to the ballpark, and nothing at all was settled.

"George," his wife, Carol, said as he walked to the car, "if your son committed a murder, would you stand by him?"

"Of course I would," Sparky said. "I'd be there every day."

And she said: "Then why don't you stand beside him in this? Give him your love."

Sparky thought about that. Maybe she was right.

Then he went to the ballpark and watched the Dodgers' pitcher Don Sutton throw a no-hitter against his guys for six full innings. Don Sutton! That cheater. Sparky was sure Sutton was cutting the baseball so that he could make it dive down harder. Sparky had even started his own collection of Don Sutton–engraved baseballs—you could see that he cut the ball in the same spot every time. He planned to show those baseballs to an umpire someday. But today he just watched as Sutton got out after out. Morgan popped up behind the plate. Bench hit a foul pop-up behind the plate—damn, Bench hadn't hit worth a damn since he got married. Perez hit a foul pop-up down the first-base line. Sparky's guys could not even hit the ball into fair territory.

In the seventh inning, Rose hit a harmless fly ball to center. Morgan struck out. Sutton punched the air in joy after striking out Morgan. The thirty thousand or so in the crowd went crazy. Everyone could sense it: Sutton was going to no-hit the Machine. Sparky could not believe the day he was having.

Then Sutton made his one mistake. He was so happy he got Joe Morgan out that he grooved a fastball right down the middle of the plate to Johnny Bench. Bench still knew what to do with belt-high fastballs, and he crushed it over the left-field wall. That blew the shut-out and the no-hitter. But that was the only hit for the Reds. The Dodgers still won the game. The Reds had lost four of five games.

"I wonder if we can beat anybody right now," Sparky told reporters.

Sparky knew who to blame for the bad start. Who else? John Vukovich. His third baseman. Balsa. Sure, Bench wasn't hitting. Perez wasn't hitting. Hell, nobody on the whole team but Morgan was hitting. But that didn't matter: Sparky knew all those guys would come around. But that third baseman was killing him. John Vukovich would never come around.

"Look at the third baseman they have over there," he told his bench coach and right-hand man, George "Shug" Scherger, as he pointed over to the Dodgers' third baseman, Ron Cey, the one every-one called "the Penguin." Now that was a third baseman. He hit with some power. He drove in some runs. He made the diving defensive plays. He did all the things a third baseman was supposed to do, and on top of that he was tough and strong, and damn it all, how was Sparky supposed to beat the Los Angeles Dodgers with a third base-man who was so weak he kept getting the bat knocked out of his hands?

"You tell me," Sparky said to Scherger. "How?" Scherger nodded and shrugged. He had known Sparky for more than twenty years—Scherger was actually Sparky's minor league manager back in Santa Barbara in 1953. He knew Sparky when he was wild, out of control, when he played baseball with more of an edge than any player Scherger had ever known. None of these players would even recognize Sparky back then. He always seemed a beat away from attacking someone—an opposing player, a teammate, an umpire, whoever.

Sparky had harnessed that temper, but he had not lost it. Scherger could see that Sparky was about to lose it. Truth was, Vukovich wasn't hitting too bad—he had a .294 average through the first eight games—and it was too early in the year to start panicking. But Sparky had that look, the look he'd had when he was nineteen years old and wanted to beat up the world. Vukovich was a dead man, and the poor son of a bitch didn't even know it.

On a cold April day in Los Angeles, the Dodgers pitched an old legend, Juan Marichal, in the third game of the series. Marichal had been a great pitcher in the 1960s—he won more than twenty games six times during the decade. Marichal had a most remarkable windup. *Time* magazine once ran a nine-photo sequence of Marichal's pitching delivery. In one of the photos, Marichal's left foot is above his head. In another, Marichal's arms have flailed to the side like he is conducting the Boston Pops. They called him "the Dominican Dandy." But on this day, he was thirty-eight years old, his left leg did not lift as high, his fastball did not rush in as hard. Marichal had not pitched especially well in four years; hitters whispered that the great Marichal had nothing left. Nobody knew it when the game began, but this would be the last time Marichal pitched in the big leagues.

In the second inning, with the game scoreless, Marichal walked Ken Griffey to load the bases. John Vukovich was scheduled to hit. Maybe if it had been a different day, different circumstances, Sparky would have left it alone. Maybe if the team had not crumbled against Don Sutton's pitching the day before, he would have left it alone. Maybe. But Sparky's team was in the tank. His family was breaking apart. The Dodgers were laughing in his face.

"Danny, grab a bat," Sparky yelled out to Dan Driessen. Then, turning to Vukovich, he said, "Vuke, you sit this one out."

The dugout fell silent, and Vukovich stared at Sparky for a second. At first, he thought this had to be a joke . . . Sparky was not really going to pinch-hit for him in the second inning. Managers never pinch-hit for a player in the second inning. It had to be a joke, but if it was a joke, Vukovich did not get it. Then he watched it happen. Driessen grabbed a bat and walked on the field. The public-address announcer said, "Now batting for John Vukovich, Dan Driessen." All the Reds players were looking at Vukovich—this was really happening. Sparky Anderson was pinch-hitting for him before he even got his first at-bat of the game. Vukovich had never even heard of such a thing, not in high school, not in Little League, not ever. His whole body felt hot, he knew his face was red, and he could almost taste blood.

Vukovich just stood there with his mouth open. What to do? Talk to Sparky? Yell at him? Hit him? Throw a bat? He only knew that he had to do something. Vukovich knew that he was a weak hitter. He knew that Sparky saw him as the weak link in the Machine. But this was something more, this was personal, this was Sparky just kicking sand in his face. Vukovich looked at Sparky again, for just an instant. Then he grabbed his bat, and he started screaming. He walked into the tunnel, and he shouted curse words in an order that did not form sentences, and then he meticulously smashed every lightbulb in the tunnel leading back to the clubhouse.

Back on the field, Dan Driessen fouled out to third base.

The Reds pummeled Marichal in the third inning. Pete doubled. Johnny singled him home. Tony Perez homered. Cesar Geronimo singled. Dave Concepcion singled. Ken Griffey doubled them both home. Sparky still seethed in the dugout. Vukovich showed him up. This punk third baseman who couldn't hit water if he fell out of a boat showed him up. It was unacceptable. It could not be tolerated. Sparky, above all, believed in order. That was why he could not stand to see Lee with long hair. That was why he treated stars better than he treated the other players. When Sparky went out to the mound to take out a pitcher, there was a right way to do it. The pitcher was supposed to put the baseball in his hand softly—like he was handing over important documents—and then walk to the dugout without saying a word. And if a pitcher ever mouthed off, ever, well, Sparky did not like it.

"I still feel good," the kid pitcher Pat Darcy said to Sparky once. Only once.

"Yeah?" Sparky snapped. "You feel good? You'll feel better in the shower." And when that game ended, Sparky gave the kid the verbal beating of his life. It wasn't personal. Darcy just needed to learn.

Now, this no-hit third baseman was going around breaking light-bulbs, acting like he'd actually done something in his life. Sparky stewed on the bench. Then watched the lead fade. In the fourth inning, the Penguin hit a two-run homer for the Dodgers. "You see?" he shouted at Scherger, but loud enough for everyone to hear. "You see what a third baseman is supposed to do? How in the hell am I supposed to win without a real third baseman?"

The Reds made the score 6–2 in the seventh inning. The Dodgers came back in the bottom of the inning against that kid Darcy. Dodgers outfielder Jimmy Wynn, who had the colorful nickname "the Toy Cannon," crushed a grand slam to tie the score.

"No, I wasn't trying to hit a home run," the Toy Cannon said after the game. "But I have to admit it did enter my mind."

Mike Marshall shut out the Reds in the top of the ninth. Steve Garvey hit the game-winning single in the bottom of the ninth. The Reds lost again. They dropped into fifth place.

"I'm going to kill our third baseman," Sparky said as he walked through the dark tunnel back to the clubhouse.

Sparky decided to wait until the next day before confronting Vukovich. It was a bad decision; his ulcer kept him up all night. Then Sparky arrived at Dodger Stadium early, and he sat in the visiting manager's office, and he stewed. When Vukovich walked in for the meeting, Sparky wondered if he should let him close the door. He wanted everyone to hear what he was about to say.

"There's one thing you better get straight, kid, and I mean get it straight right away," Sparky began. "I run this ball club."

Vukovich sat there and stared at Sparky. He knew going in that he had to take his medicine. He still knew he was right, knew that what Sparky had done was, in the baseball vernacular, "horseshit." But when it came down to it, Vukovich was still a no-hit third baseman who loved baseball and only wanted a chance to play. He wasn't going to win any fights with Sparky Anderson.

"I'll pinch-hit for anyone anytime I think it can help me win a ball game," Sparky shouted. "According to my statistics sheet here, you don't happen to be a star in this game yet."

Vukovich thought: *More horseshit.* Sparky knew damn well that you don't pull a man for a pinch hitter in the second inning. Now he was going to rip Vukovich's batting average . . . pure, unadulterated horseshit.

"You won't give a guy a chance to prove anything," Vukovich shouted. "You will kill a guy's confidence."

"I'm not here to build your confidence," Sparky roared. Vukovich sat back and reminded himself to shut up. He had to take it. He had no choice. Sparky was unloading. "I'm here to win a baseball game, and if I think I can win by pinch-hitting in the *first inning*, then, by God, I'll pinch-hit for you in the first. So you just play your position. . . ."

Vukovich sat there, drained, and just waited for the battering to end. But it would not end; Sparky went on and on. When Sparky finished—and it seemed like it took him hours to finish—he asked Vukovich if he had anything else to say. Vukovich had plenty to say. But he did not say a word. He walked out into the clubhouse, and his teammates avoided his gaze.

"You know," Shug said to Sparky after the meeting, "the kid does play good defense at third base."

"I don't give a damn about defense right now," Sparky shouted.

That night, Vukovich started at third base, and Sparky—perhaps feeling bad—waited all the way until the eighth inning to pinch-hit for him. The Dodgers tied the game in the bottom of the ninth. The Dodgers scored the game-winning run in the eleventh when Reds first baseman Dan Driessen made an error. Marshall pitched three scoreless innings to get the Dodgers victory.

"We can't do anything right," Sparky said.

The Reds could not do anything right, but they did get one break in the early part of 1975. Two days after Marshall beat the Reds for the last time, he pitched against San Francisco. On the third pitch of the game, he threw a curveball and then collapsed in agony. He needed help leaving the field. He told the doctor that it felt like someone had stuck a knife in his side. He would pitch only twice in the following six weeks. He was not indestructible.

HOW ABOUT THAT PETE ROSE?

April 20 to May 17

> *So please play for me a sad melody.*
> *So sad that it makes everyone cry.*

— B. J. THOMAS, "ANOTHER SOMEBODY
DONE SOMEBODY WRONG SONG"

April 22, 1975

CINCINNATI
REDS VS. GIANTS

Team record: 7–8

Johnny Bench could not remember a time before he wanted to be a hero. Like most ballplayers, he got that from his father. Ted Bench was one helluva ballplayer in the army. Ted was squat—a filled-out five-foot-nine—but he had this arm you would not believe. Ted was a catcher, and every time he uncorked a throw to second, he would hear the sighs of the crowd. Some people saw that arm in action and told Ted that he ought to pitch, but Ted Bench did not think anyone should tell a man what to do with his life. Ted quit high school as a senior because his baseball coach put him on the bench for a few days. Later, Ted would tell his sons, the coach tried to put him in a game.

"Get in there, Bench," the evil coach said in the parable.

"Naw," Ted replied. "I don't wanna go in. If you don't start me, I can't go in." And with that, the story went, Ted Bench quit the team, quit school, joined the army, and wowed the hard men of the Greatest Generation with his rocket arm.

The lesson in the story was for the boys to figure out. For a while after he got out of the army, Ted still had some vague dream of playing big league ball, but he was twenty-six, and he already had two sons, and he had bone chips floating around in his elbow. He came back to Oklahoma with his wife, Katie, looked for steady work, and finally found some driving a truck for a propane company in a little town of six hundred called Binger. On the side, Ted played sandlot baseball on diamond-hard fields covered with rocks and sand. He planned to raise a big league ballplayer, planned it even before he got married. His oldest son, Ted Jr., had the heart of a ballplayer, but he lacked the talent. His second son, William, might have had some talent, but there was something missing. Johnny had everything. Even when Johnny was a toddler, he could throw. Yes, sir, he was the one. Ted went to work on him right away. Ted would hit high pop-ups to his son in Oklahoma cornfields. Ted would have Johnny practice his throw to second base again and again and again until every throw landed on the corner of the bag. Johnny would always remember Saturdays, going with his father to Helms Grocery, buying a gallon of Neapolitan, and racing home to catch the *Game of the Week* on their black-and-white TV.

"There he is, John," Ted would say, and he would point to the screen at Mickey Mantle, the great Yankees outfielder who had grown up in Oklahoma.

"I'm going to be a professional baseball player too," Johnny would say.

"Yes, you are," Ted said.

Johnny first alerted the world to his baseball destiny when he was in the second grade and the teacher asked the ubiquitous question: "What do you want to be when you grow up?" Johnny never could figure out why every other boy in the class offered what seemed to him mundane ambitions—policeman, fireman, teacher, farmer.

There was something about growing up in a small town, something comforting and confining all at once, something that Johnny Bench would spend his life celebrating but, even more, running away from. Johnny announced that he intended to play baseball for a living. And every school year—in school essays, in class speeches—Johnny would remind every teacher and every student in his class that his goals had not changed.

Ted started a youth baseball team—the Binger Bobcats—and he made Johnny his catcher. He made Johnny a catcher for practical reasons: that was the easiest route to the big leagues. There were never enough good catchers in this world. Johnny loved it. He was good at it. He would block balls thrown in the dirt and catch pop-ups behind home plate, and when he made those practiced throws to second base, eyes would bulge. "That boy of yours is gonna play in the big leagues," people would say to Ted.

"Yes, he is," Ted said.

None of it was easy, of course. The Benches were just getting by— Ted only had enough money to keep the Binger Bobcats going for a couple of years. When he ran out of sponsorship money, he drove Johnny twenty miles to Fort Cobb to play. When Ted could not drive him to Fort Cobb, Johnny and his brothers and friends played baseball games using Milnot milk cans as balls and broken bats sliced in half. And when brothers and friends were not around, Katie would watch in wonder as Johnny stood out in the driveway and, for hours at a time, threw chunks of gravel up in the air, and hit them with a chipped baseball bat.

Ted and Johnny talked so much about him playing in the big leagues that soon it became almost plain, mundane, like planning a family vacation. Johnny never doubted that he would play in the majors. When he was in school—Johnny would always remember this—he got a C in penmanship. It devastated him. For one thing, Johnny Bench did not get Cs in anything—he had to be a success in everything or else he felt like a failure. But more, much more, he could not afford C-level penmanship. Johnny intended to sign a lot of autographs in his life.

So here's what he did: Johnny went down to Ford McKinney's Texaco station there in Binger, and he practiced signing autographs. Over and over again, Johnny would sign his name—rounding out the top of the J, making sure the H and two Ns were precisely the same height and width, adding an extra swirl in his B. He signed his name again and again, and then, when he had the letters just right, he started handing out his autographs to people around town. "Keep this," he said. "I'm going to be famous." He liked doing that so much that he did it again the next week. And then again. After a while, Ford McKinney had a shoe box full of Johnny Bench signatures. Years later, he would say he still had them around somewhere.

That was the Johnny Bench everyone in Binger knew: the cocky kid who signed autographs at the gas station and believed without a doubt that he would play major league baseball, and then he would be a major league star, and then he would marry the prettiest girl in the world. It had to happen that way. It was preordained. The Reds drafted Johnny in the second round in 1965 and offered him a measly six grand and some school tuition, a pretty insulting offer. But Reds scout Tony Robello knew just how to make the deal happen. He said: "John, if you make it, you will have more money than you could ever want." That was something Johnny Bench understood. He signed the contract. He knew that he would make it.

He played the next year for the Class A Peninsula Grays in Newport News, Virginia, and from the start he was something to see. He hit long home runs—ten of them over the HIT A HOMER HERE, WIN A FREE SUIT sign—and he showed off his gun of an arm, and he told people, "Forget Babe Ruth. Remember Johnny Bench." At the end of the year, in one of the quirkier moments in minor league baseball history, Peninsula actually retired Johnny Bench's uniform number. Minor league teams did not retire uniform numbers for one-year players, but then, none of them had ever seen anything quite like him. Anyway, Johnny took it all in stride. Retire his jersey? Why not? He smiled and waved to the crowd and then took his ten free suits and went up to Triple A Buffalo. He played less than a year there and hit twenty-three more home runs. Then the Reds called him up to the big leagues. Johnny's first day, he announced to the catchers on the team that he had not come to be anyone's backup; he had come to be the new starter, he had come to be baseball's biggest star, and they might as well know that right up front. They hated him immediately.

Hated him . . . but what could they say? Johnny may have been an arrogant little jerk off the field, but on the field he was Mozart. He wasn't just playing baseball better than any of them; he was revolutionizing baseball. Catchers through the years had caught pitches with both hands, using the right hand to secure the baseball in the glove. The Chicago Cubs' Randy Hundley, who made it to the big leagues a couple of years before Johnny, was the first major league catcher to catch one-handed. But Johnny Bench made one-handed catching an art form. He had huge hands—he could hold seven baseballs in one of them—and he would scoop pitches out of the dirt like he was a shortstop picking up a ground ball. He could get the ball from his glove to his throwing hand so fast, it seemed like a card trick. He moved like a dancer around the plate on bunts. And when he had a bat in his hand, he hit long home runs to left field.

There was something else about him too—maybe "conviction" is the right word. He knew better. There's a story Johnny would tell often involving a pitcher named Gerry Arrigo. Johnny was a rookie, and Arrigo was pitching one day against the Dodgers. Arrigo was not throwing his fastball with any authority at all that day—as ballplayers say, he was throwing meatballs. Johnny kept signaling Arrigo to throw his curveball instead, only Arrigo kept shaking off those signals. Johnny walked out to the mound, told Arrigo that his fastball did not have any heat, and Arrigo told him to pipe down and get behind the plate. Johnny shrugged, went behind the plate, and called for another curveball. Arrigo shook him off. Johnny called for the curveball again. Arrigo shook him off again. Then Johnny called for the fastball, Arrigo threw it, and Johnny reached out with his right hand and caught the ball barehanded.

"You should have seen his face," Johnny said.

In a way, that was the look on all their faces when they saw Johnny Bench play ball. He won the Rookie of the Year Award. Then he started in the All-Star Game. In his third year, 1970, he had the greatest year a catcher ever had. He hit 45 home runs. He had 148 RBIs—that was another record for catchers and would remain a record into the next century. That year only 62 brave souls tried to steal a base against him, and he threw out almost half of them. He carried the Reds to the World Series, and he was a phenomenon: the subject of a feature story in *Life* magazine, on the cover of *Sports Illustrated*, the fastest-rising star in the game.

Baseball stardom was not enough. Johnny sang in nightclubs. He went to Vietnam with Bob Hope. He met with presidents. He hosted his own television show. He became friends with stars, like the singer Bobby Goldsboro, who hit it big in 1968, during Bench's rookie year, with a song called "Honey." He dated models and a *Playboy* centerfold, and once took Miss World USA Lynda Carter to a golf tournament. It wasn't a real date, but word got out. Lynda became pretty upset, come to think of it. She thought Johnny had leaked it. He scoffed. Johnny did not have to leak anything. He was the most famous baseball player in the world. In 1972, when he had a growth removed from his lung, he had received thousands of letters in the hospital. When he married Vickie, he received almost as many letters from broken-hearted women.

He was twenty-seven years old, and he had everything. And then, on this day in Cincinnati, everything changed. Fifth inning, score-less game, San Francisco's Chris Speier singled to left field with a runner named Gary Matthews on second base. Johnny stood at home plate and waited for Pete Rose to get the ball and throw it home.

Rose got to the ball, and he threw home—Rose did not have a strong arm. The ball slowly made its way to the plate, and so did Matthews, who was six-foot-three, weighed about two hundred pounds, and was called "Sarge." Johnny could see that the baseball and Sarge were going to get to the plate at almost precisely the same time; he was in a tough spot. He wanted to catch the ball, get out of the way, and tag Matthews as he rushed by—nobody pulled that bullfighter maneuver better than Bench. But he did not have time. Instead, he stood in front of the plate, and he leaned forward to catch the ball, and he tried to protect himself. Sarge crashed into Johnny and sent him flying backward.

That's when Johnny Bench felt a whole new kind of pain. It was sharp and biting and deep inside his left shoulder. He groaned. Then he got up—nobody, not even the people who hated Johnny Bench, ever questioned his toughness. He stayed in the game. He waited for the pain to go away. Only it did not go away. And what Johnny Bench did not know that day in Cincinnati was that the pain would subside, and it would recede, but it would never go away. He would play the rest of the 1975 baseball season in agony.

Bottom of the ninth inning, same game, and Joe Morgan danced off second base. The team was in the tank, but Joe was playing great. He felt great. He had spent the off-season punching a speed-bag every single day. "What are you, training to fight Muhammad Ali?" his pal Pete Rose sneered.

"Maybe I'll knock you out," Morgan said.

He felt fast. He felt light. Float like a butterfly. Sting like a bee. Baseballs cracked off his bat; the sound was louder than before. It seemed like every ground ball he hit scooted past a diving infielder. He saw the pitches so much more clearly; he had heard hitters talk about being in this zone where even the hardest fastballs seemed to be floating to the plate, as if underwater. Now he understood. He had walked fifteen times in sixteen games. He had reached base every single game this season. He was on his way to something historic, a season for the ages. Only the rest of the guys were playing lousy.

"Come on," he shouted after he hit his double and took his lead off second base. Tony Perez came to the plate. This was exactly the kind of situation Doggie loved: man on second base, see the ball, hit the ball. Only Doggie struck out—he wasn't hitting worth a damn. Up stepped Geronimo, and Geronimo wasn't hitting either, and Morgan just knew he was going to die at second base.

Then something happened, something even Joe Morgan with his brilliant sense of language had a hard time explaining. The game slowed down. He had this feeling of destiny. He knew what was going to happen before it happened. Joe watched San Francisco pitcher Charlie Williams throw the ball in the dirt, and the ball bounced off rookie catcher Marc Hill. It was a wild pitch, and Joe took off for third base. Only then, suddenly, he slowed, no, more, he almost stopped about twenty feet from third base. He watched Hill grab the ball, and he watched him look toward third, and then he watched him throw the ball. It was exactly as he saw it. Hill's throw was wild, and it skipped past third base and into left field. Morgan raced around third and scored the winning run.

"I could have made third easily," Joe told the reporters afterward. "But I deliberately held back . . . I was hoping Hill would do just what he did."

It was absurd. Morgan was saying that he had purposely tricked Hill into making a bad throw to third base so he could score the run. The Giants players, when they heard that, went mad—they ripped Joe, they said he was an arrogant son of a bitch, and he had gotten lucky, and there was no possible way that he had really slowed down just to beguile Hill. Joe loved it. He had gotten into his opponents' heads. He had controlled the game.

"If Joe Morgan keeps up his current pace," Sparky said, "he'll be dead in another month."

Saigon fell as the Reds began their game in San Francisco. South Vietnam surrendered. Everyone knew it was coming. The few days leading up to it, the United States had evacuated the last Americans out of Saigon. "This closes a chapter in the American experience," President Gerald Ford told America. And with that, the Vietnam War was over.

Nobody seemed to know quite how to feel about losing a war. A big yellow headline, "Hanoi's Triumph," blared on the cover of *Time* magazine, and underneath was a photograph of smiling young North Vietnamese soldiers outside Danang carrying AK-47s. The cover of *U.S. News & World Report* was even gloomier, if possible. It featured a collage of sketches featuring everyday and entirely unhappy Americans doing things like shopping for groceries, working construction, and wearing cowboy hats. The headline was "Mood of America." And the conclusion, trumpeted in red ink, was a quote from a cafeteria manager in New Orleans with the unlikely name of A. L. Plaswirth III: "Things have got to get better."

It had been only eight months since Richard Nixon had resigned the presidency in Watergate shame. Unemployment was skyrocketing. The price of everything was going up too fast. And then there was news that using ordinary spray cans was destroying the earth's ozone layer. The number-one song in the land was B. J. Thomas's "Another Somebody Done Somebody Wrong Song."

"We aren't playing for shit," Sparky Anderson told Scherger. This was the beauty of being a major league baseball manager: nothing else in the world mattered during the season. Sparky liked reading the papers—later in his life, during the season, Sparky would like watching the same reports again and again on the twenty-four-hour news channels—but during this season he felt like the news didn't have anything to do with him. Even baseball news that did not involve the Machine —it was in the papers that the San Francisco Giants, the Reds' opponent that day, might go broke—did not concern Sparky. People never could understand how insular a manager felt during a baseball season. The soap opera *Days of Our Lives* went from a half-hour to an hour. Rich Little hosted *The Tonight Show.* *The Wiz*, a rhythm-and-blues version of *The Wizard of Oz*, won seven Tony Awards. American and Soviet astronauts trained near Moscow for their spacecraft linkup in July. It was just noise to Sparky. Static. The only thing that mattered was the game, and his emotions swung wildly from the first inning to the last.

"Hey, there he goes!" Sparky shouted in the fifth inning when Tony Perez cracked a double down the left-field line. Joe Morgan scored. Johnny Bench scored. It was good to see Tony hitting—maybe this would get the Big Dog going. The Reds had tied the Giants 2–2 in front of a Tuesday evening crowd of, well, let's see—Sparky poked his head out of the dugout and looked around—in front of five thousand fans or so. Maybe less. Probably less.

"That a baby, Georgie Boy," Sparky shouted in the seventh when George Foster launched a triple in the right-center-field gap. That scored Morgan again. The Reds led the Giants 3–2, and Sparky felt pretty good. Foster was hitting the ball pretty good. Sparky had to admit it. He needed to find a way to get Foster into the lineup more. Things were looking up.

Then it was the eighth inning, the Reds leading by that one run. Sparky put Vukovich in at third base for his defensive skills. He put his brilliant defensive center fielder Geronimo into the game. He put in the perfect relief pitcher for the moment, Pedro Borbon. God, Sparky loved Borbon. The guy was half crazy, everybody on the club was just a little bit scared of him, but Borbon always wanted to pitch. If Sparky needed a pitcher at two o'clock on Christmas morning, he could pick up the phone and call Borbon. He was just the right guy to hold this one-run lead. Then, with one out, San Francisco's Chris Speier singled off Borbon. Damn it. Speier was followed by some guy named Ed Goodson, and he singled too. Damn it. Sparky stomped out to the mound to yank Borbon, who was obviously not the right guy at all. He pointed to the bullpen and then pointed to his left arm, meaning he wanted Will McEnaney to come in and pitch. Sparky hated Pedro Borbon.

"Bust 'em up, kid," Sparky said to McEnaney as he walked back to the dugout.

God, Sparky loved Will McEnaney. True, McEnaney lived a bit of a wild life. He had been thrown off his high school baseball team back in Ohio for doing all kinds of stupid kid things. And all through the minor leagues, he was always busting curfew and sneaking women into his room and Lord knows what else. But when he got to the mound, he attacked, he threw strikes, he believed that nobody could get a hit off him. Sparky appreciated it.

A bunt moved the Giants' runners to second and third. Sparky smiled—a bunt, eh? San Francisco's manager, Wes Westrum, wanted to get into a little chess match with ol' Sparky? Well, that was fine. Wes was a good player in his day; he'd played on a couple of All-Star teams back when he was with the Giants in the 1950s. But, Sparky knew, Wes was no match for his own strategic excellence. Sparky had McEnaney intentionally walk Gary Matthews, and Will McEnaney struck out Von Joshua. Take that, Wes. Two out.

One more time Sparky walked out to the mound. Will had done his job. He called for one more pitcher, a right-hander this time, Clay Carroll, to finish off the job. God, Sparky loved Clay Carroll. Everyone called him "the Hawk" because of that hook in his nose. Year after year, Sparky had Carroll come into games and get important outs—the previous five years Sparky had called for Carroll more than three hundred times. And this time, he was giving Carroll an easy assignment: all he had to do was retire a no-hit rookie named Horace Speed. Colorful name. Speed was actually slow, one of the wonderful quirks of baseball. Speed had just been called up to the big leagues, and he was about to get sent down, and there was no way that he was going to get a hit off Clay Carroll. And he didn't.

Instead, Carroll's fastball slipped out of his hands, and the ball hit Horace Speed.

"He just hit that son of a bitch," Sparky said in wonder. And he stared at the field. And he said again, "He just hit that son of a bitch." He watched Speed jog to first, which allowed Chris Speier to jog home with the tying run. Incredible. Sparky hated Clay Carroll. He hated Will McEnaney. He hated Pedro Borbon. He hated all his pitchers. In the ninth inning, with the score tied, with Clay Carroll still pitching, some guy named Chris Arnold got a single. Who in the hell was Chris Arnold? Two batters later, Chris Speier came up one last time, and he ripped a double to left field, scoring the winning run for the Giants. Sparky sat in the dugout, numb. The war was lost. The country was in shambles. He hated everybody in the whole damned world.

May 2, 1975

CINCINNATI
Team record: 12–11

Sparky had to do something about his weak third baseman. The club was spinning in the mud. There were a couple of reporters out there writing that if Sparky didn't get this thing turned around quick, the Reds were going to fire him. The general manager, Bob Howsam, told Sparky not to worry, but isn't that what they tell dying patients too? The writers had to be getting it from somewhere, right? Even sportswriters didn't just make up stuff like that.

He had to do something about Vukovich. But what? He had this crazy idea—crazy, but it just might work. He just needed an opening. And now, like fate, he saw that opening. He saw Pete Rose before the game taking a few ground balls at first base. This was the moment.

"What are you doing there, Peter Edward?" Sparky said as he walked out on the field.

"Aw, just breaking in this new glove for Fawn," he said. Fawn was Pete's daughter.

"Yeah," Sparky said. Then he looked longingly over toward third base. "I sure wish you were playing over there instead."

"Where's that?" Pete asked. "You mean third base?"

"I sure could use you there," Sparky said. "Give me a chance to get Danny Driessen and George Foster in the lineup more."

"Are you serious?" Pete asked, and he looked over at third base.

This was it. This was the moment. Sparky knew he was taking a big chance. Back in 1966, a Reds manager named Don Heffner had moved Rose to third base. And it was a disaster. Rose was just twenty-five at the time, and he was a second baseman who had just hit .300 for the first time in his big league career. He had just made his first All-Star team. He was just beginning to make his mark in the game. Heffner utterly misread him. When Pete asked why he was being moved to third, Heffner told him to shut up. He was moving to third because that's what the manager wanted. Mistake. Rose had never responded well to authority, except the authority of his father. Rose moved to third, but he hated it. He hit .200 the first three weeks of the season, and he was miserable, and he was not afraid to say it. Heffner finally moved Rose back to second base, but it was too late. Heffner got fired two months later. Pete Rose's succinct scouting report of his old manager: "He was an asshole."

Sparky hoped that this time would be different because he wasn't telling Pete to move to third base. He was coming to Pete with his hat in hand. If Sparky knew Pete Rose, that would make all the difference. "So what do you say?" Sparky asked.

Pete did not hesitate. "Well, if you think it will help the club, sure. When you thinking?"

Sparky said: "Tomorrow."

And Pete said three words: "Tomorrow? Damn. Okay." Then he ran into the dugout for a moment and reemerged.

"What did you get there, Peter Edward?" Sparky yelled.

"A cup," Pete yelled back as he ran toward third base. "I'll help the club, but I'm not going to risk my family's future for you."

More than thirty years later, Pete Rose thought back with wonder to that moment. "Who else would just agree to play third base in the middle of the season?" he asked. "Just like that. Who else? You name me one star player who would do that. I was an All-Star in left field. I hadn't played the infield in, what, five years?"

Eight years.

"Damn right. Eight years. Now you tell me, who would agree to just switch positions to help the club? Do you know any great player that would have done that? I'll bet you could not name a single great player who would have done that."

He smiled in that challenging way . . . go ahead, name one. He was probably right, though. Rose was the oddest kind of player. He was undeniably and admittedly selfish—he played for glory and fame and money and statistics. But he was bizarrely selfless and generous too. In his career, he moved around to six different positions (and was an All-Star at five of them). He invited rookies to stay at his home. He always picked up the check. Will McEnaney would always remember that on his first day in the big leagues, Pete Rose walked over to him and said, "You can't wear those shoes." Rose then pointed to the shoe boxes in his locker and told Will: "We probably wear the same-size shoes. Go ahead, help yourself. Take as many as you want."

When Sparky approached Pete to play third base in 1975, it wasn't by accident and it wasn't spur of the moment. He'd been thinking about it for a couple of months, going back to spring training, ever since he saw John Vukovich swing a bat. Sparky knew all about what had happened with Don Heffner. He could not afford to alienate his team leader. But Sparky had this instinct about people. He figured that if he asked Pete Rose to play third, if he could appeal to Pete's generous side without trespassing on his pride, then Pete would jump at the chance to play third base.

"Sparky could just get us to do stuff," Pete would say all those years later. "I don't know what it was. We just liked the guy, I guess. It wasn't just me. Johnny did stuff for Sparky. Joe did stuff for Sparky. Tony did stuff for Sparky. I don't know if there was another manager who could have brought all those egos together.

"I knew Sparky was using me when he asked me to play third. But that was the thing. He *asked* me. He didn't tell me, because that wouldn't have worked. He asked me, and he explained to me why he wanted to do it, and that's all I ever asked. Sparky knew how to handle people. He knew more about psychology than Freud."

Pete then said something that probably explained Sparky better than anything else.

"Sparky," he said, "reminded me a lot of my dad."

Sparky wanted to keep the Pete Rose experiment secret for as long as he could. He did not want anyone to know, not even his general manager, Bob Howsam. He had a good reason for this: there was no way Howsam was going to let him play Pete at third base. Howsam had made his thoughts clear on that subject time and again: he believed that Pete did not have a good enough arm to play third base. Sparky did not disagree with that, but he believed the situation had gotten dire. The Reds were playing lousy. And he had to do something.

There were two advantages to playing Pete at third base. One, he could get Balsa off the field. But the second thing, the most important thing, was that he could put Danny Driessen out in Pete's old position, left field, and Danny Boy could really hit. What a story. What a discovery. Danny Driessen did not even play baseball in high school down in Hilton Head, South Carolina. He was just a talented kid goofing around with baseball on weekends down south. Then he worked up the nerve to send Howsam a letter asking for a chance to play professional ball.

Howsam signed him—all it cost was a plane ticket and a Cincinnati Reds yearbook. Danny was eighteen years old then, rawer than a fresh bruise, and when he went to the minor leagues in Tampa, he didn't hit worth a damn. He was homesick. He felt alone. It happens to young baseball players. Some never get over it. But Danny's second year, back in Tampa, he hit .327. It turned out he was a hitting prodigy—he only needed to be fooled by a pitch once and the next time he would crush it. He moved up to Double A, and he hit .322. They moved him up to Triple A Indianapolis, and he hit .409 in his first forty-seven games—he hit the ball so hard that the Reds simply could not keep him in the minors anymore. They brought him up to the big leagues, and in one hundred games he hit .301 there too. Even the players on the Machine were awestruck.

"Let me just say this: Driessen can hit," Bench told the *Sports Illustrated* reporter who had come to do a story on Driessen, a story with the headline "Reds Rookie Is a Tough Cookie."

Rose was even more astonished, and he offered the greatest compliment he could ever offer another man.

"He hits about like me," Rose said.

Oh, Danny Boy could hit, but boy, Danny could not field. Sparky tried him at third base in 1973 and 1974, but he was so bad there that even Sparky couldn't put up with his defense. The Reds lost one game because Danny simply forgot to step on the base for the third out. The Reds lost when baseballs comically skidded between his legs. Danny looked like a natural first baseman; that was the biggest reason why the Reds had tried to trade Tony Perez. But Doggie was back at first base again ("You no take my job," Doggie had told Danny with that smile on his face). There was no place to play Danny, and it drove Sparky mad. "Who would you rather have hit with the bases loaded, Danny or Vukovich?" he asked reporters repeatedly. That was the genius of this move. Pete Rose would go to third base. Danny Driessen would go to left field. The Reds would take off.

And the move was indeed genius . . . though Sparky had the wrong reason. It would not be Danny Driessen who turned around the Reds' season. There was someone else—a right-handed hitter who didn't smoke, didn't drink, didn't fool around, a powerful-looking man who read the Bible every day and quietly stewed on the bench. George Foster prayed daily for a chance. And he was about to get that chance.

May 3, 1975

CINCINNATI
REDS VS. BRAVES
Team record: 12–12

"You were born at the wrong time, Pete," Tom Callahan would tell Pete Rose. Callahan understood that feeling of being from a generation not quite your own. Callahan wrote the sports column for the *Cincinnati Enquirer*, and he was still young, just twenty-seven. He felt older. He felt like he should have written columns long before, when sports titans walked the earth, when Babe Ruth hit colossal home runs for sick children, when Luis Firpo knocked Jack Dempsey through the ropes of the boxing ring, when Red Grange scored five touchdowns and passed for a sixth against Michigan. Maybe that's why Callahan felt himself drawn to Pete. Rose played like he belonged to another time—he ran to first base on walks, he brazenly slid into second base to break up double plays, he showed up every day with this feverish enthusiasm that came right out of the 1920s.

"You know who loves you, Pete?" Joe Morgan would say all the time. "Women who are in their eighties. Those are your fans.

Because you play like the ballplayers they used to watch when they were young."

Of course, lots of guys played baseball like the old-time players. But Pete, he lived like old-time players, he seemed to live in that mythical simpler time, when ballplayers ate steaks every night (Rose had his medium rare with a baked potato and iced tea) and signed autographs for kids (Bench grew tired of signing autographs; Rose never did) and sneaked girls up into their rooms (Pete was never especially coy about it) and loved the game unconditionally. Whenever Callahan wanted to find Rose after a game, he would go to Pete's house and find him sitting in his car and listening to a West Coast game on the radio. Whenever Callahan wanted to find Pete on an off-day, he would just go to the track—Pete always loved going to bet on the horses and the dogs at the track. Pete loved the action, sure, but beyond that he seemed to love the smoke and haze and whiskey and shady characters and old gamblers and lost money. Pete didn't smoke or drink himself—fast cars, fast women, and fast horses were enough vice for him—but he still liked being around the smoke and gin.

He loved old stories. Waite Hoyt was a hard-drinking old Yankees pitcher who knew the Babe and Ty Cobb and all the rest of those old baseball greats. He had also been a radio announcer for the Reds back in the early 1970s, and Pete would talk to him for hours. Pete would ask him to repeat the same stories again and again. Later, Callahan would hear Pete tell those stories, word for word, facial expression for facial expression. It was eerie. A few years later, when Pete Rose was chasing Ty Cobb's record for most hits, the *New York Times* sportswriter Dave Anderson asked Rose how much he really knew about Ty Cobb. Rose, being Rose, indelicately answered, "I know everything about Ty Cobb except the size of his cock."

Of course, the *New York Times*—"the Old Gray Lady"—could not report it quite that way. So the quote was delicately repackaged like so: "I know everything about Ty Cobb except the size of his hat." Rose was furious. He knew damn well that Cobb's hat size was $7\,^5/_8$.

This was Kentucky Derby day, and Pete Rose did not wake up thinking about playing third base. No, he woke up thinking about Foolish Pleasure, the superhorse that was running that day at Churchill Downs. Rose prided himself on being able to pick the Kentucky Derby winner. As it turned out, he was absolutely right: Foolish Pleasure would win the Derby, passing Avatar and Diabolo, who would bump into each other down the stretch. Pete would win some money on that. Then, like a guy snapping out of a dream, he remembered that he was playing third base that day for the first time in almost ten years.

He picked up the phone and called George Scherger.

"Sugar Bear," he said, "what are you doing today?"

"Thought I'd go fishing," Scherger said.

"Naw. Why don't you come out to the ballpark and hit me some ground balls at third base?"

"Damn it, Pete," Scherger said. "What time?"

"Early. How about one P.M.?"

"Damn it, Pete," Scherger said, and he hung up the phone. He'd be there, of course.

Sparky considered calling Bob Howsam to tell him that he would play Pete Rose at third base. He decided against it. For one thing, he was the manager of the team. He had to be allowed to run the team the way he knew how. As the old line goes, it's always easier to ask for forgiveness than permission.

Second, though, he was desperate. Sparky tried to hide this from everyone, but the Holiday Inn manager, Jeff Ruby, could see it in his friend's face. Sparky had convinced himself that if he did not do something, something drastic, this team would lose, and he would get canned. "They'll fire me in a heartbeat, bubula," Sparky said over breakfast. Ruby thought Sparky was being a bit melodramatic, and he said, "They'd never fire you, Sparky." But worry creased Sparky's face.

The Reds had lost as many as they had won, they trailed the Dodgers by four games (and were even behind the Atlanta Braves—the stinking Braves!). Sparky knew he had the best team going. But he also knew that the best teams sometimes faltered, and then managers got thrown out on the street.

Sparky watched Pete take some ground balls before the game. He looked okay. He wasn't smooth, he wasn't agile, and, of course, Howsam was right about his weak arm. But Sparky had to believe that Pete would work hard enough; he would not embarrass himself over there.

"What's news, Sparky?" That was Chief Bender, the Reds' director of the minor leagues. Chief was a good baseball man—he'd been in the game for twenty-five years. There had been a good pitcher known as "Chief Bender" in the early part of the century, and Chief was often confused for him. He didn't seem to mind. He never tired of baseball. He went to a game every day—major league game, minor league game, it didn't matter. He had to be around it.

"I'm playing Rose at third today," Sparky said.

Chief's face reddened. He looked hard at Sparky, as if he was trying to determine if he had just heard an inscrutable joke. Sparky was not joking.

"Well," Chief began slowly, "Bob's in Arizona."

"Chief, I'm gonna tell you something," Sparky said, and there was a bit of snap in his voice now. "It doesn't matter where Bob is. You know we haven't won yet, and we're starting off slow this year. I look at it this way: it's me or nothing right now. I'm gonna play him at third base."

Chief gave Sparky that hard look again. Then he sort of shrugged and walked off. It was Sparky's funeral.

Ralph Garr was Atlanta's leadoff batter that night. He was fast, and he had slapped and run his way to a .353 batting average in 1974, the best batting average in the National League. Garr had a unique talent for hitting baseballs precisely where he wanted to hit them. He saw Pete Rose at third base, and he smiled.

Up in the radio booth, Reds announcer Marty Brennaman watched closely. Sparky had told Marty that Rose would play third base, but Marty did not believe him. Now he was out there. Marty watched as Garr cracked a ground ball to third. Rose took a step to his left, kind of lost his footing, grabbed the ball, stumbled slightly again, steadied himself, threw the ball across the diamond. "He got him," Marty told his radio listeners. "How about that Pete Rose?"

The Reds won the game 6–1. Gary Nolan pitched nine innings and allowed only one run—his best pitching performance since he came back from the shoulder surgery. Pete had a key hit, and he did not make a single error. Sparky had this feeling that everything was about to change.

Early the next morning, at his second home in Arizona, Bob Howsam picked up his morning newspaper and saw what he thought was a misprint. The box score showed Pete Rose playing third base. He called up Chief Bender.

"I see Rose at third," he said. "That's a mistake, isn't it?"

"No, Bob," Chief said. "Sparky put him at third base."

"Oh, my God," Howsam said.

May 4, 1975

CINCINNATI
REDS VS. BRAVES
Team record: 13–12

Every few years, people would widely decide that baseball was about to die as the national pastime. This was one of those times in America. The nation was changing—for the better, for the worse, nobody knew—but people seemed to agree that baseball moved too slow for a modern America. "Baseball is in trouble," said James J. Kilpatrick, the man on the right in the point-counterpoint segment of the television news show *6o Minutes*. "It's too old-fashioned and needs some rule changes to make the game more exciting." It was pretty jarring to have Kilpatrick—the traditionalist who was only beginning to come around on desegregation—call a sport "too old-fashioned."

But that was the popular opinion in 1975. Baseball was a sport of the past. And football—professional football specifically—was the sport of the time. Football had everything that baseball lacked— violence, danger, a ticking clock. Comedian George Carlin, who had gained some fame after being arrested for performing his "Seven Words You Can Never Say on Television" routine in Milwaukee, traveled around with a new routine about baseball and football.

"You know football wants to be the number-one sport," he told audiences. "And I think it already is, because football represents what we are. Europe Jr. We play Europe's game. What was Europe's game? That's right. 'Let's take their land away from them.' . . . Ground acquisition. And that's what football is. Football is a ground acquisition game. You knock the crap out of eleven guys and take their land away from them."

Then he itemized a few of the differences between baseball and football. Football, he said, is technological. Baseball is pastoral. Football is played in a stadium, baseball in a park. In football you wear a helmet, in baseball you wear a cap. In football you get a penalty, in baseball you make an error ("Whoops!" Carlin would shout). It was a great bit, but it was more than that. America was not the same country it had been twenty years earlier, before civil rights, before two Kennedys were assassinated, before Vietnam, before Kent State, before Watergate. Carlin wondered, lots of people wondered, if America had the patience for a pastoral game played in a park. He wondered if baseball was as outdated as candy kitchens and ice-cream socials.

The people who ran baseball worried too. "I think you will see teams disappearing in the near future," the baseball commissioner and acting voice of doom, Bowie Kuhn, told reporters. Kuhn was always predicting the end of the world, but he had a point. The economy was troubled. The nation was changing. Baseball responded with Tootsie Rolls.

The first *Baseball Encyclopedia*—all 2,338 pages—was published in 1969. It weighed more than six pounds, and it was exorbitantly priced at $25, but it was a marvel. It was the first book to have the statistics of every single player in the history of Major League baseball. The *Baseball Encyclopedia* set free the minds of many baseball fans across America, and one of those was a college student named Mark Sackler. He decided, for fun, to take a mechanical calculator and total precisely how many runs had been scored in the history of the game. He found that more than one million runs had been scored, and he thought that was interesting. And he forgot about it.

A few years later, he got his first electronic calculator, and he decided to add up all the runs scored again. This time, though, he only added up the American and National Leagues—he did not worry about the runs scored in the Federal League and the Union Association and all the other defunct leagues. He found something interesting: the one millionth run would be scored in baseball in 1975. He was working in radio then, and he got together with a promoter, and they tried to sell the one-millionth-run idea as a big celebration for baseball. At first, they tried to get McDonald's to sponsor the event, but McDonald's owner Ray Kroc was ambivalent about baseball. He owned the perennially ghastly San Diego Padres, and he was not especially happy about it. He had paid $12 million for the team, and in his first game as an owner—the first game of the 1974 season—he raced up to the press box in the eighth inning, grabbed the public-address microphone, and shouted: "I have never seen such stupid ball-playing in all my life." McDonald's did not get behind the one-millionth-run promotion.

But the Tootsie Roll people did. They felt like it was time to expand the company. Tootsie Roll, like baseball, had been around since the turn of the century, and like baseball, the candy reflected another time. In 1896, a man named Leo Hirshfield opened a small candy shop in New York, and he created small chocolate-flavored rolls that he sold for a penny apiece. He named the candy after the nickname he had for his daughter Clara—he called her Tootsie.

The company grew over the years and moved to Chicago. "Things couldn't be better at Tootsie Roll," Richard R. Harshman, the vice president for marketing at Tootsie Roll Industries, told reporters. The time was right to strike with a big campaign. And what would be better than connecting with baseball? They hired Stan "the Man" Musial, one of baseball's most beloved players, a man who had scored 1,949 of those almost one million runs. He unveiled a contest: fans would guess which player would score the millionth run. Tootsie Roll Industries would give out 496 prizes to customers who named the right player. The company also would give the player who scored the run one million pennies ($10,000 was around what the average family made in a year) and one million Tootsie Rolls. "I think it's a great promotion, I really do," Stan the Man said. "What could be more American than baseball and Tootsie Rolls?" Musial said his lines with feeling. Everyone involved expected the nation to get swept up in the excitement.

And strangely, there was excitement. The Seiko Company installed counters in each ballpark to let fans know precisely how many runs had been scored. A giant scoreboard was installed in front of the Time Building in New York so people could follow along. And as the big day approached, there was a countdown center set up in New York with phones connected to every major league ballpark. The public relations people in each city were responsible for shouting out who had scored a run the instant a player stepped on home plate. There must have been one hundred people roaming around the countdown center. Musial was in there. The old Yankees announcer Mel Allen was running the teleconference. And Mark Sackler sat in the middle with a calculator and a score sheet. It was Sunday, and it was raining in New York, so nobody was standing outside watching the giant scoreboard. This was the day when someone would score the one millionth run.

Davey Concepcion woke up excited. He had this strange feeling: he thought he might score the run. And if he scored the run, he would be famous. And Davey Concepcion wanted nothing more than to be famous.

That was something he had been born with. His father had wanted him to be a doctor in Venezuela, but Davey could not even stand the sight of blood, and anyway, nobody cheered doctors. He had watched the great Venezuelan shortstop Luis Aparicio play on television, and he said to his family: "I can do that." He quit school to work for a bank, though his actual job was to play shortstop for the bank baseball team. He was tall and skinny, and in those younger days he could not hit much. But he was a wonder playing shortstop. No ground ball seemed out of his reach. The Reds signed Davey in 1967. He made it to the big leagues in 1970. He made the All-Star team in 1973. "Davey," Sparky said, "can be a big star in this game."

The only real problem was that Davey felt quite certain he already was a big star in the game, and he was never shy about saying so. "I'm just like you and Bench and Pete," he told Joe Morgan, who shook his head.

"No, you're not," Joe said, without a touch of humor. "We're stars. You're not."

And that exchange would be repeated again and again in the Reds clubhouse. Davey was so earnest and so nakedly hungry in his pursuit of stardom that he left himself wide open for jabs. One day he walked proudly into the clubhouse wearing a flashy suit, one that he felt spoke to his status as a player. "You look like Bozo the Clown," Pete said, and everybody called Davey "Bozo" for a while.

One day, Philadelphia shortstop Larry Bowa walked over and said, "Hi, Elmer."

"Why do you call me Elmer?" Concepcion asked.

"I figured that was your first name," Bowa said, "since every day I pick up the paper and the first thing I see in the box scores is 'E—Concepcion.'"

Everybody called Davey "Elmer" for a while after that.

But the kid would not be deterred. He believed himself destined for greatness. His first child was born one week before the millionth-run day, and that just added to Davey's self-faith. Something really good was going to happen for him. And he felt sure that it would be the one millionth run.

Davey was out in the field playing shortstop when he saw the Seiko scoreboard turn to that beautiful sequence of numbers—999,999—and he tried to do some calculations in his head. He was due to bat third in the bottom of the fifth inning. He really might have a chance to score that run. Atlanta's Dusty Baker flew out to center field. Concepcion raced into the dugout and shouted, "Come on! Let's go! Come on. I have to get up there."

The first batter up for the Reds was pitcher Don Gullett, and he dutifully grounded out to third. The Seiko still showed 999,999. Pete stepped in; Concepcion watched him closely. It would be just like Pete Rose to hit a home run and score the big run. The guy had a knack for doing things like that. But Pete grounded out to second. Concepcion ran to the batter's box. He faced Phil Niekro, the Braves' famous knuckleball pitcher. Concepcion had never hit a home run off of Niekro. This was the time. The pitch fluttered in, and he swung hard, a bit wildly. He felt the impact, ball hitting bat, and he heard the crack of the bat, and he knew. He got it.

The ball sailed to left field, and Concepcion started running hard. The crowd—a packed house, more than fifty thousand—went wild. The ball soared over the fence, but Concepcion was taking no chances. He sprinted around the bases, as fast as he could go, and he touched home plate, and he shouted, "For my baby! For my baby!" The Seiko scoreboard turned to 1,000,000. The dugout was madness, Reds players shouting and hugging and waving Concepcion to get in there so they could mob him. He was Dave Concepcion, Tootsie Roll hero, millionth-run man, and it was beautiful.

Back in New York, at the millionth-run countdown center, there was a problem. The Cincinnati Reds had fallen off the conference call. Nobody was sure what had happened, but no matter what they tried, they could not get the Reds back on line. The only thing they could do was have someone designated to call the Reds directly and just repeat what he was being told.

Everyone was paying attention to the situation in San Francisco. The Houston Astros had Bob Watson on second base. Houston's catcher, Milt May, was at the plate, and if he singled, Watson could be the one millionth run. May, though, homered. So Watson began to trot home when he heard people from his dugout scream, "Run!" He ran home and touched home plate.

"Bob Watson just scored!" the man in San Francisco shouted.

Everyone stood up and cheered, but just as they stood up the man on the phone to Cincinnati shouted, "Dave Concepcion just scored!"

Everyone sat back down. Wait a minute. Watson seemed to score first, but nobody was entirely sure. The man on the phone to Cincinnati had to repeat the news, so there had been a delay. They replayed the tape to see what had happened. There was no question there had been a slight gap—four seconds or so—between the instant the man in San Francisco said that Watson scored the run and the moment when the time guy in New York relayed the news that Concepcion had scored. A ruling had to be made.

They ruled that Bob Watson had scored the one millionth run in baseball history.

The run made Bob Watson semifamous—or anyway, the answer to a trivia question. He unhappily donated his shoes to the Baseball Hall of Fame ("I had just broken them in," he would say). He said his fan mail doubled ("from four to eight"). Watson donated the million pennies and million Tootsie Rolls to charity. *Sports Illustrated* wrote a story about him. Years later, Watson would become the first black general manager in baseball, and later the first black general manager of the New York Yankees.

"I was glad to hear he's a clean-living athlete," said Richard Harshman, vice president in charge of marketing and sales. "We have to keep the image—good for kids, good for Tootsie Rolls. I know he's not blond and blue-eyed, but he's my idea of an All-American."

Meanwhile, back in Cincinnati, Davey Concepcion heard the boos. He looked up at the scoreboard and saw that Bob Watson scored the run—and that he had scored run number one million and one in baseball history. It broke his heart. "Tell them to send me a Tootsie Roll anyway," he said. "I come so close."

Many years later, the *Baseball Encyclopedia* would make numerous adjustments and changes to its statistics. It turned out that neither Bob Watson nor Davey Concepcion scored the one millionth run. It was some anonymous player who never got any acclaim or Tootsie Rolls.

May 14, 1975

PHILADELPHIA
REDS VS. PHILLIES
Team record: 18–15

Sparky's ulcer was burning again. He drank glass after glass of warm milk at night to soothe it, but nothing would calm the pain. The Reds still weren't playing worth a damn.

"No one cares who finishes second," he told Bob Hertzel, the baseball writer from the *Cincinnati Enquirer.* "This team can finish second on its ability alone. That's the easiest thing in the world. This team has to finish first. It has to want it so bad that nothing will stop it."

Maybe that's what sent Sparky over the edge: this team didn't want it as much as he did. What else could it be? He had the best second baseman in the game, Joe Morgan. Now he had Pete Rose at third base. Johnny Bench was the best catcher in the world. (Though Johnny was still griping about his shoulder hurting. Sparky didn't get that. The X-rays had come out negative.) Doggie wasn't hitting worth a damn, but he would come around. Davey was one helluva shortstop. He had super young outfielders. There was no way his team should lose.

And yet, the Reds kept getting beat. The night before in Philadelphia, cold night, rainy, some kid named Tom Underwood shut them out. Tom Freaking Underwood shut out the Cincinnati Reds. Funny, they had faced Underwood in 1974, first game of the kid's career, and the Reds pummeled him, smacked him around for six runs in one-third of an inning. After that game, Sparky told reporters: "That may be a blessing for the kid . . . it will show him it isn't too easy here in the big leagues." Sparky was still tasting those words. It sure looked easy for the kid last night, didn't it? Every time Underwood threw low, the Reds swung high. When Underwood threw a fat pitch, right over the plate, the Reds didn't swing at all. Sparky couldn't figure it at all.

This night, they had faced Steve Carlton, damn fine pitcher, threw a great slider. In the first inning, Joe Morgan got picked off first base. In the second, Doggie doubled to lead off the inning, and the Reds could not drive him home. In the third, Pete Rose hit into a double play. In the fourth, Morgan doubled to lead off the inning, and the Reds could not drive him home then either.

Sparky felt that old rage coming on. He wanted to hit somebody. His stars were ripping away at each other, like always. Hey, Pete, you ever planning on getting another hit? Hey, Joe, you awake now? Hey, John, you got something against RBIs? They were laughing, like it was funny. Meanwhile, his young players, they looked scared out of their minds. His team was busting apart. Yes, Sparky wanted to hit somebody.

In the fifth inning, Reds rookie starter Pat Darcy got into some trouble. Sparky jogged out to the mound, which made Darcy feel better. Sparky had a routine. If he jogged to the mound, that meant he only wanted to talk. But if Sparky walked to the mound, that meant he had made up his mind, he was going to yank the pitcher, bring in a reliever, no doubt about it. Pitchers often told jokes about Sparky, and the punch line was usually: "Start jogging, you son of a bitch."

Sparky jogged out and told Pat he needed to get some damn people out because the team wasn't hitting. It was a strange one-way conversation—Sparky did not seem the slightest bit interested in talking about Darcy and pitching. He wanted to rant about his lineup, his ulcer, and his bad feelings about things. This went on for a short while, until home plate umpire Terry Tata walked out to the mound to break up things and get the game going again.

"You ready to play ball?" Tata asked.

"I'm not talking to you," Sparky snapped at Tata. "When I'm talking to you, I expect to hear from you."

That's when Sparky Anderson got thrown out of the game. The

Reds lost 4–0 again, the second consecutive day they had been shut out. Sparky stayed up all night, guzzling milk and cursing the best baseball team on earth.

In the morning, Sparky felt better. Things always seemed better in the morning. The guys were just trying too hard. That's what it was. Sparky just needed to calm everyone down. Every so often, when things were going bad, Pete would come up to him and say, "Why don't you have a team meeting today and yell at me?" Pete Rose was one helluva kid. Today Sparky would just have one of those yell-at-Pete meetings. Loosen the guys up a little bit before the doubleheader. Everything would be fine.

Then Sparky walked into the clubhouse, and he saw the guys ripping each other some more—"Hey, Tony, I can bowl better than your batting average"—and he lost it again. He ordered the pitchers out of the room. He wanted to talk directly to his stars.

"What in the hell is wrong with you guys?" he shouted. "You think this is a comedy show? You think this is the Dean Martin celebrity roast? I want the ripping to stop right now." He spoke from his heart. The Reds needed to support each other. They were a family. They were the Big Red Machine, working together, gears and belts and chains all cranking in the same direction. The season was almost a quarter over, and they were stuck in third place, they were losing ground to the first-place Dodgers, they needed to wake up and start playing ball like a team again.

"I know that you are the best team in baseball," Sparky said. "You need to act like it."

The Reds played a doubleheader. In the first game, the Reds led Philadelphia 3–2 going into the ninth inning, but Cesar Geronimo dropped a line drive in center field, and then "Downtown Ollie" Brown hit a three-run homer to win the game for the Phillies. In the second game, "the Bull," Greg Luzinski, hit a long home run for the

Phillies, and the Reds lost again. Sparky did notice that the players didn't rip each other in the dugout. They didn't say much of anything at all. The whole place felt dead.

May 16, 1975

Team record: 18–18

Bob Howsam refused to believe that things were this bad. He was a professional optimist; he had spent his whole life believing in the best-case scenario. Back in 1959, a group of very rich men—oil men, a hotel magnate, an industrialist—started a new football league called the American Football League. They asked Howsam to join in, even though he did not have—as he often said—two nickels to rub together. What the hell? He joined. He founded a football team he called the Denver Broncos. When people asked Howsam how exactly he intended to keep that team going without money, he said, "Things will work out." Things worked out for the Broncos, but not for Howsam: he had to sell off the team after one year. He had tried every promotional trick he could imagine. He even had his football players wear socks where the lines stretched vertically rather than wrapping around. He thought these would make the players look taller. If so, the socks made them look like taller circus clowns.

That was Howsam. He believed that if you studied the situation carefully, if you worked hard, if you put together the best plan, if you stayed positive, things would work out. That's what he thought back in '72 when he traded for Joe Morgan. Nobody liked that trade when he made it. Look now. He got Morgan, of course. He got Jack Billingham, a mediocre pitcher for Houston who won nineteen games for the Reds in both 1973 and 1974. He got Cesar Geronimo, a brilliant defensive center fielder who, according to Reds batting coach Ted Kluszewski, had a terrible swing. But Geronimo came to the Reds, and Klu worked with him, and Geronimo hit pretty well. Things just worked out.

Now Howsam felt sure that the Reds would come around. Sitting in his office back in Cincinnati, he would write out the Reds' lineup, write out the opponent's lineup, and then decide which team had the better group of players. He always tried to be a harsh judge of his own team. But he kept coming up with the same answer.

Today the Reds were playing the Montreal Expos, and so the Howsam scouting sheet looked something like this:

First base: Tony Perez is much better than Montreal's Mike Jorgensen.
Second base: Joe Morgan is much, much better than Larry Lintz.
Shortstop: Davey Concepcion is much better than Tim Foli.
Third base: Pete Rose is better than rookie Larry Parrish.
Left field: George Foster is better than Larry Biittner or Bob Bailey or whoever the Expos decide to put out there.
Center field: Cesar Geronimo is better than Pepe Mangual.
Right field: Ken Griffey is better than Tony Scott.
Catcher: Johnny Bench is better than any catcher in baseball, and better than the Expos' rookie catcher Gary Carter.

So that was eight for eight in favor of the Reds. Sometimes the Reds won seven of the eight positions, or six of eight. But every time Bob Howsam worked out the calculation, the Reds came out ahead. He tried to be impartial and logical about it—the Reds were the best team in baseball. He knew, absolutely knew, full confidence, that the Reds would come around and win.

"I'm an optimist," he told the newspaper guys.

That day, the Reds' lineup that had won all eight positions in Bob Howsam's office lost to Montreal 4–2. Through thirty-seven games, the Reds had lost more than they had won. Also, Joe Morgan got slashed by spikes on a slide and had to go to the hospital. Also, Pete Rose made his first error at third base. Reporters were saying that the Machine was falling apart. Sparky Anderson was doing what he could to keep his ulcers from smoldering. Bob Howsam sat in his office and tried to stay positive. And Johnny Bench grabbed the Reds' young radio announcer, Marty Brennaman, and together they went out into the Montreal night.

May 17, 1975

MONTREAL
REDS VS. EXPOS
Team record: 18–19

Johnny Bench looked like he had lost several fights. He had a fever of 104, or anyway that's what he told Sparky as he walked into the dark and cramped manager's office at Montreal's Jarry Park Saturday morning. He said that there was no way he could play, and he limped back out toward the training room. Sparky nodded. Sure, why not? Bench was out. Morgan had gotten fourteen stitches in his shin the night before, and he was out too. The team had lost six games in a row. The Reds were only a half-game ahead of the Padres. Sure, why not?

Marty Brennaman walked into the office, and he had the biggest smile on his face. Marty was thirty-two years old, but he was still a kid in a lot of ways. It was only his second year in the big leagues. He had been chosen from more than two hundred applicants to be play-by-play announcer of the Big Red Machine, and he was thrilled by it all. Sometimes Sparky got a kick out of that excitement. This wasn't one of those times.

"What's going on, Marty?" Sparky grumbled as he looked down over his lineup, with Johnny Bench's name scratched off.

"Oh, I went out with Bench last night," Marty said. "And we had the damnedest time."

That woke up Sparky. He looked up from his lineup card, and he had this look on his face, and Marty Brennaman knew—instantly knew—that he had just screwed up. He had just broken the most basic rule of baseball: you never tell a baseball manager about the night before. Sparky had this crazy, almost demented, little smile on his face, and he said: "Is that right?"

Marty swallowed hard. He did not know that Johnny had begged out of the game with the flu. He did not know that Sparky had just come up with an idea, the idea that was going to change the whole damned season. Marty did not know anything. He sat there and looked blankly back at Sparky, and then all of a sudden he heard a commotion in the clubhouse. He watched Sparky race out into the madness.

Joe Morgan had walked into the clubhouse. And he was yelling. Joe had spent much of the night in the hospital, getting those fourteen stitches in his shin. He had done some thinking.

"Screw you, Perez!" he shouted.

"Screw you, Rose!" he shouted.

"Screw you, Bench!" he shouted.

Then he looked at Sparky Anderson, the manager, the man who had wanted them to treat each other with respect. He pointed his finger at Sparky.

"And screw you too!" he shouted.

Sparky looked hard at Morgan. And then, that smile reappeared, the smile that he had flashed back in the office with Marty Brennaman. And then he started laughing. Then they all started laughing.

"When you gonna play again?" Doggie yelled at Joe. "That little scratch on your leg gonna keep you out of the lineup for a month?"

"Screw you, Doggie!" Morgan shouted once more. "I'm playing today."

And that's when Sparky saw his chance. His moment. He had done all of these little things that he felt sure would make the team better. He had moved Rose to third base. He had finally moved George Foster into the starting lineup; George was hitting even better than Danny Driessen. Sparky had moved players up and down the lineup. He had begged and threatened and challenged, and the team just kept coasting along. The team needed a spark, something that would bring them all together.

This was the time. He stormed into the trainer's room where Bench was trying to sleep.

"Bench!" Sparky screamed. "I don't care if your fever is two hundred and one. You're gonna catch, and if we play thirty-five innings, you're gonna catch every damn one of them. Do you hear me?"

And he stormed back into the clubhouse and shouted: "That goes for all you! I'm sick and damn tired of hearing that the Big Red Machine is dead. That's what they're saying out there. That we're dead. Well, let me tell you something, we ain't dead. We're gonna win this thing. We're gonna win because this is the best damn team in baseball."

They were all looking at him now.

"You see that little man?" he said as he pointed at Joe Morgan. "That little man's gonna play tonight. He had fifty stitches put in his leg, and he's playing today. He's playing, and so there ain't nobody in this room that has an excuse. We got too many guys here who don't want to be part of the action. We got too many guys here waiting around for somebody else to do the job."

Now he was going good. He had forgotten how liberating this was, the chance to just unload all his feelings, to get it all out.

"If Cinderella's slippers fit, put them on!" he yelled. "If they don't, get the hell out of the way. Because we are gonna win. I'm telling you that right now. We are gonna win, and we will go right over the top of you guys that don't want to play."

In the tenth inning, with the score tied, Ken Griffey stepped to the plate to face a Montreal pitcher named John Montague. Sparky had moved up Griffey to the second spot in the lineup, and he told Griffey: "Hit the ball on the ground and run your ass off." Griffey could do that; nobody in the game was faster. Of course, Griffey thought he could do a lot of other things too, if the club would give him a chance. He could hit with some power. He could steal some bases. But the orders were clear: "Hit the ball on the ground and run your ass off."

Griffey saw a fastball coming, and he swung hard, and he saw that he had hit it up in the air. But he had hit it good; the ball sounded deep and resounding cracking off the bat. He ran hard to first, he thought it might hit the wall, but it soared over. Home run. Griffey was the hero. He jogged around the bases, and he felt good. Two batters later, Johnny Bench stepped to the plate, and he felt a little bit better—he was no longer shivering, anyway—and he saw a Montague slider, and he swung hard too. "It's about time I hit something," he told reporters afterward, while Griffey looked on and imperceptibly shook his head. Bench had hit a home run too. And the reporters surrounded him.

"Everything's changed," Sparky said. Sparky felt it now. The season had changed. The Machine had been started.

"What did Sparky say in the team meeting?" a reporter asked.

"I can't tell you that," Pete said with a big smile. "All I can tell you is that it was a dandy."

YOU MARK MY WORDS

May 18 to June 16

> *You're a shining star, no matter who you are.*
> *Shining bright to see what you can truly be.*

—EARTH, WIND, AND FIRE, "SHINING STAR"

John Vukovich knew it was coming, knew it in that suppressed way that men know they will die. But he still was not ready for it. Sparky Anderson called him into the office, sat him down, and said, "I'm sending you down to Indianapolis." That was the minor leagues. Vukovich looked hard at his manager's face: was he enjoying this?

"That's not fair," Vukovich said quietly.

"You ain't hitting," Sparky said.

"I was hitting .294 when you took me out of the lineup," Vukovich said.

"You ain't hitting .294 now," Sparky said.

That was true—Vuke had managed only three measly singles in the previous month. He had played his usual exquisite defense, and anyway, how was he supposed to hit when his own manager had no faith at all in him? "You never gave me a shot," he told Sparky.

"I know you feel that way," Sparky said. "But it just ain't so."

Vukovich left the office, walked out to the clubhouse, and packed his things. "I didn't deserve it," he told the few reporters who wanted a reaction. Then they all went up to the tall new relief pitcher who walked into the clubhouse. The kid was twenty-four years old, but he looked to be about half that age. He had the unlikely baseball name of Rawlins Jackson Eastwick III.

"I've got a job to do," Rawly said. "I'm here to help this team win."

George Foster found that he enjoyed being interviewed. He did not expect that. He had always thought of himself as the strong silent type—a man who did not drink, did not smoke, and let his black bat do the talking. It was like those words from Ecclesiastes: "A time to rend, a time to sew; a time to keep silence, and a time to speak." But George had been smacking the Ecclesiastes out of the baseball for most of the season. He had just homered in his last game.

"If I were traded," Foster was saying to columnist Tom Callahan, "I'd grow a mustache right away. Just to see how it'd look."

He watched Callahan feverishly write down the quote—well, why not have some fun with it? Callahan was writing about the Reds' no-facial-hair policy again. Reporters never seemed to tire of writing about the Reds' rules and regulations. The Reds had traded away pitcher Ross Grimsley after he started growing his hair long, leading Grimsley to say, "Sparky's two-faced." Bobby Tolan had been a star for the Reds in the early 1970s, but he also started to rebel, and the Reds banished him to San Diego. The Oakland A's, who had won the three previous World Series, were a wild-looking bunch, men with full mustaches and crazy nicknames, and they represented the times. The Reds, as they saw themselves, represented a better time.

"I'd probably let my hair grow," Pete Rose admitted. "They want us to look good, but you'll get a lot of arguments whether we look good."

Sure, Pete thought the rules were goofy. He especially could not understand the rule against having a beard or mustache. One time, when he felt like busting chops, he asked Sparky: "Hey, do you think Jesus Christ could hit a curveball?" Sparky looked at him, and Pete repeated: "No, I'm asking you seriously: do you think that Jesus Christ could hit a curveball?" When Sparky finally admitted that, yes, he did believe Jesus could hit a curveball, Rose shook his head and shouted: "Not for the Cincinnati Reds he couldn't—not with that beard."

But even though he thought the rules were goofy, he kept his hair short. They all did.

"We respect Sparky," Johnny said as an explanation that was no explanation. "The reason I wanted out of the army reserves was because I didn't like all that 'yes sir' and 'no sir.' But I take it from Sparky."

Johnny paused. "I don't have to take it. But I do."

They all took it, and not one of them could explain *why* they took it. They were tough guys, all of them, but when it came to these rules—rules about how they looked, how they dressed, how they acted—they were as dutiful and accepting as children in grammar school.

Johnny Bench was in agony. It had been more than a month since Gary Matthews had smashed into him at home plate, and Johnny's left shoulder still throbbed like it had in the moments after the collision. He took painkillers every day. He slept on his right side. Still, it hurt like hell when he tried to lift his left arm high. He thought about resting for a few days. But he couldn't rest. He was Johnny Bench.

They booed him now in Cincinnati, every time he hit a weak grounder to the shortstop, every time he struck out, every time he failed to be their Superman. Sure, the booing hurt. The fans had no memory, none at all. Johnny led the league in runs batted in just last year. He had won the Gold Glove as the best defensive catcher every single year since he arrived. People who knew, baseball people, they were already calling him the greatest catcher in the history of baseball, the greatest, and he was just twenty-seven years old. Still they booed.

It was getting to the point where baseball was no fun at all. He played with a busted-up shoulder in front of a bunch of ungrateful fans. Married life wasn't going too well either. Vickie constantly complained that they never had any time together, that he was gone all the time. Well, what did she expect? He was Johnny Bench, baseball star, famous American. He wasn't going to come home during the day and put on his Mister Rogers sweater and live some sort of regular guy life. She knew that. She had to know that. Everybody knew that.

But she didn't know that. Some reporter had asked Rose if Bench's marriage was affecting him—like the guy knew anything about it—and Rose said: "He's hitting about .240." The quote got into *Sports Illustrated*. Got everybody in the clubhouse laughing. But it wasn't funny, Johnny *was* hitting about .240 (actually .256, which wasn't much better), and his marriage was already on the rocks, and he heard every last one of those boos. He heard people mocking his $175,000 salary. He heard it all. It wasn't funny.

"No, I don't believe I'm overpaid," Johnny snapped when asked about overpaid athletes. "I don't think any ballplayer is overpaid. . . . Jimmy Connors plays two tennis matches and winds up with $850,000. Muhammad Ali fights one bout and winds up with five million bucks. . . . Me? I play 190 games, if you count exhibitions. And I'm overpaid?"

Then it was May 24, a warm Saturday afternoon in Cincinnati; the midwestern humidity was beginning to roll in. The Reds had won three games in a row, but they trailed by two runs in the sixth inning when Johnny Bench came up to face Philadelphia relief pitcher Gene Garber. Johnny banged a long home run to left field, and he ran coolly around the base, and he heard the tentative cheers, and he shrugged.

The Reds trailed by one run in the eighth inning when Johnny Bench came up to face Garber again. He banged another long home run to left field, and he ran coolly around the bases again, and now the cheers were louder. Sure, they loved him when he hit home runs.

American journalists were expelled from Vietnam. Bobby Unser beat favorite A. J. Foyt to the finish line at the Indianapolis 500, though the larger story was Tom Sneva's fiery crash—his car tumbled and exploded in flames. Somehow, he walked away. The Alaska pipeline work was halted for environmental reasons. The Golden State Warriors won the NBA championship, though few around the country noticed—NBA games drew such low television ratings that the games were often shown on tape delay. President Ford announced that the U.S. government would impose an oil tax that would raise gas prices by a penny or two a gallon. Gas was running about 55¢ a gallon.

In London, the daredevil Evel Knievel announced his retirement unexpectedly. Knievel had come to London to jump thirteen London buses on his motorcycle. Wembley Stadium was packed with people. Knievel had created his own legend. He was, according to myth and newspaper interviews, a former bank robber and a man who sold insurance policies to people in mental institutions. He had led elk-hunting expeditions into Yellowstone Park. Evel Knievel said he got his name in a Montana jail when he happened to be the next cell over from notorious criminal Awful Knofel.

Knievel invented this persona, not just as a daredevil who wore gaudy full-body suits and jumped various objects on a motorcycle, but as a man's man, the toughest hombre in America. The story goes that for his first televised jump—the one that made him famous—he walked into Caesars Palace in Las Vegas, slapped a $100 chip on the blackjack table, busted out, downed a shot of Wild Turkey, grabbed two showgirls, and walked out into the sunlight. He climbed on his motorcycle, made it growl, raced up the ramp, took off, and soared over the famous Caesars Palace fountains. Evel would say it was beautiful up there, a view no other man had ever seen, a feeling greater than sex, and it would have been better still if he had not lost power in his motorcycle just before takeoff. He crashed on top of a van, flipped over the handlebars, skidded about a quarter-mile, crushed his pelvis and femur, and descended into a coma. When he emerged from the coma, he was an international sensation.

He had tried many stunts, many of them spectacular failures, such as the time in 1974 when he crashed while trying to jump some sort of aircraft across Snake River Canyon in Idaho. But people still needed to see Evel Knievel. More than seventy thousand people showed up in London to see him attempt to jump thirteen single-deck buses. There was a point behind the number thirteen—Evel Knievel believed in tempting fate.

He pushed his 750cc Harley Davidson to about 100 miles per hour, raced up the ramp, soared about 140 feet (a new world record, his people would later claim), and clipped the thirteenth and final bus. His motorcycle tumbled over and over, and when it stopped, Knievel was stretched out on the ground, motionless, apparently unconscious. For five minutes, maybe ten, Evel Knievel did not twitch. A couple of medics brought out a stretcher and started to carry him away. But then, Evel Knievel shakily stood to wild cheers. Frank Gifford, the great former football player and ABC announcer, pleaded with Knievel to get on the stretcher. He would not. "I walked in, I walk out," he shouted. Two assistants walked him over to the platform where a microphone was waiting.

"Ladies and gentlemen of this wonderful country," Evel Knievel said. "I have got to tell you that you are the last people to see me jump. I shall never jump again, and that is the truth. I am through."

Five months later, Evel Knievel jumped fourteen buses at King's Island in Cincinnati.

May 26, 1975

Team record: 25–20

For the first time all season—but not for the last, nowhere close to the last—Sparky Anderson knew that the Machine would win. The Reds trailed Montreal 4–0 in the second game of the doubleheader, but the score didn't matter. Nothing mattered. His team had just won its fifth game in a row to start off the doubleheader, and the guys had that look, the one Sparky had been waiting for all season. They would not lose. They could not lose.

He sat back and watched. It was the fifth inning. He wondered how his Reds would win this time. Would they hit a couple of home runs? Would they steal a few bases? Darrel Chaney led off the inning with a single. Then Pete Rose walked. And Ken Griffey walked to load the bases. That brought up Joe Morgan, the little man, and Sparky could see the panic on the face of Montreal's pitcher, Steve Renko. He walked Joe Morgan too.

Sparky smiled. Few people appreciated walks as an offensive weapon in 1975. Owners—as Rose had found in his negotiations—did not pay for walks. Fans did not cheer walks. They did not even list walks in the statistics on the back of Topps baseball cards. In that time when being a man meant jumping buses, few had any use for a batter walking to first base.

But Sparky Anderson loved walks. He loved getting the runners on base, but even more, he loved the way that walks psychologically broke down pitchers' spirits. The Reds led the league in walks in 1972 and 1974. They were leading the league in walks again. Sparky looked toward the mound—he saw in Renko's body language the effect the walks were having on him. Sparky thought of the old baseball line: Renko looked like a kid standing in the rain. Sparky turned to Ted

Kluszewski, the Reds' hitting coach, and said: "Here comes a grand slam." And Johnny hit a grand slam.

"It's like I told the fans at our luncheon the other day," Sparky said to reporters after the game. "Before it's all over with, a lot of people are going to be jumping back on the bandwagon in Cincinnati. You mark my words, okay? You mark my words."

While Rose and Morgan and Perez and the rest of the hitters would sit in the clubhouse and insult each other, many of the Reds pitchers would gather in a different part of the clubhouse and discuss their favorite topic: theories about why Sparky Anderson hated them. There was no doubt that he did. Someone on the team—probably Jack Billingham, a tall right-hander from Florida who had led the team in victories each of the previous two seasons—had started calling Sparky "Captain Hook," because of the coldhearted way he would hook a pitcher in the middle of a game and bring in whatever reliever came to mind. Then he would hook that reliever and bring in another. Sparky used more relief pitchers than any manager before him. Pitchers were as disposable as razor blades.

As time went on, they came up with increasingly more complicated reasons for Sparky's hatred of pitchers, but nobody could improve on Billingham's theory: Sparky hated pitchers because he could not hit them. It was a theory Billingham would hold on to; even thirty years after the Machine broke up, Billingham would sit in the crowd at various events and listen to Sparky Anderson talk about his amazing baseball team. About halfway through Sparky's spiel—having noticed again that Sparky had not mentioned a single pitcher—Billingham would shout out (with a bit of delight in his voice): "Hey, Sparky, it sure is amazing how you won all those games without a single pitcher on the team."

It was true, Sparky had little use for pitchers in general (and Billingham in particular—Sparky thought Billingham was too casual in his pitching approach). But Sparky loved a young left-handed pitcher named Don Gullett. He was an athletic prodigy from a small Kentucky town called Lynn, along the Ohio River somewhere between Ashland and the Shawnee State Forest. Baseball scouts had a heck of a time finding it. But Gullett was so good, they did find it. Gullett was one of those kids touched by God; he could do everything. He could throw a baseball hard. He could make jump shots from all over the basketball court. He could run through defenders on the football field. Gullett was also intensely private, but if you caught him on the right day, you might get him to talk about the day he scored eleven touchdowns and kicked six extra points while playing for McKell High School. It seems his coach had gotten mad at the coach at Wurtland High—the Wurtland coach had made some remark in the paper after the last game that his team had shut down Gullett—and so, as Gullett said, "he sort of turned me loose."

Cliff Alexander, the legendary old scout who had helped discover the Hall of Fame left-handed pitcher Sandy Koufax, was working for the Reds then. He made his way out to Lynn, and he saw Gullett throw a seven-inning perfect game. Gullett struck out twenty of the twenty-one batters he faced. His scouting report: "Better at eighteen than Koufax." The Reds drafted Gullett, signed him, and Sparky fell in love the first time he saw Gullett pitch.

"Mark my words, this guy stays healthy, he's going to the Hall of Fame," Sparky told reporters. That was back in 1971, when Gullett was just twenty years old. Sparky did tend to get carried away, but there was no missing Gullett's pitching talents. He was left-handed, and he threw hard, and he had pinpoint control. He won sixteen games in 1971. No twenty-year-old lefty in fifty years had won sixteen games in a season. The last lefty pitcher to win so many at such a young age was a wild young kid out of a Baltimore orphanage named Babe Ruth.

———————

"Well, I'm not Babe Ruth," Gullett said. He didn't say much. That was another reason Sparky loved him: pitchers were meant to be seen and not heard. Gullett didn't make excuses. He didn't play defense lawyer when he had a bad outing. He just took the baseball, and he threw hard fastballs, and he won baseball games.

"He's like Koufax," Sparky told columnist Tom Callahan before the season.

"Sparky," Callahan would grumble, "he's not like Koufax. The guy has never even won twenty games in a season."

"He will win twenty this year," Sparky said as he waved off Callahan's doubts. "He's like Koufax." Sparky was starry-eyed, like a junior high school girl daydreaming about the Bay City Rollers. Callahan was not as impressed. He thought Gullett was talented but limited. He preferred other Reds pitchers. He preferred Gary Nolan's precision, or Jack Billingham's ability to pitch well in big games.

But on the last day of May, Gullett faced the St. Louis Cardinals, and he was on, and even Callahan had to admit that when Gullett was on, he was a force of nature. Joe Morgan hit a two-run homer in the first inning off a thirty-nine-year-old and fading Bob Gibson, and Gullett took over from there. He pitched nine shutout innings. The Cardinals never even managed to get a runner to third base against him. "That kid's hot," Gibson said after the game, and Sparky could hardly contain his glee.

"I wouldn't trade our guy Gullett for any pitcher in baseball," Sparky said. "He's the best there is. The very best there is."

The Machine had won nine of ten, they had moved to within a half-game of the Los Angeles Dodgers, and pitcher Pedro Borbon looked like he wanted to kill somebody. It was a natural look for Borbon, though he looked especially wild-eyed as the rain fell in Pittsburgh. Pedro had heard that someone on the Pittsburgh radio team was calling him "Dracula" on the air, and he did not like it one bit. "I go get him," he said to a couple of the guys in the clubhouse. They nodded and laughed and watched Borbon walk out of the clubhouse and out into the rain.

"Where'd Pedro say he was going?"

"To kill somebody."

"Okay. What are we playing, seven card?"

If the Machine had been a television sitcom, then Borbon would have been the crazy uncle. Everyone had a favorite Borbon story. There was the time Pedro went around the clubhouse and talked about Bernardo, his grandfather in the Dominican Republic. Pedro insisted that he was 136 years old. There were the times he would sit in front of his locker before games and play strange drumlike rhythms on his right biceps—he could play numerous songs. And there were times—his teammates' favorite times—when Borbon would come up with ways to show off the strength of his amazing arm. In 1969, when Pedro was a rookie with the California Angels, for kicks, he stood at home plate and threw the ball over the center-field wall at Fenway Park in Boston. In 1972, he stood at second base and tried to throw the ball off the Astrodome roof in Houston. ("And I almost did it," he would say.) He panicked pitching coaches and managers, but Pedro knew his right arm was indestructible. He hardly even had to warm up before coming into a game. "This arm," he said as he flexed his arm muscle and made the drum sound, "is always ready. I pitch every day if they let me."

That was the fun side of Pedro Borbon. There was another side. He had a fierce temper. After the famed 1973 playoff brawl with the Mets—the one Pete Rose started with his violent slide into New York's Bud Harrelson—Borbon realized he had mistakenly put on a Mets cap. He tore it to shreds with his teeth. One winter in the Dominican, a minor league manager named Tommy Lasorda tried to take him out of a game. Borbon wheeled and threw the ball over the center-field fence.

The "Dracula" nickname came after a different fight. The Reds and the Pittsburgh Pirates brawled during a game in 1974. Most baseball fights end up with a couple of guys playing pat-a-cake and the rest of the players watching. This fight was unusual: hard punches were thrown, players got knocked down, and Pittsburgh's Daryl Patterson, a thirty-year-old pitcher trying to revive his career, made the mistake of pushing Borbon aside. Borbon promptly sucker-punched him, pulled Patterson's hair, and then bit him on the side. Patterson had to go get a tetanus shot.

"Like a dog!" Borbon said with, perhaps, an inappropriate amount of glee. He enjoyed the attention. But he did not enjoy the Dracula nickname that came with it, and during the rain delay in Pittsburgh he ran outside and found Nellie King, the Pirates radio announcer.

"You know my name?" he shouted at King.

"Yes," King said. "Pedro Borbon."

"Borbon. Yes. Borbon. Not Dracula."

"I never called you anything but Borbon," King said calmly.

Borbon was confused. He knew the Pittsburgh radio man had called him Dracula. Something was not adding up. And then he thought: *Maybe it was the other Pittsburgh radio guy, Bob Prince, who called me Dracula.*

"You tell the other guy I no like it," Borbon said.

"I don't carry messages," King said. "Tell him yourself."

Borbon considered this. Then, with impeccable logic, he said, "Maybe I punch you in the nose."

King, a six-foot-six former pitcher, looked down at Borbon (who stood six-foot-two), just shook his head, and walked away. Borbon shrugged. He had made his point, whatever he had intended that point to be. Rain washed away the game.

June 4, 1975

Team record: 30–21

American sports had turned upside down overnight. On the front page of the morning papers, there was the news that President Ford had signed a new law called Title IX. The law required that all public schools and all colleges give equal athletic opportunities to women, except in the case of contact sports like football.

Nobody seemed sure what this meant, but panic was in the air. "This may well signal the end of intercollegiate athletic programs as we have known them," said Michael Scott, a lawyer for the National Collegiate Athletic Association. Football coaches screamed that American sports were doomed.

And that wasn't even the big news in the Cincinnati Reds clubhouse. No, bigger, much bigger, was a story coming out of New York: Pele, the great Brazilian soccer player, had signed to play for the New York Cosmos. His price: $4.7 million.

There had never been a contract like it, certainly not in team sports. The Reds players were not quite sure what it meant, but they all had this idea that the world was changing. Johnny Bench found himself almost daily defending his $175,000 salary, even though he played hard for it, he played hurt for it, and he made the All-Star team every year. Now here was a soccer player—a great soccer player, yes, but still a soccer player—signing for almost $5 million. Americans didn't even like soccer.

Yes, Johnny and the rest sensed that something significant was happening. Things would change dramatically in baseball after the 1975 season. The baseball players' union would use a couple of pitchers—Andy Messersmith and Dave McNally—to challenge baseball's "reserve clause." The clause basically came down to one sentence that stated if the player and team could not come to terms, then the "Club shall have the right by written notice to the Player to renew this contract for the period of one year on the same terms." Union head Marvin Miller could not believe that this one sentence essentially bound players to their teams until they were traded, sold, or released. The sentence very clearly said "one year." The owners claimed that the team's right to renew the contract repeated in perpetuity, but Miller thought that wouldn't hold up in a court. And sure enough, an arbitrator named Peter Seitz ruled that Messersmith and McNally were free agents.

"I'm not a new Abraham Lincoln freeing the slaves," Seitz would say.

"Baseball cannot function under the Messersmith decision," baseball commissioner Bowie Kuhn would gripe.

"Things in baseball will never be the same," Bob Howsam said.

Baseball survived fine, but Howsam was right: things never were quite the same after 1975. Salaries skyrocketed. Players had the right to become free agents after six years, and they were able to drive up their value. The average salary in 1975 was about $44,000. Four years after Seitz's decision, the average salary in baseball was about $120,000. By 1989, it would be about half a million a year. By 1992, it would be more than $1 million.

And in many ways, it all could be traced back to the enormous contract that Pele signed with the New York Cosmos. The contract told baseball players they were shooting way too low.

Pete wasn't hitting worth a damn, and it was ticking him off. Sure, he was happy that the club was beginning to win—the Reds had moved into a first-place tie with the Dodgers. But, realistically, no, Pete wasn't happy, he could not be happy when he was not hitting. His batting average, as he knew better than anyone, was .293. Back in Cincinnati, Pete sat at the kitchen table every morning and worked out his batting average. His wife, Karoyln, would watch him happily when he did that. Karolyn and Pete had married in 1964, and she knew better than anyone his faults and vices. She figured he cheated on her when he was on the road. But he loved those bright mornings, after he had cracked three or four hits the night before, and he would sit at the table like a schoolboy doing his last-minute homework. And when the numbers came out right—when he found himself well above the .300 mark—his smile had to look, more or less, like the one Pythagoras had on his face when he came up with his math theorem.

But this wasn't one of those bright mornings. Pete did the math in his hotel room in Pittsburgh. He had 61 hits in 208 at-bats—and that came out to a .293 batting average no matter how many times you ran those numbers through the long-division grinder.

"Hey, Rose," Morgan said to him, like he often said to Pete as he walked into the clubhouse. "What's the batting average looking like these days?"

"Fuck you," Rose said. "That's my goddamned batting average."

Morgan smiled. Rose did not. A .293 average. Jesus. Pete had already spent the whole winter living with last season's .284 batting average, and that was hard enough. Pete Rose knew what he was. He was a .300 hitter. That was what he was born to be. That was what his father, Big Pete, had raised him to be. When Little Pete was eight years old, Big Pete went up to his Knothole League coach—they called Little League "Knothole League" in Cincinnati—and said: "I'll make you a deal. You have to promise to let my son switch-hit. And I mean, you have to let him switch-hit every time, no matter what. If you do that, I promise Pete will give you everything he's got, and he will never miss a game. Never. We'll even leave him here when we go on vacation."

That's how it was: Big Pete happily sold his son into baseball servitude in exchange for the right to switch-hit. And more, Little Pete happily went. He never missed a Knothole League game or any other game. He never stepped foot out of Cincinnati until he went to

Geneva, New York, to play his first year of minor league ball. By the time he went to Geneva, Pete could switch-hit like a son of a gun.

Pete hit .300 every single year from 1965 to 1973, nine straight years. People wondered why he cared so much about his statistics; well, they were more than numbers to him. Big Pete (as Harry Rose) worked with numbers every single day at the bank, every day, boring and dry numbers. With that in mind, Harry Rose did not raise his oldest son to just be a major league baseball player. No, Harry Rose raised his son to hit .300.

Pete Rose jogged out to the field for batting practice and worked the math out in his mind. The Reds were playing Pittsburgh. And he knew that if he got two hits in his first two at-bats, that would make him 63-for-210, which would come out precisely to a .300 batting average. If he managed to go three-for-four, he would leave the game with a .302 average. The only thing that mattered was to get that average back up where it belonged. He needed three hits.

First time up, Jerry Reuss, a tough left-handed pitcher, threw Pete a hard-sinking fastball, the kind that caused most batters to swing over the top and bang ground balls into the dust. Rose was not like most batters. He cracked a hard line drive to right, a base hit for sure, only then Pittsburgh's first baseman, Bob Robertson, caught the ball. He was oh-for-one.

Next time up, Pete hit an easy ground ball to second base. He was oh-for-two. Third time up, he needed a hit, needed one badly, only this wasn't looking like the day to get it. Reuss was throwing a no-hitter. And Rose hit another easy ground ball to second base. He was oh-for-three.

Davey Concepcion finally smacked a single off Reuss's shin in the seventh that broke up the no-hitter and, at the same time, knocked Reuss out of the game. Rose came up in the eighth with the Reds down 2–1, and he faced righty relief pitcher Dave Giusti. That meant Pete could go back to hitting left-handed, which was good. He felt more comfortable hitting lefty. It didn't matter on this day. Pete topped the ball again and grounded out to second base. He was zero-for-four.

The Reds lost the game. More to the point, Pete's average dropped to .288. Back in the hotel room, he did the math. Now he needed four hits against the Cubs on Friday to get his average above .300. Pete was losing ground.

Davey Concepcion kept getting the strangest calls from people back home in Venezuela. They only wanted to hear his voice. Seemed that a radio station in Caracas had reported that Davey had been assassinated. He had no idea how a rumor like that could have started, but the people who called him sounded so convinced that after a little while Davey began to feel uneasy, like maybe his life really was in danger. He was not sure, though, why anyone would want to assassinate him.

"Maybe it's because of the error you made a couple of days ago," Johnny said helpfully.

Weird things were happening to the Machine. The kid reliever Will McEnaney was pitching in an exhibition game against Detroit when suddenly this sharp pain pounded in his chest. He felt sure that he was having a heart attack. Not that it surprised him exactly. Will did like to live life. He smoked two packs of cigarettes a day. He enjoyed the nights. But the chest pain scared the hell out of him. He kept on pitching and hoped that the pain would just go away. It did not. It lasted the whole time he was in the game. It pounded while he was in the clubhouse. It cut through him on the plane ride. It was a damned long heart attack. When he woke up the next morning, the pain was gone—and in gratitude he promptly quit his two-pack-a-day cigarette habit. And he did not pick it up again for days.

A few days before that, Philadelphia Phillies pitcher Jim Lonborg hit Tony Perez with a pitch and fractured Doggie's thumb. Doggie could not swing the bat, the pain was excruciating, though the pain was probably not as intense as the agony he had to endure on the bench while listening to Pete and Joe rag him.

"Hey, Doggie, how's that boo-boo?" Joe said every day, five times a day.

"I think Doggie's just so happy with his .215 batting average, he just doesn't want to risk it," Pete said.

"I'm a little guy, Doggie," Joe said. "It's hard for me to carry your sorry ass."

"Hey, Joe, what is the area code in Cincinnati?" Pete asked.

"It's 513," Joe said.

"Divide that in half, and you still are hitting better than Doggie."

Tony would then say something in Spanish that defied translation.

"Hey, Doggie," Davey said the day of his assassination rumor. "They're saying back home that I'm dead."

"Join the club," Doggie said. "We all dead."

And that day, Concepcion hit a two-run double and George Foster hit a home run. Don Gullett pitched a complete game and allowed one run. The Machine won again.

June 8, 1975

CINCINNATI
REDS VS. CUBS
Team record: 32–22
First place by one and a half games

Joe Morgan had that same feeling. He was about to change the game again. Lots of people around baseball despised Joe Morgan.

They thought him arrogant. And hey, not everybody on the Reds loved Joe either. Ken Griffey and George Foster, for instance, thought him distant. He spent much of his time off the field alone in his room, listening to jazz, reading the adventure comic books that allowed him to escape. "George and I kept waiting for him to take us under his wing," Ken Griffey would say years later. "But it never happened."

Still, they could not help but admire the way he played baseball. Joe had no weaknesses. If Pete had learned ferocity from his father, Joe had learned completeness from his dad. Leonard Morgan had played semipro baseball, and he told his son, again and again, that the secret to success was the ability to do everything well. They would go to minor league baseball games in Oakland, Leonard and Joe, and the father would express his disdain for those players who hit home runs but did not seem to care about their defense, or those who could run fast but did not seem to take pride in their hitting. "Be everything," Leonard would say.

The Reds trailed Chicago 1–0, seventh inning, first game of a doubleheader, and the Cubs' pitcher, Rick Reuschel, had allowed just one hit, a little ground ball up the middle to Cesar Geronimo. Reuschel was overpowering the Machine. Morgan worked Reuschel for a walk.

Then the game began. Morgan danced off the bag, shifting his weight from his left leg to his right, then his right leg back to his left, and he inched a little bit closer to second base, and he had that smile, the Joe Morgan smile, the one that said: *Oh, yeah, I'm about to steal second base, and there's nothing you can do about it.* That smile was yet another reason people didn't like Joe.

But he was right. There was nothing that anyone could do to keep him from stealing. On the bases, Joe Morgan was an artist at work. Reuschel threw over to first base to chase Morgan back to first base. Morgan looked back at Reuschel, and his smile grew larger, now it said, *You poor man, you think throwing over to first base will stop me? You cannot stop me. I have spent hours studying you, hours looking over your every physical quirk, how your left leg twitches, how your shoulder slumps, how your back leans. I have studied you, and I know when you will pitch. You cannot fool me. I'm already at second base. It's futile for you to throw over here.* Reuschel threw over to the bag again, and Morgan dived back in.

"This guy knows he can't pick me off, right?" Joe said to Cubs first baseman Andre Thornton, and he dusted himself off. But Reuschel did not seem to know that at all. In fact, Morgan noticed that something in Reuschel's face had changed. He was no longer so sure. He wore this look of weary apprehension, as if he was waiting for something to happen, a balloon to pop, a gunshot to go off. He started to throw over to first base again, only this time the umpire raised his arm.

"Balk!" the umpire said as he pointed at Reuschel.

Morgan jogged easily to second base. He had done what he wanted to do. He had broken something in Reuschel. Pitchers, Joe believed, were fragile creatures. When they felt good, powerful, invincible— when they got in the flow, as the saying went—they pitched easy and you couldn't do much against them. But when you got underneath that somehow, when you made pitchers nervous even for a second, you had them. Reuschel looked back at Joe, and then he threw a fat fastball to Johnny Bench. And Johnny turned on it, crushed it, hit it just to the right of the left-field foul pole. That was a home run. The Reds won again. They won the second game of the doubleheader too. And when the day ended, the Reds were all alone in first place.

Gary Nolan won that first game. He pitched all nine innings, allowed only one run, and found that he had adjusted to his new life and his new arm. No, he could not throw his fastball by hitters anymore. But he could outsmart them. He was 6–3 with a 2.55 ERA. He was pitching as well as he ever had before.

In a strange way, it was even more rewarding now because, for the first time really, he was using his mind to outsmart hitters. He found that they would get themselves out if he gave them half a chance. Throw them a low pitch and they would beat it into the ground. Throw them a high one around the eyes and they would swing right underneath it. Throw them sliders when they wanted fastballs and fastballs when they wanted sliders, pitch inside when they looked outside and pitch outside when they looked hungry and eager and angry. It wasn't easy, no, but it was fundamental. The only way they could beat him, Gary figured, was if he made a mistake.

Years later, after his playing days were done, Gary became a pit-boss at Vegas casinos and later worked at a casino in his hometown of Oroville. He found that it wasn't much different from pitching. He would stand in those casinos, and he could not even hear the clanging of the slot machines. They faded into deep background, the way crowd noise did when he pitched. He would look at his clients for only a few seconds and size them up. He found that he could instantly tell something about them. Something in the eyes. He could tell if they were desperate, tell if they were hiding something, and it was second nature to him. Though he rarely thought about it, he knew that it came from pitching, from sizing up hitters, from guessing what they wanted and then throwing something else at them.

"You know what's funny?" Gary would say as he thought about what came of his life. "I never have gambled. I've been around it all this time, and I've never even been tempted to gamble myself. I guess it's because I don't see the point of it. I know how it always turns out."

His walkie-talkie buzzed. There was some issue on the floor. He was needed.

"I guess," he said, "I never saw much use for losing. I guess I learned that from Pete Rose and Johnny Bench and the Cincinnati Reds."

June 13, 1975

Team record: 37–24
First place by three and a half games

Frank Sinatra always said that he was for whatever would get you through the night. Sparky Anderson was for whatever won a ball game. He believed in voodoo, curses, horoscopes, and dreams. He believed in hot streaks, cold streaks, gut feelings, and four-leaf clovers. People out there did not know, could not know, how helpless a manager could feel in the dugout. There were only a few things he could do. And Sparky would do all of them. He would yank pitchers like they were weeds in his backyard. He would devise all kinds of strategies. He would shout out encouraging words, and a few discouraging words when they were needed. But, really, there was only so much he could do, and so he came to count on signs, witchcraft, lady luck, and that was why, in the eighth inning, with the Reds losing to the Cubs 8–6, Sparky moved to a new spot in the dugout. And just when he moved there, Tony Perez hit a line drive single to start the inning.

"Oh, oh, Larry," Sparky said to pitching coach Larry Shepard, "I found the spot. I found the lucky spot." He lifted up his right leg. Cesar Geronimo hit a ground ball single up the middle.

"Oh, yeah, Larry," Sparky said, "this is definitely it. I have found the spot."

Funny thing how baseball works. A manager can spend countless hours working out his game plan, teaching his players, breaking down matchups, but in the end he will find himself sitting in one spot in the dugout with his right leg in the air.

"Atta boy, Davey," Sparky shouted when Concepcion hit a sacrifice fly. Now his Machine trailed by only one run. And just as Sparky was thinking that it sure would be nice to steal this game—*Georgie!*—George Foster hit a long home run. The Reds led. And then Pete Rose hit a home run. And then Ken Griffey hit a single, and what followed was crazy—the Cubs' second baseman, Manny Trillo, threw the ball to his pitcher, Oscar Zamora, but Oscar was not paying attention. He never even saw the ball go by. It rolled behind home plate, and Ken Griffey ran to third while the Cubs chased around like kids on a Little League diamond. Griffey scored when Joe Morgan hit a single. "Hey, Larry," Sparky yelled out. "Is this a lucky spot or is this a lucky spot?" The Reds had eleven runs.

Then, in the ninth inning, Sparky sat in his spot again, one leg up, and Cesar Geronimo hit a double past a diving center fielder with the unfortunate name of Rick Monday. George Foster walked. That crazy pitcher Pedro Borbon stepped up to the plate. "If he gets a hit, I quit," Sparky said. Borbon had gotten one hit all year. Borbon hit a line drive single to right field.

"Hey, Greek," Johnny Bench shouted to third-base coach Alex Grammas. "Get back in here. You're the new manager." And then to Sparky: "And don't you be calling us for tickets when we're in California."

Everyone howled. Everyone slapped backs. Everyone bent over in laughter. And Sparky stayed in his hot spot, and Pete singled, Griffey singled, Doug Flynn singled, Bill Plummer doubled, Doggie singled—when it was all over, the Reds had eighteen runs, they had their seventeenth victory in twenty games, they were pulling away from the Los Angeles Dodgers, everything was beautiful and alive and oh so lucky.

"You can bet," Sparky said to reporters after the game, "that I'm starting in my hot spot tomorrow."

Yes, a manager so rarely gets a moment like that, so rarely gets to stand on the mountaintop and look down and think: *Hey, it looks pretty good from up here.* But Sparky had that moment in Chicago. And here it was, three days later, back in Cincinnati, and Sparky was having another moment just like it. His Reds led Atlanta 9–1. His best pitcher, Don Gullett, had given up just four hits. The Los Angeles Dodgers were fading from sight. How could he describe the moment? Nothing could go wrong. Nothing. There would be problems tomorrow, no doubt. There would be headaches to come. But today, for once, Sparky could rest easy.

What a joy it had been watching this game. In the very first inning, he got to see one of his favorite things in baseball. He had gotten to see a runner try to steal a base on Johnny Bench. They almost never tried anymore, that's how frightened they were of the Johnny Bench arm. But this time Atlanta's Ralph Garr led off the game with a walk, and Garr could really motor—they called Garr "Road Runner"—and so Sparky leaned forward on the bench and hoped to see something good.

He saw Garr take his lead, and he watched Garr lean toward second. Then Garr twisted his cleats in the dirt and began his sprint. He got an okay jump—he must have gotten a step or two going before Gullett released his pitch—but an okay jump was not good enough to beat Johnny Bench. There had been catchers with great arms before him. And there had been catchers who could jump out of their stance and throw the ball quickly. And there had been catchers who had a knack for throwing the ball accurately, making it land right on the corner of the bag. But there had never been a catcher, never, who could do all those things like Johnny.

Bench saw Garr take off, and by the time the pitch hit his glove, Garr was already in full motion. Johnny caught it, switched the ball into his right hand, and threw with such force that his catcher's mask twisted and then fell off. Sparky thought the ball was never more than five feet off the ground. It hit Joe Morgan's glove in just the right spot—Morgan did not even need to move his hand. Garr slid into the tag. He was out. And it was beautiful.

Sparky got to see Joe Morgan do a little bit of everything. What a beautiful thing it was to manage the little man. In the first inning, he rifled a single off of a Phil Niekro knuckleball to score Ken Griffey. Then he stole second base. In the third inning, he drilled a double down the right-field line, again scoring Griffey. Johnny then doubled him home. In the seventh, Joe drew a walk—that was his fifty-seventh walk in fifty-nine games. Incredible. Then, in the eighth, Joe hit a home run, scoring Griffey for the third time. What a man.

And of course, Gullett pitched another gem. He made one mistake, he gave up a home run to Cito Gaston, but other than that, he breezed through the Braves lineup. It was so easy that Sparky was able to rest Bench and Pete and Joe in the ninth inning. He wanted to sit close to them. It was all so perfect, so wonderful, and for once Sparky Anderson wanted to enjoy the feeling. God had blessed him with this job, and God had blessed him with these great players. And there on the mound, his favorite pitcher—Gullett—gave up a single to Atlanta's Earl Williams, then another single to Marty Perez, then another to Vic Correll.

"You better go get him, Skip," Johnny Bench said with that smirk on his face, and he chewed hard on his blend of tobacco and bubble gum. And for a moment Sparky did think about taking Gullett out of the game, but he decided not to do that. Gullett still looked strong. He still threw hard. What the hell? Let the kid finish the game.

"You're going soft, Sparky," Joe said, and Sparky felt like a million bucks. He loved when they teased him. He rocked a little on the bench and watched Sugar Bear Blanks step up to the plate. Sugar Bear had been a pain in the ass all year. He had beaten the Reds twice already with big hits in the final inning. Well, what the hell— he could hit a home run to Toledo and it wouldn't matter now. Gullett wound up and pitched, and Sugar Bear Blanks did not hit a home run to Toledo. Instead, he lashed a line drive at Gullett's knees. Gullett reached down with his glove and his pitching hand. And like that, there was this sound, this sickening thud. And Gullett was on the ground and he was . . . was he screaming? Yes. He was screaming, "My thumb! My thumb!"

Sparky ran out to the field, but he was in a daze. It had happened too fast. His mind could not quite get around it. But sure enough, there was Gullett writhing in pain on the ground. There was no doubt about it. He had broken his thumb.

"There's nothing we can do to cover up," Sparky told reporters in his office. The locker room was silent—none of the usual ripping. "That right there is the best pitcher in the National League. I've told you all this before: if he don't get hurt, he's going to be in the Hall of Fame."

The reporters asked him what he planned to do, but Sparky was not ready to talk about that. Also, he did not know. He could only sit there and look out, glassy-eyed, and blame himself for not pulling Gullett when he had the chance, for not seeing this coming, for feeling too good. That was the real mistake. You never felt too good. That's how you hurt the ball club.

Next morning, Sparky sat at breakfast at the Holiday Inn with his friend Jeff Ruby. He looked strangely happy. Ruby could not quite figure it out. Ruby could feel his own face flushed, and he suspected that he had this panicked look on his face, because he felt panicked. "So you're telling me that Gullett is out?" he asked.

"Yep," Sparky said. "I'd say he'll miss two months for sure. He might miss the rest of the season."

"This is horrible," Ruby said. "We're in real trouble now."

Only Sparky kept on smiling, and kept on eating his breakfast, and he did not seem in trouble. Ruby couldn't quite figure it out. In private moments like this, Sparky always panicked. He *always* worried. Now he looked like a man who had just inherited money. Maybe he was just trying to put a happy face on the situation. Maybe he was trying to pretend that his best pitcher had not just broken his thumb. Maybe he was delirious from another night without sleep.

"Sparky, what are you going to do now?" Ruby said.

And with that, Sparky put down his fork, like he had been waiting for the question all along. And he said: "Bubula, I'll tell you exactly what's going to happen. Now they're all going to find out what a real genius I am."

June 17 to July 28

> *You're gonna need a bigger boat.*

—POLICE CHIEF MARTIN BRODY (ROY SCHEIDER), *Jaws*

June 18, 1975

CINCINNATI
REDS VS. BRAVES

Team record: 39–26
First place by two and a half games

"Businessman Special" in Cincinnati. Bob Howsam came up with the nutty idea to bring back afternoon games for those fans who wanted a little old-fashioned weekday baseball. He had this image in his mind of a stadium filled with men in business suits, all of them wearing hats, like it was 1938 all over again.

"A baseball game is like a Broadway show," he would say in interview after interview. Yes, it was all a show, and that was why he insisted on the players wearing uniforms precisely the same way, why he would never allow his catchers to stand in the on-deck circle while wearing their shin guards ("It just looks terrible," he told Sparky), why the Cincinnati Reds batters were never to be seen wearing their baseball caps underneath their batting helmets. It was all a show, and it had to be precise.

"He treats us like we're a fucking chorus line" is how Johnny Bench described it. And there was something to that: Howsam had this image in his mind, this brilliant image of what baseball in Cincinnati should look like. And the more other teams spiraled away from that image, the more certain he felt that the Reds stood for something bigger than baseball.

For years, the "Businessman Special" crowds in Cincinnati were sparse and grumpy—it was a fine idea in theory, but in reality few people really had the freedom in the 1970s to knock off work and head out to the ballpark. Plus, it was damned hot and humid in Cincinnati in the summer; there was a good reason Cincinnati was the first major league team to play under lights back in 1935. There was nothing in baseball quite like the midwestern fire of St. Louis and Cincinnati and Kansas City in the afternoons.

But Howsam stuck with the idea. And here it was, a Wednesday afternoon against a terrible Atlanta Braves team, and more than thirty thousand people poured into Riverfront Stadium. They were not all wearing suits like Howsam had envisioned, but it was still beautiful. The town was falling for this team again.

Nobody could believe the heat. You could actually see it lifting off the field in waves, like desert heat in the movies. Johnny Bench had been playing in Cincinnati for almost eight years, and he had never felt this sort of oven burst as he walked out of the clubhouse and onto the field. He knew before the game even began that he would lose five pounds before it was over, maybe ten pounds. He was edgy. They were all edgy—they were playing the Braves, who were no match, who did not even belong on the same field. "Let's play quick," Johnny muttered to his pitcher, Jack Billingham.

With the score tied in the third inning, Bench came to the plate, and he swung angrily and ripped a hard ground ball down the third-base line. The ball smashed right into the knee of third-base umpire Lee Weyer. And while he hopped around in pain, the ball bounced out to center field. It was ruled a ground-rule double, two runs scored, and Bench stood at second base with a big smile he could not quite hide. Well, at least someone else would feel a little bit of pain on this preposterously hot day.

"You ever hit an umpire before?" Joe asked in the clubhouse after the game.

"Wanted to," Bench said. "But never did."

The Reds won again, and Weyer sent the baseball into the clubhouse and asked Bench if he would sign it. Bench, the kid who had practiced signing autographs at McKinney's Texaco station back in Oklahoma, had grown out of the habit; he did not like signing autographs. But he happily signed this one.

"What did you write on it?" reporters asked him.

"Sorry," Bench said.

Everybody was talking about *Jaws*, the movie. Lines were stretching around movie theaters. Movie critics were calling it the scariest movie ever made. "MAY BE TOO *INTENSE* FOR YOUNGER CHILDREN," the poster warned. SUPER SHARK was the headline on the cover of *Time* magazine. A movie had never quite taken over America like this one . . . but then, a movie had never before opened up in 409 movie theaters around the country simultaneously. It was the first summer blockbuster in Hollywood history.

The timing was perfect: as summer began in 1975, it seemed like everyone wanted something to take them away, something bloody and jolting and utterly unreal and yet, at the same time, too real. Movie reviewers at newspapers wrote two reviews of the movie—one reviewing the movie itself, another reviewing people's reactions. In a couple of weeks, *Jaws* would be shown in 675 theaters—more theaters than any movie ever—and there would be a new *Jaws* movie poster telling people to "See what you missed the first time after closing your eyes."

Pete Rose had his own summer release—he had written a diary of the 1974 season with the *Cincinnati Enquirer*'s Bob Hertzel. The book was called *Charlie Hustle*. Pete hated the book. Well, he didn't hate what was written in the book—as he told friends, he didn't even read it. No, it was just that he had become convinced that the book was bad luck, that it was part of the reason he did not hit .300 in 1974. The book had distracted him. Pete had always just lived. Now, though, he found himself watching things and thinking, *Yeah, that will be a funny thing to put in the book.*

There was this one time in 1974 when he was in a slump—he'd gone two games without a hit—and he went into the clubhouse after the game.

"We'd better guard the pool tonight," Joe Morgan said. "Pete might just jump out of his window into it. We'll find him floating, facedown, in the morning."

"Don't worry about that," hitting coach Big Klu said. "He won't hit that either."

That was funny stuff, and Pete wrote it down. But maybe it was bad luck to tell everybody about it. Maybe he should have kept his focus on the game. Or maybe Pete just felt like he gave away too much of himself. The critics were not especially kind. The book apparently had made him seem shallow and driven by his numbers and, well, obsessed. There was his description of the charms of San Francisco: "Sophisticated? Lovely? Filled with charm and excitement? Bull. Candlestick Park is a sad excuse for a ballpark."

Oh, yeah, the critics had a ball with that. Well, what was everybody laughing about? Candlestick Park was a pit. Sure, he was stat-driven and obsessed, Rose knew that, but maybe that was his secret, maybe that was why he hit .300 every year, maybe that was why he made himself into a ballplayer when everybody kept telling him he was too slow and couldn't throw and didn't have any power. Maybe he should not have written the damned book. Anyway, he just wanted to get away from 1974. His slump was over. He had gotten hot. He just wanted to get up there and hit.

Saturday night in Houston, in the stale, air-conditioned air of the Astrodome, he stepped into the batter's box. He stared at J. R. Richard, a twenty-five-year-old man-child who stood six-foot-eight and could throw a baseball one hundred miles per hour but had only the vaguest notion of where it was going. This was Pete's kind of pitcher, his kind of challenge. "I hear you can throw hard, kid," he shouted at Richard. "Let me see a little bit of that heat." Richard reached back and fired his best fastball. Pete whacked a line drive for a base hit. Best feeling in the world, ripping a hard fastball.

"I thought you were supposed to throw the ball hard," Pete said next time he stepped up to face Richard. "That didn't seem too hard to me." Richard threw his fastball as hard as he could, maybe even a little harder, and Pete ripped it into the gap for a double. There was no way to throw a fastball past him when he felt like this, when his eyes felt sharp, when his whole body felt as sensitive as a tuning fork. He was hitting .319. He felt alive.

The game went on. The Reds thought they won in the top of the tenth when they scored twice, but the Astros scored two runs in the bottom of the inning to keep the game going. The game stretched on and on, and in the fourteenth inning Rose came up again, only this time he faced Joe Niekro, the brother of the great Braves pitcher Phil. The Niekros threw knuckleballs. And unlike fastballs, knuckleballs just pissed off Pete Rose. Hard fastballs, like J. R. Richard's fastball, spoke to Pete Rose. He thought baseball should be like a gunfight at high noon, two men under a high sun, facing off, one winner and one loser, one quick and one dead. Pete wanted a pitcher to throw his best fastball, and he would swing his best swing, and they would see who was the better man. Pete felt pretty certain that he was the better man.

Only Joe threw that knuckleball, which danced and dropped and rose and turned, and that wasn't right. That was like bringing a boomerang to the O.K. Corral. "I'd rather try hitting a hummingbird than a knuckleball," Pete the author had written in *Charlie Hustle*. He had faced Joe Niekro one time in six years. He struck out.

"Just swing hard," he reminded himself. This was Rose's strategy against the knuckler—swing hard so that even if he made an out, at least he would not foul up his swing for the next two weeks. Niekro fluttered the knuckleball his way, and Rose lashed at it, and he smacked a double. The next batter, Ken Griffey, singled in Rose for the game-winning run.

"I feel reborn," Pete told reporters after the game.

"Have you seen *Jaws* yet?" he was asked.

"I *am Jaws*," he said.

June 24, 1975

Team record: 43–27
First place by three games

The genius sat on the bench and watched his starting pitcher, Pat Darcy, very closely. It was the eighth inning, and Darcy had pitched a beauty. The Reds led the Atlanta Braves 3–0—all the runs coming on Joe Morgan's home run off a Phil Niekro knuckleball—and Darcy had baffled the Atlanta hitters all night long. It was a Sparky Anderson kind of pitching performance. The Braves had not even moved a runner to second base since the first inning. Sparky's ulcer was calm. He felt at ease.

Then Darcy made the critical mistake—he walked Rowland Office, the Braves' leadoff batter in the eighth inning. Sparky saw that some of those pitches were high. Sparky had this theory about high pitches—high pitches, if allowed to continue, became long fly balls, and then became home runs. He walked slowly to the mound to go take Pat Darcy out of the game.

"Good game, kid," Sparky said, and Darcy wanted to say something back, something like, "You're taking me out now? I'm pitching a shutout." He wanted to say something like, "No, I have a lot left, I'm throwing good, I have to finish this thing." He wanted to say a lot of things. But talking, he knew, was strictly prohibited. He handed Sparky the baseball and walked slowly to the clubhouse. Fred Norman came into the game.

Starting pitchers in 1975 expected to finish their games. In 1975, they finished about one-fifth of the games they started (compared to three decades later, when starters finished only one in forty games they started). They expected the chance to get out of their own jams, to finish what they started. Some pitchers would shout their managers off the mound. Some would refuse to give up the baseball. But it wasn't like that in Cincinnati.

And more, Sparky Anderson had come up with the genius plan. With Don Gullett out, he was going to change pitchers whenever he felt it in his gut. Sparky knew that his pitchers hated him. He knew that they felt underappreciated. And he did not care, not even one bit, because Sparky felt like he understood pitchers. Yes, he did. He understood better than they did when they were losing their stuff. He understood that the quickest way to lose a game was to stick with a pitcher too long because of personal feelings.

And the game was changing. He was changing it. That's why he was smiling at that breakfast with Jeff Ruby, because it all became clear to him. He had this great bullpen of pitchers. He had Will McEnaney, that flaky lefty who didn't seem to fear anything. He had Pedro Borbon, his crazy righty who would pitch every single day if he could. He had Clay Carroll, the Hawk, his veteran righty who had pitched in more games than any Cincinnati Reds pitcher ever and who knew how to get batters out. And finally, he had the new kid, Rawly Eastwick, who liked painting and reading and doing all sorts of intellectual things that Sparky didn't understand or trust, but on the mound he was all ballplayer—Rawly had the kind of arrogance that made him believe that nobody could hit him.

Sparky understood in that moment that it was his bullpen that would make the Reds champions. Sure, he cried the night Gullett got hurt—cried for Gullett himself. The kid probably would have won the Cy Young Award if he'd stayed healthy. But by morning, there were no more tears. Sparky saw the future. The bullpen was the future.

"Why did you take out Darcy?" Morgan asked back in the dugout, mostly because he wanted to get Sparky going. And of course, he did.

"You want to know why?" Sparky said, and he said it loud enough for everyone to hear. "I'll tell you why. Because if you want to stay in the game, it's like dance steps, boys. You need to play the song in your head like a waltz—one-two-three, one-two-three, one-two-three. You play it like that, and I'll just sit right here in the dugout and enjoy it. But you start going one-two-three . . . four-five, well, we'll see you later. We'll get somebody else out there who wants to get somebody out."

Fred Norman got out of the eighth inning unscathed. He started off the ninth by allowing a walk and then a single. Sparky made his slow walk out to the mound again. He pulled Norman out and put Pedro Borbon in. Borbon got a double-play grounder and foul fly ball, and the game was over. Three pitchers—and two were ticked off—but the Reds won, and that was all that mattered.

"Just follow my lead, boys," Sparky said happily as he walked back into the clubhouse.

———————

Lee Trevino, the only professional golfer out there who consistently could beat Jack Nicklaus, was struck by lightning while sitting under a tree at the Western Open in Oak Brook, Illinois. Tennis players Jimmy Connors and Ilie Nastase yelled at a man in the crowd at Wimbledon, causing quite the stir in London. A woman named Nancy Fitzgerald won the Indianapolis city golf tournament, though she was eight months pregnant at the time.

The newspapers tried to calm the shark fear by pointing out, helpfully, that only fifty people each year were killed by sharks in the whole world, while more than three hundred died in the United States alone from bee and wasp stings. There was no reported surge in bee and wasp panic, however. People all over the country still reported shark nightmares after seeing *Jaws*. "I'll never go swimming again," Martha Lecaroz of Saugus, Massachusetts, told the United Press International senior editor assigned to report the mass hysteria that *Jaws* was causing. On Cape Cod, the movie-line recording warned that adults should not see it before they went swimming.

The papers reported that a nineteen-year-old woman named Cheryl Petit was expected to live a normal life after doctors replaced her defective heart valve with one made of pig tissue. President Ford signed a bill into law that would help middle-income people get financing to buy homes. Jewel thieves in Paris pretended to be delivery boys and stole more than $4 million worth of diamonds from the ex-wife of the Revlon cosmetics emperor.

And Joe Morgan tried to adjust to his new life as the best player in baseball. He liked the attention, but he did not know how to deal with it. Funny thing, he had spent so much of his life bitterly fighting back at the perceptions. He signed with the Houston Colt .45s, he always said, because the scout, Bill Wight, approached him after a game in college and said, "You're a really good player." Other scouts had come to talk to him, but all of them called Joe a good *little* player. And it was that word, "little," that bit of condescension, that inspired Joe Morgan. He would face down that patronizing word for the first ten years of his career. He hit with power, he stole bases, he intimidated pitchers in any number of ways. And still people saw that five-foot-seven ballplayer with the tiny glove that looked like it was a toy out of a Cracker Jack box. And it inspired him more.

Now, though, they could not help but see his greatness—and what was left to prove? What was left to drive him? Morgan had uncharacteristically clipped something out of the morning paper—he was among the league leaders in batting average, home runs, runs, runs batted in, and stolen bases. All five categories. He wanted to send that clipping to his father.

"I have never seen anyone, and I mean anyone, play better than Joe has played this year," Sparky told reporters. Nobody argued. Joe was on another level.

"All I want to do is get the most out of what I have," Joe told the writers who, more and more, gathered around him. Now the writers noticed how thoughtful he was, how well he spoke about the game, how much he loved to talk. He told them a story about a game he played his second year. He made an error in the tenth inning that cost Houston the game. He said that he actually started crying, right there in the dugout, and when he walked to bat in the bottom of the inning the fans booed him mercilessly. "Don't let it get to you," the Dodgers catcher Johnny Roseboro told him. "You'll hear a lot of cheers before it's over for you, kid."

That did not make him feel too much better. He walked into the clubhouse after the game, still despondent, his head hanging, and a coach named Jimmy Adair told him: "If you go out and give the best you got, you don't ever have to come in the clubhouse with your head down."

And while the reporters scribbled down the story, Joe said: "That's why I don't worry when Johnny Bench or Pete Rose get more publicity than I do. I know I've done my job."

It was the perfect story. He was able to get his point across—that Bench and Rose got more publicity than he did—without sounding bitter. He was able to explain what mattered to him ("Give the best you've got") without sounding insincere. He was able to tell people how much the game mattered to him ("I was in tears"). Joe had a great sense of words.

And they had to listen to him now, had to appreciate him. A warm Friday night against San Diego, he came up in the eighth inning with the Reds trailing 2–1 against a San Diego pitcher named Dave Freisleben. He hit a home run to tie the score. He came up again in the eleventh inning with the score tied and two outs. This time he faced a pitcher named Danny Frisella, and he banged a single. He stole second. He scored the game-winning run when Danny Driessen hit a line drive that barely skimmed over the right-field wall for a home run.

"What were you thinking?" they asked him after the game.

"You don't think," Joe Morgan said. "You just play."

June 30, 1975

CINCINNATI
REDS VS. ASTROS
Team record: 48–28
First place by seven games

Ken Griffey never forgot the red jacket he got. That was his signing bonus: a red jacket and five sanitary socks. It was not a Reds jacket. There was no logo on it, no lettering, no sign at all that it came from a major league team. The Reds handed out better-looking jackets to kids on "Jacket Day" at the ballpark. This was just a cheap red jacket, the kind you could buy at a thrift shop for 99¢. That's what the Cincinnati Reds thought of him.

Still, he smiled. Ken Griffey always smiled when he played ball. So what if the Reds took him in the twenty-ninth round? So what if they did not even waste a telephone call to tell him that he was drafted? So what if they just sent him a cold letter telling him to report to Bradenton, Florida?

"Hey, Mom, I got drafted," Ken shouted out when he got that letter.

"Oh, my God, no," his mother shouted back. It was 1969. The Vietnam War was raging.

He went to Sioux Falls, South Dakota, in 1970, where he stayed in a hotel so cheap and dirty that he had his infant son Ken Jr. sleep in the open top drawer of the dresser—high above the rats. He came close to quitting the game then, and he would have quit except that he found an apartment that was moderately cleaner. Anyway, he was not the quitting type. He had grown up in Donora, Pennsylvania, twenty miles south of Pittsburgh, and (as he would hear again and again his entire baseball career) the hometown of the great Stan Musial. A dark gray smog hovered over his hometown and his childhood—the same smog that killed Musial's father two years before Ken was born.

Ken played baseball on the barren field at Highland Park, where they used bricks for bases, a scrap of cardboard for home plate, powdered milk for the baselines. The Reds only drafted him because of an old scout named Elmer Gray, who had been watching kids play baseball around Pittsburgh for more than two decades. Elmer happened to bring a stopwatch to Ken's high school game. It wasn't unusual. Elmer always brought his stopwatch to games—he felt like that was his most important scouting tool. He loved players who could run. He loved to tell the story about how, in 1960, he tried to sign a raw but fast young outfielder named Joe Namath. He had it all worked out, but when he brought the contract papers over to the house, Namath was gone. The University of Alabama football program had taken him into hiding. Joe Namath went on to football glory. "We never saw him again except on TV," Elmer told *Sports Illustrated*. "And then it was another guy. It was Broadway Joe."

Ken Griffey was the fastest thing Elmer had seen in a baseball uniform since the young Broadway Joe. Griffey could not hit a lick—

he had this crazy-looking swing. He could not throw all that well either. But holy cow, he could run to first base about as fast as anyone you ever saw. Nobody else knew about Griffey. Nobody else cared about him. "Draft him low," Elmer Gray recommended. "He might become somebody."

Griffey made it through Sioux Falls, and the next year he led the Florida State League in hitting. The year after that he led the Eastern League in hitting. The year after that, he led the American Association in hitting. The Reds finally called him up, and he hit .384 in twenty-five games. He was so fast that any ground ball he hit softly to the left side of the infield was a single. So that became his art form. While other hitters hated getting jammed—hated having the ball hit the bat too close to their hands—Griffey would get jammed on purpose. The ball would just drip off the bat, like drops of water out of a leaky faucet, and by the time the third baseman or shortstop or pitcher could get to the ball, Griffey would already have run past first base. He moved so fast—as they all said—he blurred.

And all the while he smiled. People thought it was because he loved the game so much, and that was exactly what he wanted them to think. He did love the game. More, though, he did not want any of them to know what he was thinking. That was his business. He had a lot of thoughts. He could see the way Johnny Bench would look through him, like he was not even there. He was aware that Joe Morgan ignored him, maybe was even a touch jealous of him (because Joe, as good a base runner as he was, could not run with Ken Griffey). He heard them mock him, his batting style, his quiet personality. They thought it was funny. He did not often find it funny. But that was okay. He would not let them in. He would not let them see. He would not let anything affect him. He smiled all the time.

"You just shut up and do your job," Johnny told him one day, "and we'll make you a star." Ken nodded and smiled.

"Just remember your place," Joe told him. Ken nodded and smiled.

He smiled when Sparky Anderson moved him all over the lineup. He batted Ken seventh or eighth or second or sixth, wherever he felt like it. In baseball, a man's place in the lineup was a sign of respect. Pete *always* batted first, Joe *always* batted second or third, Johnny *always* batted cleanup, Doggie *always* batted fifth. Their place in the lineup was their place in baseball. It was their business card. Pete wasn't "Pete Rose, Baseball Player." He was "Pete Rose, Leadoff Hitter." Ken, meanwhile, was a man without a spot in the line, a man without a country. Sparky moved him up and down the lineup like he was an afterthought.

And then, one day, Sparky told Ken he would hit second, a huge promotion. But even that came with a caveat.

"Kenny," Sparky said, "I'm moving you up to the number-two spot in the lineup. That's because I think you're a great hitter. But there's one thing you need to know: from now on, I don't want you stealing any bases. You got Joe Morgan hitting after you, and he's the best damn player in the game of baseball, and he doesn't like when people steal bases when he's batting. It distracts him. So you don't steal."

Griffey smiled even then, even when Sparky took away his greatest gift, his speed. He could have stolen eighty bases if they would have just let him, he felt sure of that. They took that away so that Joe, who was already a big star, who was already making more than $100,000 a year, could feel more comfortable. That was how it went with the Big Red Machine. The stars ruled. And the turds just did what was asked of them. Ken's job was to get jammed and run hard to first base, and that's what he did. He was a team player. And he smiled.

Then, with the Reds trailing Houston 6–2 in the bottom of the eighth inning, he came up with the bases loaded, and he bashed a triple to deep left field, a triple that scored three runs. The Reds tied up the game, and then in the twelfth inning, with the score still tied, he crushed another ball to left, this time a double. Two batters later,

Johnny Bench hit a long home run, and the Reds won in extra innings for the third time in four nights. The Reds were seven games ahead of the Dodgers. They were pulling away.

The reporters crowded around Johnny Bench. He was the designated hero.

"Yeah, I was tired," Bench told the writers. "I wish we could make a trade where I could be a designated hitter for a week." Everyone laughed. Ken Griffey looked on and smiled.

July 1, 1975

CINCINNATI
REDS VS. ASTROS
Team record: 49–28
First place by seven games

The Machine had not made a single error in more than two weeks, and Doggie was not going to let anyone forget it. "Hey, I was talking to Pete, and he said you are going to make that first error," Doggie said to Joe Morgan.

"Don't listen to that asshole," Pete shouted across the room.

"You said it, you know you said it," Doggie said.

They had gone fifteen consecutive games without an error. That was a record, but a bizarre one. Baseball is a game of bizarre records—consecutive-game hitting streaks, most home runs hit in a month, most games in a row with a walk, and so on. Nobody on the Reds quite knew what this record meant. It was impressive, sure, going that long without making an error. But what did it *mean*? The players understood that there was something odd about the whole error concept. For a player to get an error, a man in the press box—called, pretentiously enough, the "official scorer"—had to determine that a player should have caught that ball or picked up that grounder or made a better throw. The official scorer, of course, would not appreciate that the ball was spinning so rapidly that you could hear it buzzing. He probably would not care that the sky was so empty and vast that the baseball simply disappeared into it. He could not appreciate that there was a fast runner racing to first base, which changed the whole dynamic of the play. No, the official scorer sat up high, judge and jury, and he alone would rule that a player did not do his job well enough, that he made an error, and this was the silly thing that the Reds had managed to avoid for fifteen straight games.

But silly or not, the players on the Machine simply hated making errors. Pete could barely tolerate a hitless night, but he could not tolerate making an error. He would go home and sit at the kitchen table and stare at the wall for hours. In Los Angeles once, he dropped a pop-up when someone threw a beer at him just before the ball landed. He was so upset about it that later, when a friend suggested that he should have caught the ball, Pete picked up a biscuit, threw it at the guy, and said, "Catch." The friend reached up to catch it, and just before he could pull it in Rose threw a glass of water in his face. The friend dropped the biscuit.

"That's why I didn't catch it," Rose shouted. They all felt more or less like that. An error left bad feelings.

So the Reds players were proud of their record, proud that they were playing flawless baseball for longer than any team had ever played. But they all knew that the streak would end. And none of them wanted to be the one to end it.

"Actually, I sure it will be you, Pete," Doggie said. "You cannot play third."

"You need a bulletproof vest over there," Joe said.

"Hey, it won't be me," Pete said. "I've only made two errors over there. It will probably be Bozo."

Concepcion looked up from across the room and shook his head. He simply could not imagine anything more mortifying than being the one to break the streak.

In the fifth inning that night, with the score tied, Houston's Bob Watson hit a line drive single to left field. Danny Driessen was playing out there. It had to be Danny Driessen. He grabbed the ball and tried to throw home, only he didn't quite grab the ball—it fell out of his hands and dropped to the ground. Two runs scored. Watson ended up at second base. And that was the error that broke the streak.

"You the man, Danny!" Doggie shouted after the game. The Reds won in extra innings—fourth time in five days. It was getting eerie. This time they scored three runs in the ninth inning to tie the game. They won in the fifteenth when Joe Morgan cracked a single that scored Pete Rose. But as far as the Reds were concerned, there was only one hero.

"Danny, you save us all," Doggie said. "Now we don't worry about errors no more. We have the record. We can relax and play ball."

Sparky Anderson would say later that it was no brainstorm. He did not have a brilliant dream or a eureka moment while lying around at the pool. He had just tried so many different lineup combinations that it was inevitable that he would come across the right one. And so, on Independence Day 1975, he unveiled what would become the most famous lineup in baseball history:

1. Rose, 3B
2. Griffey, RF
3. Morgan, 2B
4. Bench, C
5. Perez, 1B
6. Foster, LF
7. Concepcion, SS
8. Geronimo, CF

Sparky did not think much about it then. Nobody did. Seemed like everyone was talking about the upcoming "Battle of the Sexes" horse match race between the filly Ruffian, who had won every one of her ten races going away, and the thoroughbred Foolish Pleasure, the Kentucky Derby winner. President Ford went to Camp David, the presidential retreat, and said that the nation's third century should be an era of individual freedom. A bomb hidden inside an old refrigerator killed thirteen in Jerusalem. Johnny Bench's old friend Bob Hope became only the third American—after Presidents Herbert Hoover and Harry Truman—to receive the Philadelphia Freedom Medal. The Reds beat the San Diego Padres 7–6, and every single player in the lineup got a hit. The lineup change went largely unnoticed.

But this was historic: the Reds almost never lost when Sparky Anderson entered that lineup. The lineup had everything. Rose gave the lineup will, Griffey gave it speed, Morgan gave it a little bit of everything. Bench gave the lineup power, Perez gave it big hits, Foster gave it home runs, Concepcion gave it great plays at shortstop, Geronimo gave it defensive grace in center field.

There had never been a lineup quite like it. Yes, the famed 1927 New York Yankees had four Hall of Famers in the lineup—including Babe Ruth and Lou Gehrig—and had averaged more than six runs per game. The "Boys of Summer" Dodgers of the 1950s had Jackie Robinson, Duke Snider, Pee Wee Reese, and Roy Campanella and were a beautiful blend of power and speed. But the lineup Sparky Anderson put on the field on July 4, 1975, had something more. The Reds' lineup had power and speed too. More, though, there were three African Americans in the lineup, three Latin Americans, two white Americans—and Johnny Bench had Native American blood. They were the Great American Ball Club.

"We had black players on our team?" Johnny Bench would ask many years later. "We had Latin American players on our team? I never noticed that. I promise you, none of us ever noticed that. We made fun of each other. We made fun of the way players talked. We made fun of the way players looked. But when it came down to it, we were Cincinnati Reds."

He paused here for emphasis.

"We were," he said, "the Big Red Machine."

July 6, 1975

SAN DIEGO
REDS VS. PADRES
Team record: 53–29
First place by eight games

Everyone loved Ruffian. The papers called her the modern-day Black Beauty. She was almost entirely black, with just a touch of brown around her nose. And as a racehorse, she was invincible. The first time she raced she won by fifteen lengths. The next nine times she raced she won wire to wire. Lucien Lauren—the trainer of the great Secretariat, widely viewed as the greatest racehorse ever—wondered if Ruffian was better.

Everyone was looking for the next battle of the sexes. More than ninety million people around the world had watched the 1973 exhibition tennis match between Bobby Riggs and Billie Jean King at the Houston Astrodome. In 1975, states were debating the merits of the Equal Rights Amendment. The new Title IX rule was sparking arguments between men and women too. And, yes, the question was fascinating: could Ruffian beat the greatest thoroughbred, Foolish Pleasure, in a female-versus-male race at Belmont Park on that Sunday afternoon? The *Chicago Tribune* called it a battle of Anthony and Cleopatra.

"Any woman who wears a Foolish Pleasure button at a time like this ought to be ashamed of herself," a fan, Pat Menafra, told the *New York Times*.

More than fifty thousand people were in the stands when the race began, and Ruffian worked her way to an early lead. It was expected. Ruffian had always shown brilliant early speed, and Foolish Pleasure's talent was coming from behind. Still, it was electrifying to see Ruffian pulling away, first a quarter-length ahead, then a half-length, still pulling away. Then tension built. And then, suddenly, Ruffian wobbled. "I heard a crack," said Braulio Breza, the jockey on Foolish Pleasure. Ruffian stumbled into Foolish Pleasure, brushed him three times. Then he rushed by while jockey Jacinto Vasquez had Ruffian pull up. She had broken down. Vasquez would later say he never heard a racetrack so quiet.

The doctors rushed in to save her. She had shattered two sesamoid bones in her right leg. If Ruffian had been another horse, the doctors would have put her down right away. But she was Ruffian. Six veterinarians attempted to operate and put her in a cast. And everyone hoped.

While a nation waited to see what would happen to Ruffian, Joe Morgan booted Tito Fuentes's ground ball in San Diego. He kicked the dirt. The Reds already led 3–0—Joe already had a run scored and an RBI—but he did hate errors. They all did.

In the second inning, Morgan botched another ground ball, this time hit by San Diego's Johnny Grubb. The Reds led 6–1 by now, but still Joe felt miserable. Two errors in one game. He could not believe it. And as he looked around the infield, he noticed that all the other guys, well, they were laughing at him. Man, they were going to give it to him in the clubhouse.

In the fourth inning, with the Reds leading 8–2—Morgan had two runs scored and two RBIs—Johnny Grubb came up again. He hit another ground ball to Morgan. And one more time, Morgan booted it. He had committed three errors in a single game.

"Congratulations," Bench told him back in the dugout, and he threw his hat at Joe. "You pulled off the hat trick."

The Reds won the game 13–2, but Joe did not want to go back to the clubhouse. He felt miserable, and anyway he knew the guys would be there waiting to tear him apart. When he got in there, he noticed that none of his teammates were standing around his locker. He looked over at Doggie and Pete, waited for them to say something, but none of them said a word.

Then Morgan got to his locker and saw there was a garbage can in front of it. He looked inside and saw his glove inside.

When Ruffian came out of the operation, she immediately tried to run. This was exactly what the doctor had feared. She destroyed the cast they had set for her.

"Don't let her suffer anymore," owner Stuart Janney told the doctors at 2:00 A.M., and it was then that Ruffian was, as the papers told a shocked nation, "humanely destroyed."

July 7, 1975

CINCINNATI
REDS VS. PHILLIES
Team record: 54–29
First place by eight games

"Doggie," Pete Rose told Tony Perez, "you know the three worst things that ever happened to you?"

"What that, Pete?" Doggie asked back.

"Me, Joe, and Johnny," Pete said. Well, Pete was right. Nobody outside the clubhouse seemed to appreciate what made Tony Perez special. That's just how it was with the Machine. Newspaper reporters were in a hurry after games. They needed a fast quote, something pithy, something edgy, something wise, something that would help them make deadline. There were rules. Hal McCoy, the young base-ball writer from the *Dayton Daily News*, figured them out. If he wanted something thoughtful, he would go find Joe Morgan. Nobody could break down the game quite like Joe. "I should give you my type-writer," he would tell Joe sometimes.

If Hal needed something pithy, he would go to Pete Rose. Nobody in baseball could beat Pete when it came to thinking up the perfect one-liner. But there were politics involved. If Hal needed to talk to Johnny Bench, he could not talk to Pete Rose first. Johnny did not like that. Johnny was a good quote—thoughtful and opinionated—but if he saw the reporter talking to Pete Rose first, he would turn his back.

"John, you got a minute?" Hal would say.

"Seems to me you got all you need," Johnny would grumble, and walk off.

Hal loved talking to George Foster. He thought George had this great and subtle sense of humor that few people picked up on. He got a kick out of Davey Concepcion; you never knew what Davey was going to say. He thought Ken Griffey was quiet and Cesar Geronimo even quieter. He liked talking to pitchers sometimes. But really, Pete got it right. There were three guys in the Reds clubhouse who mat-tered to reporters: Pete, Joe, and Johnny.

And Doggie? Well, sure, Hal liked Doggie, everybody liked Doggie. But he was hard work. His English wasn't great. He fell back on clichés. It wasn't that Hal avoided Tony Perez, no, he talked to Doggie all the time. He just did not use many quotes.

"I didn't care," Doggie would say, and then again, "I really didn't care. They didn't put me in the paper much. So what? They put Joe and Johnny and Pete in the paper all the time. So what? I'll tell you what: You know when they put me in the paper? They put me in when I got a big hit. And I got a few big hits."

In the first inning against Philadelphia, on a humid Monday night in front of a half-filled Riverfront Stadium, Doggie came to the plate to face Steve Carlton. Nobody was harder to hit than Carlton. He had a blazing fastball that would rise, a curveball that would drop like a New York elevator, and the greatest slider anyone had ever seen. Carlton had learned that slider while pitching exhibition games in Japan back in '68. It looked just like the fastball only, at the last instant, it broke hard to the right. "Hitting against Steve Carlton," Willie Stargell had said, "is like eating soup with a fork."

Perez was hitting .192 against Carlton for his career. He had struck out six times against him in the previous thirteen months. And Doggie was not hitting all that great against the other pitchers either; his batting average was only .247. He shrugged. "I'm a good hitter," he said. "I'll get hot. I just need something to get me going."

This time Carlton threw his slider, and Doggie swung hard. He connected. He knew as soon as the ball hit his bat that it was something special. The ball soared down the left-field line, and Perez watched it. He knew it was a home run. But he wanted to see where it would hit.

The ball landed in the second row of the upper deck—the red seats. The red seats were famous in Cincinnati. Only one Reds player had hit a baseball to the red seats at Riverfront Stadium. That was Tony Perez. Now he had done it again, and as he jogged around the bases, people all around the stadium sat in awed silence. Up in the press box, reporters estimated how far the ball had traveled. The best guess was five hundred feet.

After the game, the reporters did gather around Perez. They asked him what kind of bat he used, and he said it was a Babe Ruth model.

"The Babe never hit one that far," Doggie said. Then he smiled. He had thought up a quote.

"Well," he said, "not right-handed, anyway."

July 11, 1975

Team record: 57–29
First place by nine and a half games

They were booing Sparky. Could you believe it? The Reds had won six games in a row. They had won thirty-eight of the last forty-seven. They had humiliated the Los Angeles Dodgers, left them nine and a half games behind, coughing dirt and eating smoke. "The players ain't worrying about LA no more," Sparky told reporters. "LA to them don't exist."

The Machine, Sparky was telling people in his double negative way, was playing baseball like it ain't never been played before. And still the fans booed Sparky every time he stuck his head out of the dugout. He wanted to laugh about it, but he was not sure it was funny. Here it was a Friday afternoon, first game of a doubleheader, big crowd, and he walked out to the mound in the seventh inning to go get his starter, Fred Norman. Well, hell, Freddie walked the opposing pitcher. In Sparky's world, when you walked the opposing pitcher, you were begging to get pulled out of the game. Anyway, it looked like Freddie was going into his mad scientist bit, and Sparky had to get him out of there before he hurt himself. Freddie was a tough little pitcher; he stood no taller than five-foot-seven, weighed no more than 150 pounds, Freddie and Joe were the two guys Sparky could see at eye level. Sparky liked Freddie. But the guy was always tinkering, trying new things, adjusting his grip, experimenting with new pitches, and that stuff drove Sparky mad. When Sparky saw that, he would mutter, "Oh, boy, Freddie's experimenting again." Then he would walk out to the mound real slow and go get him.

Anyway, as soon as he stepped on the field to go get Freddie, the crowd booed him mercilessly. It sounded like the boos were flapping around him, like low-flying bats. In a way, Sparky understood. It had been exactly a month since he let one of his starters finish a game. He was closing in on some kind of record—most consecutive days without a pitcher throwing a complete game. And the people didn't like it. He sort of understood.

But on the other hand, he didn't understand at all. Baseball was changing. How could they not see it? Sure, it was fine in the old days to let a starting pitcher keep going even when he got tired, when his arm hurt, when his fastball was shot, when his curveball was hanging. But no, Sparky was not going to put up with that. He was not going to just sit in the dugout and watch a tired pitcher blow the game. No. He had a kid warming up in the bullpen, Rawly Eastwick, and Eastwick threw hard, and he threw with confidence. He challenged the hitters' manhood. Every pitch, he seemed to be saying: "Here's my fastball, boys. Go on and hit it." When you had a pitcher like that in the bullpen, there was no damned reason to stick with a tired starter.

"Good job, Freddie," Sparky said over the boos when he got to the mound.

"I'm not tired," Norman said. He was the one pitcher who was allowed to talk back to Sparky; hell, he wasn't but eight years younger than Sparky. Freddie had played for nineteen different teams in his professional career; he had bounced around from the minors to the majors back to the minors, and he endured because of this screwball he picked up in San Diego and because he never stopped coming up with new ways to get batters out. For that, Sparky let him talk . . . a little.

"Yeah, I know, Freddie, you got us here, let's get you this win," Sparky said, and he reached out his hand. Freddie handed him the ball. The boos swirled around him.

Then Sparky waited for Rawly Eastwick to come to the mound. He handed him the ball and said, "Remember, up and in, down and away. Go get 'em." He always said something like that. Then he walked back to the dugout, and the boos started up again. Sparky shook his head. Genius is so rarely appreciated in a man's time.

Rawlins Jackson Eastwick III was a strange case. They were all strange, of course, all those bullpen guys. The lefty, Will McEnaney, was a wild one. There was this time in Indianapolis, Will had a minor league manager named Vern Rapp, a generous man who had fought in Korea. One day, Rapp caught Will in the elevator with a woman, and it was long past curfew, and it wasn't the first time.

"That's it, I'm fining you a hundred fifty bucks," Rapp said.

"I won't pay it," Will said.

"You broke a rule. You had that woman in your room."

"I did not," Will said. "She was banging on my door while I was sleeping, what the hell else was I supposed to do? I had to walk her out of the hotel."

"You're a liar. You had that woman in your room."

"No, I didn't. I won't pay that fine. You can't fine me for a woman banging on my door in the middle of the night."

Will never paid that fine. He did have a knack for getting away with things. Pedro Borbon was, of course, certifiable. Clay Carroll was crazy in his own way too. It made you think that relief pitchers, the good ones, needed a couple of screws loose.

Only Rawly Eastwick was entirely sane. He seemed too sane to be a reliever. For one thing, he painted. That one threw Sparky. His own grandfather had painted houses. Sparky's father painted planes for Douglas Aircraft. Sparky had paint in his blood.

Eastwick, though, painted on canvas. The guy was a regular Pablo Picasso. Sparky didn't know enough about art to know if the kid had any talent, but Sparky had to admit that the fruit Rawly drew looked pretty much like fruit. One of those paintings was so realistic, the kid gave it to Johnny Bench for a wedding present. Johnny liked it and said he would hang it up on his living room wall. It all just seemed a little bit weird to Sparky. And it wasn't only painting. The kid liked to read too—books and things, history and novels. He liked to talk about current events, the real current events, like busing and the Equal Rights Amendment. He took classes.

It was not like Sparky had anything against these things. He believed all people should work to improve themselves, if they could. Sparky himself, for a time, tried to improve the way he talked; he and his wife, Carol, sat at the dining room table and went over some grammar books for a while. It didn't take; Sparky had to finally just say, "Fuck it, I'm going to talk like I fucking talk." But Sparky valued education and the arts.

Still, Sparky wasn't sure that a kid who painted and went to classes and read important books would be tough enough to get out hitters in the ninth inning. But here was the thing: on the field, the kid was damned tough. He competed. Like here, as Friday afternoon turned to evening, eighth inning, the Reds still leading by a run. The Mets sent big Dave Kingman to the plate. Kingman stood six-foot-six, and he swung the bat with force, like he was trying to knock over a building. They called him "Kong." He swung and missed a lot, but when Kong connected, he hit the ball to the moon. Sparky had never seen anyone hit the ball higher than Kingman did. Some people called Kingman "Sky King." He hit home runs that could only be called majestic.

Kong was a pretty fearsome guy, the type of guy who should have intimidated a skinny rookie pitcher who liked to paint pictures. Only, Eastwick had this look of calm . . . like he *knew* what was going to happen. And, funny, he did know what was going to happen. Rawly threw his first fastball, and Kingman swung and missed. He threw his second fastball a little higher, and Kingman swung and missed again. He threw his third fastball a bit higher than that, and Kingman swung and missed a third time. Strikeout. Inning over.

"Climbed the stairs," Rawly said when he got back to the dugout, calm as could be, and Sparky just looked at his relief pitcher with a bit of admiration. Let the people boo all they wanted. Sparky knew exactly what he was doing.

July 13, 1975

Team record: 60–29
First place by eleven and a half games

It was the last game before the All-Star break, and it was time for Joe Morgan to pull off his greatest feat of the season. This was the play he would remember for the rest of his life, the singular play from his singular season. He did not hit a home run. He did not score the winning run. He did not make a special defensive play. No, he simply destroyed the will of a man. And the man was the best pitcher in the world.

They called Tom Seaver "Tom Terrific." He was just thirty years old, but already he had won two Cy Young Awards as the league's best pitcher, and he would win another one that year. He had led the 1969 New York Mets to a most improbable World Series championship. Seaver threw three different kinds of fastballs—one that rose, one that sunk, one that came out of his hand a tad slower—and he had a beautiful pitching delivery that looked like it was torn right out of a "How to Pitch" instruction book. Seaver had this great pitching mind that was always spinning, always plotting—when he had you, he really had you. He was, in so many ways, the pitching version of Joe Morgan.

Tom was terrific that day against the Reds. The Mets led the game 3–0, and the Reds had managed two measly hits, both by Pete Rose. Morgan led off the seventh inning, and he wanted badly to get Seaver. This was the ultimate challenge. Seaver was the best. And the Machine was the best. And as they say, there can only be one best. Morgan stepped to the plate and fouled off a pitch, then fouled off another. Seaver's fastball was hopping, and Joe realized that he probably was not going to be able to get a hit off Seaver. He was not going to get Seaver that way. He had to get Seaver another way. Joe let a ball go by, another, a third, he fouled off another pitch. Seaver walked him.

Tom Terrific kicked the pitcher's mound. He knew exactly what was happening. Now the game had moved to Joe Morgan's arena. Joe stood on first base and glared at Seaver; he offered that confident smile again, the one that promised he would steal second base. He took a huge lead. Seaver threw over to first. Joe slid back easily. He had studied Seaver's mannerisms on the mound. He had studied every move, every twitch, every facial expression, written it all down in the book he kept in his locker. Joe knew exactly when Seaver would throw to first base and exactly when he would throw home. He was a poker player who knew Seaver's cards.

Seaver pitched, and at precisely the right instant Joe took off for second. The Mets' catcher, Jerry Grote, was so eager to get the ball and throw out Joe that he missed the ball completely. The baseball rolled to the backstop. Joe jogged into third base. And now the look of disgust on Seaver's face was unmistakable. Two batters later, Danny Driessen doubled Joe home. And then, after Doggie struck out, Cesar Geronimo singled, Dave Concepcion singled, pinch hitter Terry Crowley walked, and Seaver was taken out of the game with the score 3–2. Pete Rose then followed with a two-run single against a pitcher named Rick Baldwin, and the Reds won again, tenth victory in a row.

Years later, Joe Morgan would remember the play, but he would remember it differently. That's how it goes for ballplayers. Details blend, memories merge. Joe remembered Tony Perez hitting a big home run after he had broken Tom Seaver. But baseball details are for sportswriters to look up. Joe remembered the feeling precisely.

"The thing about us is that we were winners," he said. Joe may have realized that this was a cliché—by the time he said this, he was the most prominent baseball announcer on television. He had won over many fans and, at the same time, had inspired many critics. A hugely popular Internet website had the rather telling name FireJoeMorgan.com. The subhead: "Where Bad Sports Journalism Came to Die." It was always Joe Morgan's fate to be both loved and despised.

But Joe was not a journalist, not really. He was not precisely an analyst either. He was someone who felt baseball. He had played the game about as well as anyone, ever, and he believed deeply that the game reflected life. He believed that the only way to succeed at baseball was to play it with spirit and fearlessness. When he said, "The thing about us is that we were winners," he wanted those words to mean something more, he wanted his audience to *feel* with him, to believe in those mystical qualities that make up a winner, to understand that what made the Machine hum was not home runs and double plays and strikeouts but something deeper, something from the heart, something that transcended the little numbers in the box score. It seemed that not enough people believed him.

"I didn't beat Seaver with my bat," he said. "I beat him with my mind. That's how we played. That's how we won."

And they did win. They won forty-one of fifty games after Joe Morgan had come into the dugout with stitches in his shin and started screaming at them all. They had broken everyone's spirits. They had built an almost impossible-to-believe twelve-and-a-half-game lead over the Los Angeles Dodgers.

"We have been destroyed psychologically by the way the Reds have been playing," Los Angeles second baseman Davey Lopes told reporters. It was like that. The Dodgers, the mighty Dodgers, were all waving the white flag—well, all of them except Steve Garvey. He had been reading Thomas Kiernan's new book, *The Miracle of Coogan's Bluff*, about the 1951 New York Giants, who came all the way back from thirteen and a half games back and beat the Brooklyn Dodgers, with finality, on Bobby Thomson's ninth-inning home run. Garvey was still thinking about miracles. But nobody on the Dodgers was listening to Garvey. Some had come to complain to Walter Alston about his holier-than-thou attitude—as Tom Callahan wrote in the *Cincinnati Enquirer*, they complained that Garvey was "visiting too many orphanages." Anyway, it has always been like that for teams that fall short of their hopes. The Reds were too good.

And the Dodgers—as the old line went—were dead.

July 15, 1975

MILWAUKEE
All-Star Game

Pete Rose sat in the dugout with his five-year-old son, Pete Jr., and basked in the awe. Yes, the Reds had broken everyone's spirits. It felt good to be on top of the world.

"You gonna throw me some?" Pete Jr. asked his father, and Pete kept looking out over the field. Everyone talked about how Pete Jr. was just like Pete, who was just like Big Pete, and it made for a good newspaper story, the passing of generations. Tom Callahan would remember watching Pete Jr., standing in the dugout with a toy bat while Big Klu pitched rolled-up socks to him. When Klu's aim wandered, Pete Jr. growled, "Hey, get this shit over, the fish ain't biting today." Oh, Pete Rose loved that story, kid was just like him, chip off the old block.

But the odysseys of fathers and sons are never simple. Pete Jr. needed his father's attention. And his father was very busy trying to be Pete Rose, author, hitter, icon, gambler, superstar.

"Yeah, I'll throw you some in a minute," Pete Rose said finally, absently. He thought about his own father; he always missed Big Pete at All-Star Games. Pete remembered that day in December 1970. He went to the barbershop to get his hair buzzed. The phone rang, his barber answered, and then handed Pete the phone.

"Dad died," Pete's sister Jackie said, plainly and too suddenly.

And then Pete said to his sister: "Dad died? You mean Mom? You mean Mom died?"

Pete realized later how callous those words sounded. But he simply could not imagine Harry Rose dying. He was too damned stubborn to die. As it turned out, it was stubbornness that may have killed him. Harry had been feeling sick at the bank, and someone offered to call him a cab. But Harry Rose didn't take cabs. He took the bus home, walked in, told his wife, "I don't feel good," and collapsed. A blood clot had reached his heart and stopped it. The doctors said there wasn't much pain, not that this gave Pete comfort. Harry Rose could handle pain. He was invincible. He was indomitable. He never called in sick a day in his life. He never missed a sandlot football game, no matter how many bones were broken. He played basketball with Pete the night before he died, and he played like always—physically, angrily, no blood, no foul.

Harry Rose was the toughest man in Cincinnati.

And when he died, Pete became the toughest man in Cincinnati. He cried for three days, and then he went about living—though he never got over Big Pete dying. One small paper—the *Abilene Reporter-News*—had a small story about Harry Rose dying, only the headline said: "Pete Rose Dies." In many ways, that's how it felt for Pete.

Baseball was always important, but it became more important after Harry Rose died. Days at the track became more precious. The bets grew bigger. The nights grew longer. Life on the road became more delirious. Pete wondered, many years later, what it would have been like—what *he* would have been like—if Big Pete had lived. All of his young life, Pete Rose had lived to please his father. Harry Rose wanted to raise a ballplayer; every birthday and Christmas, Harry would give Pete a baseball present—a bat, a ball, a glove, another bat, a catcher's mitt. "I don't think I got a single toy my whole childhood," Pete would say. Harry Rose wanted to raise a tough son of a gun, so Pete stepped in the boxing ring to impress his father. (And he got bloodied, beaten, but when the fight ended, he said, "I didn't go down, Dad," and Harry Rose smiled broadly.) Pete switch-hit because Harry wanted it, he ran hard to first on walks because Harry loved how Enos Slaughter did that, Pete hit first because Harry told him to.

"We gonna throw, Dad?" Pete Jr. asked again. Pete looked out over the field. In later years, Pete Jr. and his sister Fawn would talk about how distant they felt from their father. Fawn told the writer Pat Jordan, "My father is the world's worst father."

And when Jordan asked Pete Jr. what he'd learned from his father, an even more heartbreaking answer emerged.

"What'd I learn from my dad?" Pete Jr. asked the writer Pat Jordan. After some thought he said, "My dad told me to hit the ball where it's pitched."

Truth was, Pete Rose wasn't ready to be a father. He still felt like a son.

July 25, 1975

CINCINNATI
REDS VS. DODGERS
Team record: 64–34
First place by twelve and a half games

The games for the Dodgers series had been sold out for months, and reporters pulled out every hackneyed line they could find in the sportswriter toolbox: the Dodgers had their backs against the wall; it was do-or-die time; there was no tomorrow; it was now or never. Really, it was a whole lot less than that. There was no race. The Reds, with a spectacular six-week show, had run away from the Dodgers.

Truth was, there were no interesting races anywhere in baseball. The three-time World Champion Oakland A's were ten games up in the American League West. The Boston Red Sox were not expected to do well before the season began, but the emergence of two rookies—Fred Lynn and Jim Rice—had changed their fortunes, and they led the New York Yankees by seven games in the American League East. And the Pittsburgh Pirates—who had won the National League East four of the previous five years—had a comfortable enough five-game lead. There would not be much tension in the final two months.

So teams had to find different ways to draw fans. In Atlanta, they spread twenty-four thousand one-dollar bills on the field and had six fans try to grab as many as they could in ninety seconds. One of those fans, Peggy Stephens, entertained everyone by stuffing the bills in her blouse. In Minnesota, manager Frank Quilici hoped to spark his team and inspire some fan support by naming Rod Carew—the league's leading hitter—as team captain. Unfortunately, the Twins were in last place at the time, twenty games behind Oakland. "Today seemed like the ideal moment," Quilici said. He would be fired at the end of the season. In Texas, manager Billy Martin announced that he had been fired right in the middle of the season, and he used the moment to publicly announce that Rangers owner Brad Corbett "has owned his team for one year, and he thinks he's a baseball genius. Corbett knows as much about baseball as I know about plastic pipe."

And in Cincinnati, the Dodgers arrived for four games. Players on each team tried halfheartedly to make it sound like the games still had some meaning. If the Dodgers somehow swept all four games, they would be only eight and a half games back, and anyway, it was something to talk about.

"I don't want to win this thing by twenty games," Joe moaned to reporters, an interesting new complaint. Joe worried that the Reds would lose their edge if they won the division title too easily. In truth, he felt like the Reds already *had* lost their edge. They had been play-ing poorly since the All-Star Game (though the Dodgers were playing badly themselves). Morgan had been playing poorly. "Maybe I do too much for a little guy," he said in a weak moment. And he went on: "I'm tired. I'm always battling, but I'm going to rest somewhere." This was not something that a member of the Machine was supposed to say, certainly not to reporters. Joe knew, even as the reporter was writing down the words, that he had made a mistake, and his team-mates would make him pay.

The Reds and Dodgers played a doubleheader that Friday night, and more than fifty-one thousand packed into Riverfront Stadium to see it. In the afternoon, heat poured upward from the Astroturf; it felt like they were playing over a New York sewer grate. At night, moths fluttered in the lights. The Dodgers won the first game after a backup outfielder named John Hale smacked a double in the eighth inning to score Garvey and then came around to score himself a couple of batters later. The Dodgers' previously indestructible Mike Marshall was back after missing close to two months with that mysterious injury back in April. He felt good again. And he still knew how to unwind the Machine. He threw two shutout innings, which infuriated Pete all over again.

"We have got to *hit* that son of a bitch," Pete shouted. Pete didn't feel any of the hesitant feelings that Joe felt. He wanted to win the division by twenty games, thirty games, fifty games. He wanted the Dodgers to writhe in embarrassment. He did not want there to be any excuses left. He did not want them to say, when it all ended, "It would have been different if only we'd had Marshall all year."

Second game, seventh inning, Reds trailed 3–2, and Pete stepped to the plate with two men on base. Marshall was pitching again. "Pete Rose was the weakest hitter in that lineup," Marshall would say many years later; the war between the two raged on. "Well, he was. I could get him out pretty much anytime I liked. All he did was hit the ball on the ground and run. The only way Pete Rose could hit me was if I made a mistake."

This time, Pete moved his hands up on the bat three or four

inches—Marshall had struck him out in the first game with a sneaky fastball, and Pete was not about to let one of those go by again. Marshall threw, only it wasn't a fastball this time. It was instead a hanging screwball—meaning it was up and sitting there, tempting as low-hanging fruit. It was a Mike Marshall mistake. Pete turned on it, crushed it, a line drive homer to left field, a final blow.

"It was a big one," Pete said after the game. "The Dodgers were done before. But they're really done now."

When Joe Morgan arrived at the ballpark early the next day, a Saturday, he still felt exhausted. He had not gotten a hit Friday. To be precise, he had not gotten a hit in his previous eighteen at-bats—hell, he had not even hit the ball hard. His batting average had plummeted twenty points, his magical season was drifting away, and he was angry and disappointed and, more than anything, tired.

He walked into the clubhouse and toward his locker. There he saw two pillows, a sleeping bag, a cup of coffee, a pair of slippers, and two aspirin tablets.

There it was: his teammates' response to his "I'm going to rest somewhere" quote. Joe looked around quickly. Was it Bench? No, he wasn't around. Rose? Doggie—it had to be Doggie. Only he wasn't around either. With this team, it could have been any one of them. And so Morgan just shouted out loud, for everyone to hear, "You guys are crazy! Insane! I love it! Without this, I'd hang myself."

And that afternoon Joe banged two hits, scored a run, drove in a run, and the Reds beat the Dodgers again.

THE MACHINE
July 30 to August 18

> *They'll never see hide nor hair of Hoffa again.*
> *He'll never see the light of day.*

—Ex-gangster Mickey Cohen

For three weeks in that hot summer of 1975, while the Eagles' song "One of These Nights" played constantly on the radio, while actor Bob Newhart and singer John Denver guest-hosted for Johnny Carson on *The Tonight Show*, while President Ford tried to reassure a nation scarred by Watergate and Vietnam and a tumbling economy, while everyone wondered if Jimmy Hoffa was alive, the Big Red Machine played baseball as well as it has ever been played.

The Reds had had brilliant times before, of course. And there would be many more famous moments to come. But this was their apex, their Fifth Symphony, their *Citizen Kane*. This was the time when all the tumblers clicked into place, when Pete stretched doubles into triples, when Joe stole bases with abandon, when Johnny hit and threw, when George Foster hit long home runs, when Doggie drove in runs, when those haunted starting pitchers—Gary Nolan, Freddie Norman, Jack Billingham, Pat Darcy—were unbeatable.

For eighteen games, the Reds' whole team hit .318. For eighteen games, the Reds' starting pitchers did not lose even once. For eighteen games, the Reds won by big scores and small ones, they won easily and they won with late comebacks, they won with speed, with power, with defense, with starting pitching, with great relief, with strategy, and with pride. They lost only twice, and even those games were epic. In one loss, the Reds relaxed and blew a five-run lead. Sparky Anderson would call the other loss one of the greatest games he ever managed.

The stretch was breathtaking, no less so because it was also—in real terms—almost meaningless. The championship race was over. The Reds began the stretch thirteen and a half games up on the Dodgers and everyone else. They had the best record in baseball. They could have coasted into the playoffs. But maybe that's what separates good and great, beautiful and spectacular, contender and champion. In a baseball season, there are many muggy days, late in the season, when the race has been won or lost, and exhaustion has set in, and the bat feels heavy, and the strike zone moves, and the sound of the crowd pounds like a jackhammer on a New York sidewalk. And the great teams win on those days.

Joe Morgan and Pete Rose had an almost daily argument. Joe believed you play baseball to win, nothing else. That's how he lived, that's how he performed, that's why he wanted to be good at everything. He did not steal bases with the team up a few runs. He did not enjoy playing as much when his team was comfortably ahead (or hopelessly behind). He rested a few games every year so he could stay fresh. He did not want to beat the Dodgers by twenty games. He thrived on victory and defeat.

Pete believed something else. He believed that you play baseball to *play*. Sure, he conceded, you play to win. Sure, he conceded, you play for money. Sure, he happily admitted, you play for fame and celebrity and the fancy cars and the second glance of the woman in tight jeans. He was no monk, not even a baseball monk, not by a long shot. But there was something more. He hungered for one more at-bat, one more ground ball to field, one more chance to bring the crowd to its feet. He played to make headlines, to make history, to let everyone on the ball field know that Pete Rose was the toughest ballplayer they had ever run across. He was playing in a spring training game once, and Sparky wanted to take him out. "One more at-bat," he told Sparky, and in that at-bat he ripped a ball into the gap, and he rounded first, rounded second, raced to third, and finished it off with a vintage, flying headfirst Pete Rose slide. He got up, dusted himself off, and waved to the dugout.

"Now you can take me out," he shouted. He had given the kids a thrill.

Baseball fit his personality because it was the one game played off Wall Street that encouraged selfishness and rewarded greed and called the guy with the highest batting average "Champion."

"Pete, I'm going to give you a rest one of these days," Sparky said to him at one point in the middle of this glorious stretch.

"Well, who do we play Thursday?" Pete asked.

"Nobody," Sparky said. "We have Thursday off."

"Fine," Pete said. "Then that will be my day of rest."

For eighteen games in the middle of their remarkable season, the Reds played baseball Pete Rose's way. They played for glory. And they were damned good.

Sparky Anderson began the glorious stretch in a foul mood. His genius had paid off better than even he expected—the Reds had run away from the Dodgers with their best pitcher, Don Gullett, injured and out—but it had worn Sparky down too. The Reds had gone forty-five consecutive games without having a starting pitcher throw a complete game. That was a record, and it kept Sparky up at night. For forty-five straight games, every single night, Sparky made the slow walk to the mound to take out his starter. His starting pitchers despised him. The fans booed him. The newspaper guys mocked him. Sure, it was all well and good to say that he didn't care about that stuff, but he cared. He was not mild and unsure George Anderson pulling weeds in his backyard and letting the phone ring. No, he was

Sparky Anderson, showman, and he managed the best baseball team in the world, maybe even the best baseball team that ever was, and he wanted everyone to know it.

"Damn it, we've got to end this streak, it's killing me," he kept telling his pitching coach, Larry Shepard. "I don't care what happens, tonight the starter's going the distance." But then it would be the eighth or ninth inning, and the Reds would be up a few runs, and the starter would show the slightest sign of weakening, and Sparky would take that slow walk to the mound. He could not help himself. He could not take any chances. He really was Captain Hook.

The first game of the glorious stretch, the Reds led San Francisco 6–1 in the ninth inning, and the starting pitcher, Pat Darcy, was still on the mound. It was miserably hot in Cincinnati, fans were fainting in the stands, and Darcy was pitching on fumes. Pat grew up in Arizona, and he loved pitching in the heat, but he knew that his energy was drained. His fastball had nothing on it. Darcy gave up a single to Gary Matthews. He gave up another single to Willie Montanez. Darcy told himself: *Don't look at the dugout. Don't look at Sparky. If you look at him, he will take you out of this game.*

And it was a good thing he did not look, because he had it just right: Captain Hook was beginning to get worried. Sparky did not want this streak to keep going, but damn it, he was not going to lose a baseball game just to prove a point. He got Rawly Eastwick to start warming up in the bullpen. Damn it.

Darcy settled in, found a burst of energy. He struck out Chris Speier. He got Derrel Thomas to fly out to center field. Two out. Sparky felt good again. The kid was going to do it; he was going to end this damn streak once and for all. Then Steve Ontiveros rapped a single to left, and Sparky stood up again. "They're killing me, Shep," he said to his pitching coach, Larry Shepard. "They's absolutely killing me."

A guy named Jake Brown stepped up to pinch-hit for the Giants. He had been in the big leagues for about two months, and he would be in the big leagues for only two more months. "If this guy gets on," Sparky announced to everyone, "I'm hooking him."

Pat did not hear Sparky yell that . . . but he knew anyway. He had a five-run lead, and he was one out away from a complete-game victory, and he had pitched beautifully . . . but it did not matter. If he did not get the out, he was gone. Pat threw one of his sinking fastballs, and Jake Brown pounded it into the ground toward first base. Doggie scooped it up, touched the bag, the game was over, the streak was over, and Sparky felt free.

"You know people were fainting in the stands," a reporter told Darcy.

"Really?" Pat asked back. "Over a complete game?"

Next day, Sparky was in his office when he heard some yelling back in the clubhouse. He didn't think anything about it because the guys on the Machine were always yelling about something. Johnny Bench knocked on the door and poked his head into the office. He said that Merv Rettenmund, the Reds' backup outfielder, had to go to the hospital. What followed was pulled out of an Abbott and Costello routine.

"What happened?" Sparky asked.

"Terry Crowley stepped on his foot," Bench said.

"Oh," Sparky said. "Wait, why in the hell did he step on Merv's foot?"

"He was breaking up the fight," Bench said.

"Oh," Sparky said. "Wait, what fight?"

"The fight between Cesar and Pedro," Bench said.

"Oh," Sparky said. "Wait. What?"

Cesar Geronimo and Pedro Borbon were best friends and roommates. Their personalities meshed perfectly. Pedro was loud and loony, and he had that savage temper. And Cesar was precisely the opposite. He was as quiet as the furniture, and he always seemed at peace. Cesar, like Borbon, grew up in the Dominican Republic. When he was twelve, his parents sent him away to the Santo Tomas de Aquino Seminary to study for the priesthood. Cesar believed that he was destined to be a priest, he thought that was his calling, but at night he would listen to New York Yankees games on the transistor radio that he had slipped under his pillow.

He did not play baseball at the seminary—there was no baseball to be played. Instead, he played softball, and it was while playing softball that he developed what hitting coach Big Klu would call "a swing absolutely as bad as anything I'd ever seen in a big-league uniform." With a swing like that—"like he's trying to crush a cockroach," Pete would say—Cesar should have had no chance to sign with a professional baseball team. But he had one thing: he was born with a magnificent left arm. That was the arm that the famed Yankees scout Pepe Sada saw when Cesar showed up at a tryout camp. Sada signed Cesar based on that arm, signed him to be a pitcher or an outfielder, didn't matter, he would let them worry about that back on the mainland.

Cesar became an outfielder. He hit .194 his first year in the minor leagues. But he saw his signing as a gift from God, a sign too, and he had a fierce determination to make it to the big leagues. He taught himself how to play center field, and he played it with a beautiful grace—he looked like Joe DiMaggio out there.

They brought a little something out in each other. Cesar was the one guy in the clubhouse who seemed to know how to calm down Pedro. And Pedro was the one guy in the clubhouse who could get Cesar to talk. Only, on this day, Pedro started to make fun of Cesar, and for once Cesar came back with a few rips of his own. Pedro didn't like it. He yelled, causing the Reds players around to step in the middle. Pedro sat down at the stool by his locker. The moment passed. Only then, quite suddenly, Pedro bolted to his feet and went after Cesar. A bunch of people stepped in to stop the fight. The only injury was to Merv, one of those players who stepped in.

"Damn it, *that's it!*" Sparky yelled after he closed the clubhouse to reporters. "There will be no more ripping around here. Do you hear me?"

If they heard, they did not listen. That night, the Reds were facing a rookie pitcher named John Montefusco—everyone was calling him "the Count of Montefusco," or just "the Count" for short. The Count had won ten games, and he was among the league leaders in strike-outs. But what made him special, what made him the talk of baseball in 1975, was that he bragged and gloated and never shut up. All week, leading into the game, Montefusco guaranteed that he would not just beat the Reds, he would shut them out. And he would not just shut them out. He would strike out Johnny Bench four times in the game. When asked by reporters if it was wise to rattle the cage of the Big Red Machine, the Count smiled and said that the Machine had never seen anything like him.

"Hey, Count," Johnny yelled at him before the game. "You strike me out four times, and I'm buying you a steak dinner."

"I can taste it already," the Count yelled back.

"Hey, Count," Pete Rose yelled. "Did you hear that Morgan's not playing tonight?"

"Morgan's not playing?" the Count yelled back. "Well, then it won't just be a shutout tonight. It will be a no-hitter."

The Reds loved it. Montefusco was their kind of player. He was a beautiful inspiration for a late summer ball game. "You know the difference between us and everyone else?" Joe Morgan would say. "Everyone else talks when they're winning. We talk whether we're winning or losing."

First batter, Pete Rose, struck out. Montefusco smiled big. Then Ken Griffey doubled and stole third. (Joe Morgan wasn't in the lineup, so Griffey was free to run.) Ken scored when Johnny Bench's ground ball was mishandled by first baseman Willie Montanez.

"*Lucky!*" the Count screamed.

"You didn't strike me out, meat," Johnny screamed back.

Next inning, George Foster doubled, Darrel Chaney doubled, and Reds pitcher Clay Kirby doubled too. Ken walked. Danny Driessen singled and then stole second. Johnny Bench walked up to the plate, and he saw that the Count's face was ashen. On a full count, Johnny smashed a long home run to left field. Before the ball even landed, San Francisco manager Wes Westrum had reached the mound and taken the ball away from Montefusco. The Cincinnati crowd jeered and waved handkerchiefs and laughed as Montefusco walked toward the dugout. Before he disappeared, though, the Count of Montefusco tipped his cap.

"Are you out of the prediction business?" the Count was asked.

"Hell, no," he said. "Wait till I get 'em back in San Francisco."

There was a saying in baseball that went like so: every time Walter Alston sneezed, the rest of the National League caught a cold. Alston was the grand old man of the game—he had been managing the team since 1954, since the Dodgers were in Brooklyn, and he had won four World Series, and he had won another three pennants, and yes, it was true that pretty much every other manager in the game copied Walter's style.

So, yes, Sparky wanted to outsmart the grand old man, at least this once. And here it was, eighth inning, Reds leading 3–2, and Alston was trying everything he could to tie the score. Alston sent in a pinch hitter. Then he sent in another pinch hitter. Then, he sent in *another* pinch hitter. Sparky looked at the scorecard and smiled. Even when the Dodgers tied the score, he did not stop smiling. Walter Alston had buried himself. He had made so many moves in his desperate effort to tie the score that he had no choice but to put a second baseman, Lee Lacy, in left field. He had to put a left fielder, Tom Paciorek, in center field. He had to put his utility infielder, Rick Auerbach, at shortstop. He had to put Paul Powell, a twenty-seven-year-old with seven big league hits, at catcher. Sparky had barely heard of Paul Powell. It was a freak show out there.

"Genius, boy," Sparky said to himself. He had done it. He had his Reds way out front in first place. He had invented a whole new way to run a pitching staff, using relief pitchers in a whole new way. And now he had outflanked the great Walter Alston, and in his hometown of Los Angeles no less. Yes, Georgie Anderson had turned out all right. Sparky sat back in the ninth inning and almost laughed when George Foster hit a single to left field with Johnny Bench on second base. Bench rounded third, headed for home, about to score the winning run . . . and then something crazy happened. Lee Lacy, that second baseman playing left, fired a perfect throw to home plate and that unknown catcher Paul Powell slapped the tag on Bench.

"Out," the umpire shouted.

Well, that was unfortunate. So the game went to the tenth inning. This time the Machine's Darrel Chaney walked and moved to second base. Pete came up. He smacked a single to left field. Sparky smiled. Chaney rounded third, headed for home. And Lee Lacy fired a perfect throw to the plate. Paul Powell slapped the tag on Chaney.

"Out," the umpire shouted.

And the Reds lost the game in the bottom of the tenth inning.

"That," Sparky said to reporters after the game, "was the greatest game I ever managed." And when reporters suggested it could not be the greatest—after all, the Reds had lost—Sparky simply smiled and said: "The greatest. It just goes to show you what it is to be a manager."

Not that it mattered much. The Reds won the next day, and the next day, and again the next. Borbon and Geronimo made up; Pedro even called Cesar's parents in the Dominican to apologize. Two days later, when Pedro's third son was born, he and Cesar handed out cigars in the clubhouse.

The ripping continued. On Sundays, Pete would get on Davey about crossing himself before he hit. "Davey, let me ask you something. What happens if you make the sign of the cross and then the pitcher makes the sign of the cross? Why would God take your side? Do you really think God gives a shit about a baseball game?" Davey muttered something quietly in Spanish, something that loosely translated to mean: "Oh, you're going to hell, Pete Rose." Not that it mattered to Pete. Every Sunday, when the chaplain, Wendell Deyo, led the Reds in prayer in the weight room, Pete would sit by his locker, work over his bats, and just shake his head.

"Hey, Doggie," he said as he pointed at a player heading to chapel. "Look at this guy. I hope he's thanking God for that piece of ass he got last night because he damn sure isn't getting any hits."

Doggie was the clearinghouse for all Reds gags. He started the gags, he ended them, he was the arbiter of good taste, the man who drew the lines, the team leader who, more than anyone else, decided what was funny and what was off-limits. There wasn't much off-limits.

"Hey, Joe, you hitting so bad now that Pete say he top your average today," Doggie said.

"I don't care," Joe said.

"Wait," Pete shouted. "I didn't say anything."

"That's not what you told me," Doggie said. "I heard you."

"Hey, Pete, where your calculator?" Davey asked. "You figure your average already?"

"I don't need a calculator," Pete said. "I'll learn what I'm hitting in tomorrow's paper when I look at the league leaders. You will have to wait until Sunday, when they publish all the averages . . . if they run them down as low as you are."

Doggie caught Griffey sitting by his locker laughing. "Hey, Kenny," Doggie said. "How many infield hits you got? Never before do we have a player who get hits on ground balls to second base."

GRIFFEY: *So I have twenty-eight infield hits. How many homers do*
you have?
DOGGIE: *A weak sixteen.*
GRIFFEY: *I'll catch you.*
DOGGIE: *It take you ten years. . . . Put all your twenty-eight infield*
hits together, they might reach the fence.

Jimmy Hoffa disappeared, and investigators seemed to be looking for him, though everyone got the feeling from the start that the investigators did not expect to find him. Hoffa had led the Teamsters. He had done some shady deals. He made enemies. Witnesses had seen him standing outside a fashionable restaurant in Detroit in the early afternoon; he was supposed to meet Anthony Giacalone, better known in the papers as "Tony Jack, the reputed kingpin of the Detroit Mafia." Hoffa never made it to the lunch. The Hoffa family offered a $275,000 reward to anyone who could offer information to help find Hoffa, though in barbershops and diners across America no one expected that reward to get collected.

The New York Mets fired their manager, Yogi Berra. "I did the best I could," he said. "And I couldn't have done no better." The great old Yankees manager Casey Stengel turned eighty-five and explained why he would never want a woman umpire in baseball: "I couldn't argue with one," he said. "I'd put my arms around her and give her a little kiss." Xerox announced that it was getting out of the computer business just as two longtime friends, Bill Gates and Paul Allen, were putting together a business plan they tentatively were calling "Micro-soft." Cigarette advertisements filled *Time* magazine, including an odd photograph of a woman with a black eye. Above it was the tagline: "Us Tareyton smokers would rather fight than switch!"

The country kept changing. For years, the Staten Island Ferry had charged a nickel for a ride from Staten Island to Manhattan, but tough times forced the New York City Council to raise the price to a quarter. There was an uproar, and the Associated Press came up with a list of things that Americans could still buy for a nickel, and among those were two and a half tablespoons of peanuts from a vending machine in Alabama; a cup of coffee at the Last Chance Café in Reno; and a local phone call in Wapakoneta, Ohio, the birthplace of astronaut Neil Armstrong.

The one-year anniversary of Richard Nixon resigning over Watergate came and went, the only real news being made by Betty Ford, the first lady, who told Morley Safer of the television show *60 Minutes* that she would not be surprised if her eighteen-year-old daughter, Susan, said she was having an affair. Mrs. Ford also offered up the opinion that, in some cases, premarital sex might prevent divorce. Clergymen lined up for days after that to criticize the first lady, none more than Elder Gordon B. Hinkley of the Church of Jesus Christ of Latter-Day Saints, who said: "We deplore the deterioration of morality around the world."

On a Tuesday, the Reds beat the Giants without Johnny, Joe, or Doggie in the lineup. Cesar Geronimo cracked three hits, and his old friend Pedro pitched scoreless relief. Sparky complained. "We had a couple of guys loafing out there," he told reporters. The next day, the Machine banged out twenty hits and walked seven times in a 12–5 destruction of the Giants. They were a preposterous sixteen and a half games ahead of the Dodgers. And for the first time, people were beginning to compare the Reds with the greatest teams ever. "The Reds may go down in lore with the 1927 New York Yankees," wrote Jim Murray of the *Los Angeles Times*.

"I think this ball club can compare with any team in history," Johnny said.

"I think it's better," Sparky said, and then he added: "Because you got to remember, all those old-time records were made in small ballparks. There isn't a Chinese home run in any ballpark in the National League."

Nobody needed to ask what a Chinese home run was in 1975.

The Reds fell asleep and blew two big leads against Montreal on a Friday—their only other loss in this glorious stretch—and so they obliterated the Expos 9–1 on Saturday. Pete Rose bashed three more hits—nobody could ever remember seeing him hotter—and Clay Carroll pitched four scoreless innings in relief. They called Clay Carroll "the Hawk" for the way his nose curved like a beak. He was from a small place in Alabama called Clanton, and everyone on the club had a good Hawk story. The best one was about the Cadillac—Hawk had signed with the Milwaukee Braves back in '61, and he immediately spent his bonus money on a new Cadillac. A friend immediately wrapped it around a tree. Ever since then, the Hawk had wanted to buy a new Cadillac. After he was traded to the Reds, he had his first big league success, and his first big paycheck. And he knew just what to do.

"I'm going to buy a new Cadillac," he told Johnny.

"No way," Johnny said. That was 1971; Johnny and Pete co-owned a Lincoln dealership in town. They also co-owned a bowling alley. It wasn't until later that they decided they would be better off not being business partners.

"You want a Lincoln," Johnny said. "It's a much better car."

"No can do," Clay said. "Ever since I wrecked my first one, I've wanted a Caddy."

"Yeah," Johnny said, "but the Lincoln Continental is the only car on the market that comes equipped with its own vacuum cleaner. Think of all the time you'll save."

The Hawk thought about that: a vacuum cleaner would come in handy. It wasn't until two days later that he drove his car back into the dealership lot and screamed at whoever would listen: "I've been looking for two days and I can't find that goddamned vacuum cleaner."

The Reds did love Clay Carroll. From 1968 to 1974, he pitched in more games than any Reds pitcher ever, but things began to change in '75. The Hawk pitched about as well as ever, but Sparky didn't seem to trust him in the big moments. Nothing was ever said, but everybody knew that Sparky's favorite pitchers were now the kids: Will McEnaney and Rawly Eastwick. The only person who did not seem to notice was the Hawk himself, and every time he was called into a game, he ran in from the bullpen full speed, running so hard, as George Plimpton would write in *Sports Illustrated*, that teammates worried he would build up too much momentum and "run right past the mound, over the manager and the catcher standing there, and fetch up in a tumble in the dugout beyond."

Johnny got three hits the next night as the Reds pounded Montreal again, 11–3. Johnny's batting average moved back above .300. He still felt miserable. His shoulder throbbed no matter what he did. He tried hot pads, ice packs, cortisone shots, and none of it gave him relief. Also, he knew that his marriage was falling apart, though more to the point, it had never come together. He did not know what Vickie wanted from him. He was a ballplayer. He was a celebrity. He was a star. He could not stop being those things. And he was still a sex symbol; he could not help that either. Every day, it seemed, he got more tearstained letters from women who could not believe he had gotten hitched. There was this one young woman who adored him; she used to come out to the ballpark with her family and cheer like mad. He gave her a broken bat once, and she sent him notes after that. Then she sent him presents. Then she started sending him photographs, some of them of her in rather revealing poses. When he announced on local television that he was getting engaged, he came home to find that broken bat on his front porch. There was a rather frightening note attached too. He got a lot of notes like that, a lot of cards from brokenhearted women. He could not understand why Vickie did not appreciate that he had been the most eligible bachelor in town, maybe in the Midwest, maybe in the whole damn country, and she got him.

Johnny had always loved baseball. He loved not only playing ball but also what baseball could do for him. He loved to make gentle wisecracks about his hometown of Binger—"It's about two and a half miles past a town called 'Resume Speed,'" he would say—but the truth was that, as far back as he could remember, he had wanted out. His father, like Pete's father, had raised him to be a ballplayer. And he was going to be the best damned baseball player who ever lived. Johnny's friend Glen Campbell had a song on the radio, and the lyrics suited Johnny:

> *But I'm gonna be where the lights are shinin' on me*
> *Like a rhinestone cowboy.*

That was Johnny, a rhinestone catcher, and the offers poured in—host your own TV show, appear onstage, do a commercial, pose in a picture with Miss World USA Lynda Carter, tell a few stories on *The Tonight Show*—and he would not say no. He did not like all the trappings of fame—he loved them. He did not like getting booed—and he did not care. He did not like dealing daily with the reporters' inane questions—and it drove him mad when they did not come to talk to him first. The kid who had practiced signing his autograph at Ford McKinney's Texaco station had grown up into a man who avoided signing any autographs, even for teammates. But even so, he loved *fame*, the concept, the idea, the way people would look at him. Vickie did not understand that. She did not understand him.

The Machine obliterated the Cubs 9–3 and 12–8 over the next two days. In the second game, the Cubs actually scored four runs in the first inning, but as San Diego pitcher Brent Strom would say: "You could score four runs in the first inning and feel like you were behind. You were constantly playing in fear against those guys." The Reds scored five runs in the third inning—Ed Armbrister singled, Pete singled, Ken Griffey singled, Tony Perez singled, George Foster singled, Danny Driessen tripled, Darrel Chaney singled. They really were a Machine, an unstoppable Machine, an assembly line of hits, a force of will.

"We're the best team in baseball, there is no doubt," Johnny told reporters. When one asked about the Oakland A's—who, after all, had won three consecutive World Series—Bench scoffed. "You got to have respect for the Athletics because they're World Champs," he said. "But if you ask me, Reggie Jackson and Joe Rudi are the only guys there who could even make our team."

Well, of course, that ticked off the Oakland players. The A's star relief pitcher Rollie Fingers fired back: "Johnny Bench couldn't even carry the catcher's gear over here with the A's. I'd hate to have to pitch to him . . . he can't think behind the plate."

And that ticked off the Cincinnati players. Pete fired back. "Oakland's time is over."

And Oakland's backup catcher Larry Haney fired back: "Our whole pitching staff could make the Reds."

And Johnny fired back: "Haney should know, he has bounced from one team to another so much he should be an authority."

And Oakland pitcher Ken Holtzman fired back: "The Reds haven't even beaten Pittsburgh yet. The Pirates might beat them three straight."

The Pittsburgh Pirates came to town—and like Holtzman suggested, the Pirates were good. They had their own nickname, "the Pittsburgh Lumber Company," and they had run away with the National League East division. The Reds would play the Pirates in the playoffs. "We got something to prove to those guys," the Lumber Company's star player, Willie Stargell, said in the papers.

The Reds beat them four straight. In the first game, George Foster mashed a three-run homer in the fourth inning, then another one two innings later. He had become a star, even Sparky had to admit it. Sparky did not just admit it: he already had begun to rewrite history. He had started to say that the reason he moved Pete Rose to third base was to get George Foster in the lineup. That wasn't quite right; he did want to get Foster a few more at-bats, but he really had moved Pete to third to get John Vukovich out of the lineup and to get Danny Driessen in the lineup more. Nobody argued, though. It was just another bit of Sparky genius.

George had begun to develop his own style on the field. While almost every other hitter used the bats stained brown, so they looked like natural wood, George would wave a menacing black bat, and he would flip his bat in the air when he walked, and he would hit monstrous home runs, the sort that would make even Doggie shake his head in wonder. Then, after the game, he would have the reporters laughing hysterically.

"Why do you use that black bat?" someone asked George after one game.

"I thought someone should integrate the bat rack," he said.

"Why do you step in and out of the batter's box and make pitchers mad?" someone else asked.

"If a pitcher is mad enough, he'll try to blow the ball past you," he said. "That's what I'm looking for." And then he smiled big and with a comic's timing said: "I like that fastball."

"Where the hell did that personality come from?" Sparky wondered. If there was one thing Sparky had learned since becoming manager of the Reds it was that people would surprise you.

The Reds beat the Pirates 8–3 in the second game. Pete Rose got two hits in the first inning; that gave him 2,499 for his career—one shy of a magic number. Johnny hit a homer. Fred Norman pitched a complete game. The day after that, Doggie and Cesar hit homers, and the Reds beat the Pirates again. "We are playing free," Doggie said.

———————

On Sunday afternoon, Sparky sent out a makeshift lineup—no Johnny, no Doggie, no Davey Concepcion, no George Foster. The stage belonged to Pete Rose. Baseball is a game of numbers, and the most beautiful of those are the round numbers. Pitchers want three hundred victories. Batters want five hundred home runs. Pete Rose was one hit shy of two thousand five hundred, and it was driving him nuts. He had been one hit shy for two days.

Pete knew why. The Louisville Slugger Bat Company had sent him a special bat to use for his twenty-five hundredth hit. Pete Rose loved memorabilia. He had kept the baseballs for every numerically round hit of his career—his five hundredth hit, his one thousandth hit, his two thousandth hit, his first World Series hit, and so on. He enjoyed having a token from every big moment of his career. And he had this hunch that all these things would be worth a lot of money someday. So he was happy to use the specially made bat, except for one thing: the bat they sent was thirty-five ounces. And Pete *always* used a thirty-four-ounce bat. You wouldn't think an ounce would make much difference, but for Pete, using that damned bat was like wearing a wristwatch one size too big or a shirt with a neck size a half-inch too small. He could not get around with that heavier bat. He lashed two hard ground balls, and in Pete's estimation both of them should have rolled up the middle for a base hit. Instead, they went right to the shortstop. That bat was making him swing an instant too late.

"To hell with it," Pete said in the seventh inning, and he borrowed someone else's thirty-four-ounce bat. He walked over to Sparky and Big Klu and said, "You just watch, this time the ball will go right up the middle."

Then he stepped into the batter's box, dug in against Pittsburgh pitcher Bruce Kison, and cracked a line drive right up the middle for a base hit. While the fans cheered and the Reds scored the game-winning run, Pete Rose stood on first base, pointed to the Reds dugout, and shouted, "I *told you* it was the fucking bat."

Don Gullett returned to pitch the final game of the glorious stretch. The Reds' best pitcher had missed fifty-seven games. The Reds won forty-three of them. The Reds led the Dodgers by only three and a half games when Gullett broke his thumb on June 16, and everyone prepared for a heated and tight summer pennant race. When Gullett returned, the Reds led the Dodgers by seventeen and a half games. Sparky had been exactly right the morning after the injury, when he had breakfast with his friend Jeff Ruby at the Holiday Inn. Now everyone saw his genius.

And Gullett pitched five scoreless innings against the St. Louis Cardinals on his first day back.

"It was like he had never been away," Sparky gushed to reporters. This game was like so many of the rest. After Gullett came out, Pedro Borbon pitched. After he hit a batter in the eighth, Will McEnaney came in and limited the damage. After McEnaney gave up a lead-off single in the ninth, Clay Carroll came in. After Carroll gave up a single to load the bases, Rawly Eastwick came in. He finished off the Cardinals, the Reds won 3–2, and they were on pace to win more games than any National League team in sixty years, and they were playing the best baseball that had ever been played.

Not that anything had really changed. When the game ended, reporters surrounded Pete Rose and one asked him if Dick Wagner— the man who had cut his pay before the season began—had seen Pete's twenty-five hundredth hit. "I don't think he's ever seen me get a hit," Pete said. "All he sees is me throwing baseballs into the stands at twenty-five bucks a clip."

Clay Carroll inspired another Clay Carroll story. He borrowed a magazine from a reporter, glanced at it, and returned it. "Boy, that was quick," the reporter said. "Weren't no pictures," the Hawk replied.

The guys ripped Johnny for going oh-for-five. Joe and Pete

argued about which one of them would end up with a better batting average. And Sparky sat in the office, drank milk, and worried about things—worried that his players might let down, worried that someone would get hurt, worried that the Reds would lose to Pittsburgh in the playoffs, worried that maybe he lacked the killer instinct that separates champions from bums.

WE HAVEN'T WON ANYTHING

August 19 to October 7

> *The highway's jammed with broken heroes.*

—Bruce Springsteen, "Born to Run"

August 25, 1975

CHICAGO
REDS VS. CUBS

Team record: 84–44
First place by sixteen and a half games

Bruce Springsteen was not happy, not at all, not with the sound, not with the hype, and most of all not with the album. *Born to Run*, his new album, hit the stores on August 25, and it was a monster. He had spent fourteen hard months making it. He felt like a failure. Springsteen was twenty-five years old, and he wanted only one thing, but it was the biggest thing he could imagine: to make the greatest rock-and-roll record ever. He had spent fourteen hours a day in the studio, every day for more than a year, leaving at six o'clock most mornings, sometimes later, and still he could not get the sounds out of his head and onto the tape. His friend and coproducer, Jon Landau, kept telling him to get the record done, to set a release date, and Springsteen would growl: "Hey, man, the release date is just one day. The record is forever." The pressure was intense. Years later, Springsteen would tell the author Dave Marsh that he bought an $89.95 record player and listened to the album for the first time. He hated it so much that he wanted to kill the release.

But Landau calmed him down and talked him into releasing the album. Landau had been a wandering rock critic—a year earlier, after seeing Springsteen perform at the Harvard Square Theater, he had written one of the most famous reviews in rock-and-roll history. He wrote: "I saw my rock'n'roll past flash before my eyes. And I saw something else: I saw rock and roll future and its name is Bruce Springsteen. And on a night when I needed to feel young, he made me feel like I was hearing music for the very first time." Landau and Springsteen understood each other. They both wanted something hard to describe.

Maybe it was a little bit like that in America in 1975, with the war over and the economy dried up and Watergate smoldering, maybe it was a time to reach for something wild and bold or—as Springsteen sang in "Jungleland"—for poets to reach for their moment and try to make an honest stand. The album *Born to Run* began with a screen door slamming and ended with those poets winding up wounded and not even dead, and in the middle, as the author Greil Marcus would write, were "one thousand and one American nights, one long night of fear and love." The album would get Springsteen on the cover of *Time* and *Newsweek* the same week. Thirty years later, it would be placed in the Library of Congress as a culturally, historically, and aesthetically significant recording, there forever with John Kennedy's inauguration speech, the Beatles' *Sgt. Pepper's Lonely Hearts Club Band* album, and the evangelist Billy Graham's "problems of the American home" speech. It would become, to many, the greatest rock-and-roll album ever recorded.

But that day, Bruce Springsteen believed he had failed.

In Chicago, the Reds pounded the Cubs 11–4, Pete got three hits, Doggie drove in two more, and Clay Carroll threw perfect relief. When the game ended reporters gathered around Pete as usual, only he did not seem as happy as he normally seemed after a victory.

"Is this the best team you've ever seen?" they asked Pete.

"We haven't won anything," he said softly. "We've got to win it all."

August 29, 1975

CINCINNATI
REDS VS. CARDINALS
Team record: 89–44
First place by eighteen and a half games

Bob Gibson, that proud man, walked slowly in from the bullpen, and he had that same scowl on his face, that famous Gibson scowl, the scowl that said, "I'm going to get you out, or I'm going to kill you." He had the scowl, but he no longer had the fastball. Gibson was almost forty years old. His record was 3–9. He had pitched so poorly that St. Louis manager Red Schoendienst, who had been Gibson's teammate years earlier, put him in the bullpen, where he pitched mop-up relief. For a man with Gibson's pride, that demotion cut through him like a cold wind. Still he pitched on. Every player on the Machine understood—this would be the last time they would ever face him.

Gibson had defined baseball for more than a decade. He was big and strong and black and ferocious. He set off childlike fears in major league players—he made them feel like they were facing the fastest pitcher in Little League. It wasn't just that Gibson was bigger than anyone else (though he was big) or that he threw harder than anyone else (though he threw hard) or that he was meaner than anyone else (though he was plenty mean—he would not hesitate to hit a player who he felt looked too comfortable at the plate).

"You wanted to earn his respect" was how Joe put it many years later. Gibson once told the author Roger Angell that he had played hundreds of games of tic-tac-toe with his daughter . . . and she never beat him. Gibson once announced to parents, "Why do I have to be an example for your kid? You be an example for your own kid." Gibson was one of the rarest of players, a legend in his time, a man players measured their careers against. Every player who ever faced Bob Gibson remembered the moment.

The Reds led the game 6–1, it was the bottom of the fifth inning, and Gibson dug his spikes into the dirt. Cesar Geronimo stepped into the box, and he saw Gibson stare him down, and he felt unnerved, like the years had melted away. Gibson struck him out. "He throw hard," Cesar said as he walked back into the dugout.

The next inning, Pete Rose stepped in. "Bob Gibson is the toughest pitcher I ever faced," Pete would say after that day and many times after that. This wasn't the same Bob Gibson. But he was still Bob Gibson. The two battled, and then there were two strikes, and then Gibby threw his fastball, his pitch. And Pete swung and missed for strike three. Gibson stomped off the mound, and Pete watched him go.

"I won't miss him," Pete would say. "But the game will."

Five days later, Gibson pitched in his final game, against the Chicago Cubs. He had nothing. He walked a man, allowed a single, walked another, threw a wild pitch, intentionally walked a man. And finally, he grooved a fastball to Pete LaCock, a twenty-three-year-old first baseman who was the son of game show host Peter Marshall. LaCock blasted it, a grand slam. That was the last pitch Bob Gibson ever threw in the big leagues.

But with Gibson, there's always one more story. Many years later, he was pitching in an old-timers game. And Pete LaCock was playing too. LaCock stepped up to face Gibson, who was well into his fifties. Gibson stared him down and promptly hit LaCock in the back with a pitch.

"Ow, Bob, what gives?" LaCock asked.

"I've been waiting for years to do that," Gibson said.

September 3, 1975

CINCINNATI
REDS VS. DODGERS
Team record: 91–46
First place by eighteen and a half games

The Machine had dismantled the Dodgers in every way possible—physically, emotionally, spiritually, you name it—but they had one more message to send. It was the fourth inning, and there were two outs, and Pete Rose walked to the plate to face Andy Messersmith. Dave Concepcion was on first base.

Pete crushed a double over the center fielder's head to score Davey. Then Geronimo walked. Then Joe Morgan hit a double to right field, scoring Pete. Then Doggie singled up the middle, scoring Geronimo and Joe. Then Johnny hit a single to center. Then George hit a choppy ground ball that was botched by the Dodgers' third baseman, Ron Cey, and another run scored.

It started to pour rain, and everyone raced off the field. It rained hard for thirty minutes, then it stopped, then the Reds sent out the Zamboni machine—those Big Red Machines that general manager Bob Howsam always talked about—to dry the field. When everything was dry, a new Dodgers pitcher came in. Marv Rettenmund hit a double to score two runs. Davey walked. Gary Nolan singled in a run. Pete got hit by a pitch. Cesar reached when the catcher dropped the third strike. Joe walked with the bases loaded. It was, as the papers put it, a free-for-all.

And when it ended, the Reds had scored ten runs.

"I'm not sure what you say," Captain America Steve Garvey said. "I guess it's their year."

It was their year. Everything was anticlimax for the Machine in September 1975. The Reds officially wrapped up the National League West championship on September 7 while sitting in the clubhouse. They had beaten San Francisco an hour and a half earlier, and then they just lingered around, wrestled with each other's kids, talked with reporters, sipped beer. They were waiting to see if the Dodgers lost to Atlanta; if they did, then the Reds would be champions and it would be the earliest date a team had ever clinched. If Los Angeles won, then the Reds would have to wait to clinch tomorrow or the next day or the next. There were still three weeks left in the season. The ending was inevitable. The rest was timing.

There was champagne chilling, and the Reds players watched television. The Dodgers led 2–0 going into the bottom of the eighth inning, and then Atlanta's comically named Biff Pocoroba walked. Then the more professionally named Rowland Office doubled. The Dodgers sent in their knuckleball pitcher Charlie Hough. Then Ralph Garr reached on an error. Everybody moved up a base on a wild pitch. Darrell Evans walked. Another pitcher, this one named Dave Sells, entered the game.

"What is Dave selling?" Johnny riddled.

"Dave Sells cars," Joe said.

Dave Sells walked Dusty Baker. Then he walked Mike Lum. The Dodgers were marching to their own funeral. Atlanta led 3–2. And when the Dodgers went down meekly in the ninth inning, the Reds were champions. Clubhouse attendants rushed in with forty-eight bottles of champagne, which the players dutifully poured on each other. Broadcaster Marty Brennaman walked around in his underwear—"You guys ain't going to get *my* clothes," he shouted as he got doused.

"If I was a drinking man, I'd be set," Pete shouted as he was drowned in champagne, then beer, then cold water. Dick Wagner, the man who had cursed out the team chaplain, walked around the clubhouse warning players to stop running around with bottles in their hands . . . somebody could get hurt. They dumped a bucket of water on his head.

"We want Pittsburgh!" Johnny shouted in an effort to start a clubhouse chant. "We want Pittsburgh!" A few joined in.

"This is more subdued than past years," Dick Wagner told a reporter. And then Bob Howsam dumped more champagne on his head.

The feds finally gave up the search for Jimmy Hoffa and pronounced him dead. A woman named Lynette Alice Fromme ("Squeaky" for short), who was once a child performer who appeared on *The Lawrence Welk Show* and later a member of the Charles Manson family, pointed a gun at President Ford in Sacramento. She may or may not have pulled the trigger, but the gun did not go off. She was grabbed by the Secret Service and arrested.

Seventeen days later, in San Francisco, another woman, Sara Jane Moore, actually did shoot at the president, and she only missed because an ex-marine named Oliver Sipple happened to see the gun just as she was about to fire. He screamed, "Gun!" and grabbed her arm just as the gun went off. The bullet missed the president and bounced off the St. Francis Hotel. "I'm not a hero," Sipple said to the media. "I'm a live coward."

The Sipple story did not end . . . it took several days for President Ford to personally thank him. Why? According to Randy Shilts's book *The Mayor of Castro Street*, Harvey Milk—the openly gay politician just coming into his own in San Francisco—suspected that it was because Sipple was gay. Milk called the San Francisco newspaper and outed him. "It's too good an opportunity," Milk told the author

Frank Robinson. "For once we can show that gays do heroic things. That guy saved the president's life."

Two days later, San Francisco columnist Herb Caen quoted Milk saying he was "proud—maybe this will break the stereotype." Soon other newspapers picked up the story that Sipple was gay— "Homosexual Hero" was the headline in the *Chicago Sun-Times*—and the news made it back to Detroit, where his mother read it. She was a strict Baptist and refused to leave the house for days after reading the news. When Sipple called her, she hung up on him.

Everyone was talking about the big boxing match coming up— the third Muhammad Ali–Joe Frazier fight, which would be fought in Manila in the Philippines. "Come on, gorilla!" Ali shouted as he pulled out a toy gorilla and punched it. "We're in Manila!" Frazier seethed in furious silence. The sportscaster Howard Cosell started a new television variety show that he called *Saturday Night Live*. On *All in the Family*—the most popular show on television—Archie Bunker saved a woman's life by administering CPR. He found out later that "she" was really a man.

The Reds kept winning. They won their one hundredth game of the season in Atlanta in front of three thousand people, the smallest crowd of the year. They beat the Astros two out of three in the Houston Astrodome. They came home and beat Atlanta again. Records fell every day. They won the most games in team history. They built the biggest division lead in National League history. On the last day of the year, a Sunday, more than forty-four thousand people packed into Riverfront Stadium. The Reds were losing by two runs in the eighth inning, and the lineup was filled with backups and Pete Rose. The Machine came back. The Machine always came back that year. Pete's single in the eighth inning gave the Reds a brief lead. Cesar's single in the ninth won the game.

The final numbers staggered the mind. The Reds had won 108 games—more than any National League team since the 1906 Chicago Cubs. They beat the Dodgers by 20 games, and no team since 1902 had won by more. They scored 105 more runs than any other team in the league. They won 90 of their last 125 games, an absurd 72 percent . . . no National League team had played that well for that long in fifty years.

"There is nothing in my wildest dreams that didn't come true this season," Sparky told the reporters, a brilliant double negative to end the brilliant season. Everything had worked beautifully. Gary Nolan came all the way back from his injury—he won 15 games. George Foster emerged as a star—he hit 23 home runs. Joe Morgan played better than anyone Sparky had ever seen before. Pete Rose hit .317 and banged out 210 hits. Johnny Bench, even though he still felt awful, finished second in the league in runs batted in and stole 11 bases in 11 attempts.

"Watch out!" Johnny yelled at Joe. "I'm going to become the base stealer around here, and you're going to have to hit the home runs."

Those kids in the bullpen, Rawly Eastwick and Will McEnaney, combined for 37 saves—giving the Reds pitchers more saves by far than any team in baseball.

It all seemed beautiful. And yet, Sparky could feel that ulcer burning again. Now the playoffs would begin, and all the things they had done during the season would mean nothing. Sparky thought a lot about the 1954 Cleveland Indians; there was a team that had played brilliantly. They won 111 games during the season. They beat the mighty New York Yankees. They were in position to make history. Then they faced the New York Giants in the World Series, Willie Mays made a famous catch in the first game, and the Indians never recovered. The Giants swept the World Series. And the Indians were mostly forgotten.

It could happen. Sparky knew it. The Reds would play Pittsburgh in a best three-out-of-five-game playoff, and he felt certain that the Reds were better than the Pirates, but that didn't always matter. His team had been better than the New York Mets in 1973, but that was the series when Pete jumped Bud Harrelson, and those New York fans threw garbage on the field, and the Mets won the series in five games. There was no way in hell that Mets team even belonged on the same field as his Machine. That's how it goes in baseball, though. To Sparky, brilliance was pronounced over months, not days; greatness was found in the chill of April, the humidity of August, the long shadows of September. That's how Sparky saw it. But that wasn't how America saw it. If the Reds lost to Pittsburgh, they would be forgotten. Or worse. They would be remembered only for what they could not do, remembered as a team that melted when it got too close to the sun.

"Sparky," a television reporter began, after the final game of the season. Sparky had never seen him before, but it was that time of year—that time when new reporters who did not know a baseball from a bass drum popped up like mushrooms. "Sparky," the guy said, "are you worried that if the Reds lose to the Pirates in the playoffs you will be fired?"

Fired. He said it. Sparky stared at the guy for a moment and felt something building inside him, but that something would not fully form until late that night. In the moment, he sputtered through some kind of answer. Sparky said that he wasn't worried about his job, he was worried about this team, and he felt like he had done a good job. That night, though, while trying to get some sleep at the Holiday Inn, it hit him: he had just managed the greatest team in baseball history. He had coaxed the veterans through their ego problems, soothed the worries of the younger players, reinvented the way a manager uses a pitching staff. Sparky had led his team to 108 victories. And some reporter asked if he was worried about getting fired.

That's it, he would remember thinking. *I'm not talking to those damn reporters anymore. They twist everything around. I'm not talking. Let them find their own stories.*

And he fell off into a fitful and short sleep.

October 4, 1975

Playoff Game 1

The Ali-Frazier fight played in movie theaters all over America. They were calling it, simply, "The Superfight." Ali, as usual, described it better: "It was the closest thing to dying that I know of." Ali had pummeled Frazier in the early rounds. Then Frazier, with that big fighting heart of his, ravaged Ali's body in the middle rounds. The final rounds, though, belonged to Ali. "The fight's over, Joe," Frazier's trainer, Eddie Futch, said as he refused to let his man go out for the fifteenth round. It was savage and terrible and, the sportswriters were writing, the very essence of sports.

At the same time, Major League Baseball held a bubble-blowing competition for players leading up to the World Series. The play-offs began in Cincinnati, where the Pirates played the Reds, and in Boston, where the defending World Champion A's played the Boston Red Sox. But in the shadow of the Thrilla, baseball to many seemed so tame, passé even. "Baseball's still the national pastime," Pete Rose insisted.

Joe Morgan had told everyone about the perfect run. It went like so: Joe would walk to get on first base. He would steal second base. He would steal third base. And then he would score on a sacrifice fly hit by Johnny or Doggie or whoever. That was perfection, a run scored without a single batter getting a hit, without anyone padding their statistics, a silent and deadly run, a James Bond run. "It messes with the pitcher's mind," Joe would say.

In the third inning of the first playoff game, with the scored tied, Joe walked against Pittsburgh's starter, Jerry Reuss. Joe had specifically asked Sparky Anderson to move him from the third spot in the lineup to the second spot. It was a matter of responsibility. In the third spot, Joe felt like he had to be more of a power hitter, he had to drive in runs, he had to carry his teammates. But from the second spot in the lineup, Joe felt free. He could steal bases, score runs, destroy pitchers' psyches. He thought that his speed was exactly what the Reds needed to beat Pittsburgh. The Pirates' catcher was an affable man from Panama named Manny Sanguillen who could hit any pitch you threw him—he became famous for swatting line drives on pitches that were a foot above his head or heading for the dirt—but he did not have much of an arm. Joe knew Sanguillen could not throw him out stealing.

Sparky agreed. He shifted the entire lineup around. He moved Joe to the second spot, Johnny to the third, Doggie to the fourth, and George Foster to the fifth. And in the third inning, after Joe walked, he stole second. Then he stole third. Reuss looked uncomfortable. He walked Johnny and gave up a single to Doggie, which allowed Joe to score the almost perfect run. Reuss's mind was suitably messed up. He gave up a double to Ken Griffey that scored two more runs.

"Everything worked out like Sparky and I planned it," Joe crowed when the game ended, and it did work. The Reds scored four more runs in the fifth inning, the big hit a long home run by Reds pitcher Don Gullett. The Machine rolled to an easy 8–3 victory. Joe did not have a single hit, but he felt like the hero. He happily told reporters about messing with Reuss's head.

A few lockers down, Ken Griffey smiled. Yes, everyone was happy . . . except that, by toying around with the lineup, Sparky had moved Ken Griffey down to the seventh spot in the lineup. Ken knew he did not deserve that. He had hit .300 all season. He had been the perfect number-two hitter—he had given up his speed game to keep Joe comfortable, he had slapped all those infield hits, he had done whatever they asked. He did not deserve to be moved to the seventh spot. But he smiled just the same. As always, his feelings were his own.

October 5, 1975

CINCINNATI
REDS VS. PIRATES
Playoff Game 2

Well, if there was one thing Ken Griffey knew, it was this: if Joe
and Sparky were going to move him back to seventh in the lineup, he
would damn well steal some bases. All year, he had held back—Ken
liked to see himself as a team player, a helpful guy, a man willing
to put away his own ego for the good of everyone—but he was not
going to hold back now. He could have stolen seventy bases in 1975
if they had let him, maybe eighty. He was faster than Joe Morgan
(who had stolen sixty-seven). But they did not want that, and Ken felt
pretty sure he knew why: they did not want Ken to become a star.
The Machine already had its stars—Johnny, Pete, Joe, and, to a lesser
extent, Doggie—and there were no vacancies. Davey had wanted to
be called a star for years, and they laughed at him. George hit the ball
harder than any of them, but he could not quite break in. And Ken
knew, absolutely knew, that if given the freedom, if asked to be his
best, he could be a star too. Nobody was asking, though.

Well, now he was hitting seventh in the lineup, and he would show
them all. The Reds led by three runs in the sixth inning of Game 2,
and Ken led off against Pittsburgh reliever Kent Tekulve. He sliced
a single to left field. And then he danced off first base, danced and
danced, and he saw Tekulve's shoulders tighten. Ken took off. He
stole second base. It was easy. Poor Manny Sanguillen did not even
have a chance to throw him out. He danced off second base, danced
and danced, and again he saw Tekulve's shoulders tighten. Ken took
off. He stole third base. It was easy.

This was what Ken could be, if they would let him. Pittsburgh
manager Danny Murtaugh called to the bullpen, brought in left-
handed pitcher Ken Brett. Griffey danced off third base. He was

invincible. He was unstoppable. Brett looked nervous. He flinched. The umpire pointed at him . . . balk. The umpire pointed Griffey toward home. The Reds won again, won easily, 6–1 this time. The Pirates were helpless.

Years later, Ken Griffey sat in a leather seat in a hotel lobby in Tampa, Florida. "I'm going to be honest with you," Ken was saying. "Johnny Bench, to me, was an asshole. The last four or five years, he's gotten better. He's totally a different person. You can sit and talk to him now. He's just totally changed. Back then, he would look right through you."

He smiled and kept looking straight ahead. "Joe was an asshole too. Joe was like that too. He talked down to certain people. He didn't talk at all to me or George. I guess we weren't on his list of good people or something. That's just how it was, you know?"

Griffey had stayed in baseball. He coached for a while, and then he became a scout. He was in Florida scouting a minor league baseball game for the Reds. He said he still loved being around the game.

"I could have been a whole hell of a lot different player," he said. "I could have been a very selfish player. I could have been like a Joe Morgan. . . . Joe knew that he couldn't run with me. I could have stolen just as many bases as he did. I could have stolen more bases. Back in 1973, I was the best there was at stealing bases. The best there was.

"But that wasn't my story, you know? Sparky told me I couldn't steal bases because it bothered Joe's hitting. And after '75, I kind of lost my ability to steal bases. I sacrificed for the team. I always sacrificed for the team."

Ken Griffey went on to a very good career in the major leagues. He made three All-Star teams. He accumulated more than two thousand hits. And he played long enough that he was actually a teammate of his son, Ken Jr., on the Seattle Mariners. Junior went on to even more fame and more success. Junior hit more than six hundred home runs, and people often said that he had been born to play baseball. Ken Sr. never believed that. He remembered those days when he had to put Junior to sleep in a dresser drawer to keep him above the rats.

"Junior had the opportunity to do the things I didn't do," Ken says. "He had the opportunity to be himself. I didn't get that chance. They didn't let me be myself.

"Here's the thing: most of the guys in the major leagues at that time were selfish players. You had to be selfish then. It was about money. And it wasn't a lot of money, but you had to put up numbers to get paid. That's just how it was then. When I went to negotiate with Dick Wagner, he told me to sign or he would send my ass to Triple A. And I had hit .305."

He shrugged. Those clubhouse rips that seemed fun in 1975, maybe they stayed with him through the years. Those slights he smiled through in 1975, maybe they still cut him just a bit. A man does not talk about these things. But they still come out.

"It was fun, you know?" Ken said. "I mean, we were a great team. It was fun to be part of that team. We had fun. But it's still true. I sacrificed. I sacrificed more than anybody. I could have been a different player. I could have put up numbers. They played all these mind games with me. But I didn't let any of that bother me. Shit, I came from a little housing project in Pennsylvania, they couldn't get me with those mind games. I knew. That's the thing. I always knew. I was no fool."

October 6, 1975

CINCINNATI
Travel day

Tony Perez slept soundly. He usually slept pretty well, but he always slept beautifully after a good game. Doggie had banged three hits and a home run in Game 2 of the playoffs against Pittsburgh. How about that? Joe Morgan, as always, had been ripping him about his age.

"Hey, Doggie, how old are you *really*?" Joe asked. "Because we all know you aren't thirty-three. Hell, I'm thirty-two, and you're old enough to be my father. I think my father remembers seeing you play."

"Hey, Joe," Doggie said. "You steal all those bases, but I don't see you steal home. We still have to drive you home. If you try to steal home, Sanguillen will jump on you and punch you in the nose."

"Dog, we're going to use you up this year, then send you to the American League."

"I will go," Doggie said. "I make a lot of money over there."

And so on. Doggie loved it. They could talk about how old he was, but he felt young as childhood. He had bagged three hits and a homer against the Pirates. After the game, Tony was dead asleep and dreaming happy dreams.

His wife, Pituka, though, could not sleep at all. She had rushed out to pick up the morning paper so she could read a few stories about her husband, the baseball hero. Pituka was everything that Doggie was not . . . flame to his ice, passion to his calm. She was a leader too, a leader of the wives, but she led in a very different way. Pituka spoke her mind. She was direct. She offered advice. And she expected to be treated with respect. With Pituka, right was right, and wrong was not something to be tolerated.

And she could not believe what she saw when she opened the paper. There was hardly anything in it about Tony. He had been the star of the game—he hit a home run, he drove in three runs—and yet there was a story about the Reds' ability to steal bases, another about how Bob Howsam built the team, another about the comeback of Gary Nolan. Where was her Doggie? Where was the respect? This team had wanted to trade him away. They did not pay him as much as they paid Johnny and Joe and Pete. And now this? Pituka was enraged. She wandered over to the bed to wake up Doggie, then decided to leave him alone, then decided to wake him, then waited again. She wrestled with herself for as long as she could. Finally, she could not wait.

"Don't read this," she said as she woke him up.

"What?" Tony mumbled.

"Don't read this," she said, and she showed him the paper. "You look at it, and you don't even know you played."

Tony looked at his wife for a moment. There was deep love between them. Baseball marriages were not built for distance, but Tony and Pituka knew that they belonged together. Johnny and Vickie had hoped for a fairy-tale marriage, but Tony and Pituka lived in the real world. She protected him, and he was strong for her. Tony looked at his wife, and Pituka looked back. Her eyes were red with rage.

And then, without saying a word, Tony rolled back over and went back to sleep.

October 7, 1975

PITTSBURGH
REDS VS. PIRATES
Playoff Game 3

Gary Nolan wanted to grab all the feelings and senses of this moment—the smell of the Pittsburgh air, the midnight black of the sky, the moths fluttering in the lights, the sound of the crowd, the colors everywhere, the feeling of the dirt beneath his spikes, the sweat on his forehead, the way Pete chattered away at third base, the way Johnny pumped his fist to inspire him. He wanted to put it all away, in a bottle, no, in a jewelry box, snap the lid shut, have those feelings there to enjoy whenever he needed them. Gary was pitching in the playoffs again.

First inning, Gary faced Willie Stargell, the great slugger for the Pirates, and he threw his changeup, that fluttering pitch, and the big man swung hard but way too early. In the third, it was Richie Zisk who stood in the box. Gary again threw his soft changeup. Zisk waved the bat helplessly. Strikeout. Nolan's arm felt great. His mind felt sharp. He knew exactly what he wanted to do. In the fifth inning, with two runners on base, he threw his best fastball, and he watched Pittsburgh's Ed Kirkpatrick hit a high and harmless pop-up behind the plate. Gary then struck out his opposing pitcher, John Candelaria.

It was beautiful. In this moment, Gary felt like he did when he was eighteen. He was doing exactly what he was born to do. When the game ended, Pittsburgh's Richie Hebner would unwittingly give Gary the compliment of his life. He said: "Guys come back to the bench and say, 'Damn, I just missed it.'"

"You are pitching your *ass* off," Pete Rose shouted happily as he threw the ball to Gary with a little bit of extra strength. The Pirates' rookie pitcher, John Candelaria, was pitching his ass off too. He threw a hot fastball and a biting curveball, and he kept striking out Reds hitter after Reds hitter—Candelaria would strike out fourteen in the game. Gary retaliated by tying up the Pirates hitters in knots. Gary felt a bit like he was pitching against his own youth. And he was holding his own.

Then, in the sixth, Gary made his one mistake. He thought Pittsburgh's Al Oliver was expecting a changeup. So he threw a high fastball. And the instant he let it go, Gary realized that it was a mistake. He could see that Oliver had been waiting for that pitch. He had it timed. And he did not miss. Oliver crushed a long home run that scored two runs, and Pittsburgh led 2–1. Gary stared down at the ground. Then he heard Pete shout: "We'll get you that run back. Hell, I will personally get you that run back, Gary. Don't worry about it. Two runs are not enough to beat the Big Red Machine. No chance."

Gary struck out Stargell again. He got the brilliant young Dave

Parker to fly out to left field. He walked off the field, and Sparky met him at the top of the step. "Hell of a job, Gary," Sparky said to him as he looked in his eyes. "Hell of a job. Thank you."

Pete Rose remembered the home run he had hit in New York in the playoffs a couple of years earlier. It was an odd memory to pop into his mind now, with the Reds losing by a run to the Pirates in the eighth inning. But that sort of thing happened to Pete sometimes. A memory would emerge in his mind, and he would let it play all the way through. Pete remembered that the score was tied, and the New York fans were glaring hate at him, and their boos were spiked with daggers. They did hate him—hated him for jumping Bud Harrelson the day before, hated him for being the star of the other team, hated him for being Pete Rose, the cockiest, brashest, boldest, and toughest son of a gun around. They hated him with all the zeal with which they would have loved him had he played for the New York Mets.

All their hate, all those boos, all of it made Pete focus harder. "Those stupid sons of bitches never figured it out," Pete would say. "Boos never bothered me. I loved when they booed me. It was silence that bothered me."

He hit the home run that won that Mets playoff game, and he ran around the bases while the boos got louder and louder, and all the way around the bases he thought, *See, Dad? I showed them. I showed every damn one of them.*

Now he stepped to the plate, and it was the eighth inning, man on base, and the Pirates fans booed him, and that memory played in his mind. He had failed to get a hit his three chances against Candelaria. But Pete Rose always loved hitting in the late innings, with the game on the line, with his body warm and his eyes honed. He hit .393 in the eighth inning in 1975, and when Candelaria threw his fastball, Pete saw it good. He swung hard. He hit it hard. Pete Rose was not a home run hitter, of course, but he knew how one felt coming off the bat. He had hit another playoff home run. The Reds led. Pete was the hero again. He ran around the bases easily, happily, and he could hear his teammates in the dugout, and one (was that Joe's voice?) shouted: "Man, that must have been a piece-of-shit pitch if *Pete* hit a home run on it. The kid's done."

And then those Pirates sons of bitches scored the tying run in the ninth, and Pete suddenly wasn't the hero.

No, Eddie Armbrister was the hero, which did not surprise him at all. He had been guaranteeing all year that he would be the hero. He hardly played at all. He had gotten only sixty-five at-bats all year. He had mostly been used as a pinch runner and a defensive specialist—the turd of turds, as he liked to say—but all year long he'd be chirping at the batting cage: "Don't forget about me. I'm the key to this team. You will see. When it comes down to the end, I'll be the big man." Armbrister was from the Bahamas—just the third major league player ever to come from the Bahamas—and the guy was always happy. Always. Sparky did not get it ("What the hell is he so happy about? The guy's hitting .185"), but he realized that whatever he asked Armbrister to do, the kid did. If Sparky needed a bunt, Eddie bunted. If he needed someone to play any of the outfield positions, Eddie played them. If he needed someone to pinch-run, Eddie would run his heart out. He did it all happily, joyfully, like coming off the bench and bunting was his life's dream.

Casey Stengel, the great Yankees manager, had just died a week earlier, at age eighty-five, and the papers were all reporting perhaps his most famous quote: "The key to being a good manager is to keep the five guys who hate you from the five guys who are undecided." Sparky had his own quote about what being a manager was all about: "Every great team needs at least one guy who enjoys picking up the trash." Eddie was the happiest garbage man in baseball.

Sparky sent Armbrister up there in the tenth inning, Ken Griffey on third base, score tied. "Just give me a fly ball," he had told Eddie.

"Okay, Skip!" Armbrister said, and he smiled real big, and he hit that fly ball to center field. Ken scored, the Reds won the pennant, and Armbrister wandered around the clubhouse, champagne pouring off him, and he shouted: "I told them. I told them. Nobody listened. But I told them all. I told them, at the end, I'd be the big man. And look at me now. I'm the biggest man."

Sparky Anderson called his old friend Milton Blish back in California. Milt had been the man who put Sparky Anderson in the car business when it looked like his baseball career was over. Milt had been the man who taught Sparky everything there was to know about human nature and how to treat people and what to do about feelings. Milt was dying of cancer. Sparky had been calling him all year, and at first there was hope, but now the illness had moved past miracles. Milt was going to die soon. He wasn't ever going to sell another car. He wasn't ever going to make it back to Santa Anita to lay down a few bad bets. All that was left for him was a few minutes of comfort surrounded by a few hours of pain.

"You won it, huh?" Milt said on the phone.

"We won it, Milt," Sparky said. "The boys did it. The boys are the best."

Milt paused, and then he began to thank Sparky. Sparky cut him off.

"Milton," Sparky interrupted, "real friendship means you don't ever have to say thank you." Milton knew the line. It was what he had told Sparky over and over when he was the one doing the saving.

"I want to make an announcement," Sparky said to the reporters soon after he hung up, and there were still a few tears in his eyes. "I am dedicating this victory to my good friend Milton Blish." The reporters pulled out their pads.

"How do you spell it, Sparky?" someone asked.

"B-L-I-S-H," Sparky said. "He's an old friend of mine. One of my real friends."

"How do you spell it, Sparky?" someone else asked.

"B-L-I-S-H," Sparky said again. "He's on his back now. I call him 'Uncle Miltie.' He loves the Detroit Tigers, Los Angeles Dodgers, the Rams, and USC. I told him, 'God Almighty, Miltie, you're having a bad year.'" Sparky stopped.

"How do you spell his name, Sparky?" someone else asked.

Sparky shouted: "Milt Blish! B-L-I-S-H. Milt Blish, goddamnit." He was worn out. He did not want to answer any more questions. Across the country, earlier in the day, the Boston Red Sox had beaten the Oakland A's to win the American League pennant—that was a surprise. The Reds had been expecting to play the A's, the three-time World Champions, the team that beat them in the '72 World Series. Everyone was peppering Sparky with questions about the Red Sox, Fenway Park, the emotion of winning, the fear of losing, and Sparky simply felt overwhelmed.

"They must be a great ball club," Sparky said about the Red Sox. Someone else asked how to spell Milt Blish's name, and Sparky walked off, into his office, leaving the champagne and celebration behind.

October 10 to October 22

Here I come to save the day!

—COMEDIAN ANDY KAUFMAN DOING MIGHTY MOUSE ON
Saturday Night Live

October 10, 1975

BOSTON

Day before the start of the World Series

To the Reds players, "the Wall" looked like the Eiffel Tower or the
Leaning Tower of Pisa or some other place that they had heard about.
Most of them had never seen the Wall. It was strange, really, but
baseball was divided—American League and National League—and
there wasn't much mixing of the two. Pete had been playing ball in
the major leagues since '63—there had been four U.S. presidents in
his big league years—and he had never seen "the Green Monster,"
the giant wall that towered over left field at Fenway Park. Pete stood
at home plate and stared at it, the thirty-seven-foot wall (plus two
inches) made of wood and covered in concrete and tin. A twenty-
three-foot screen extended over the top. The wall, officially, was 315
feet from home plate, but nobody believed that. It looked so much
closer. An expert had studied aerial photographs and determined that
it was 304 feet away. It looked closer still.

"Nice little ballpark they have here, huh, Pete?" Joe asked. "Nice and definitely little."

Johnny Bench was mesmerized by it. Johnny was a dead pull hitter; that meant that he hit almost everything to left field. He flew out to the left fielder thirty-seven times in 1975, and as he stood there at home plate looking at the Wall, he tried to calculate how many of those outs would have been doubles or home runs here in Boston. It was scary for Johnny to think about what kind of numbers he might have put up had he played half his games at Fenway Park.

"Wow, you can reach out and touch it from here," George Foster said to Hal McCoy, the beat writer for the *Dayton Daily News*. And then George began tiptoeing toward the wall. "Shhh," he said. "Don't wake it up."

The Boston players mostly complained about how nobody respected them. Pitcher Rick Wise came up with the idea to have all the Red Sox players wear T-shirts with a giant letter U, and then underneath—in case anyone missed the symbolism—the word UNDERDOG written in script.

"Nobody believed in us in March, in June, in August, and nobody believes in us now," Wise moaned. "And here we are."

"Even if we won," another Red Sox pitcher, Bill Lee, said, "we'd get picked for third place in 1976."

"No one has given us any credit or thought we had talent all season," catcher Carlton Fisk told reporters. "So it's like starting new every day."

There was truth in the complaints—few had expected the Red Sox to make it to the World Series. The Red Sox had for years found their own certain rhythm: they were always good but never quite good enough. Every year since 1968, the Red Sox had won more games than they lost. Every year since 1968, they finished just off the pace. Their 1974 season was typical—the Red Sox were in first place in late August, then they lost eight in a row and faded to third place. They were thoroughbreds who could not go the distance. People in New England saw it as a character flaw. Also, the Red Sox lacked pitching.

But the texture of the team changed in 1975—they were (as the author John Updike had written about a Boston team years before) a much nimbler blend of May and December. Three dazzling young outfielders revitalized them. The twenty-two-year-old left fielder, Jim Rice, scowled and hit long home runs. The twenty-five-year-old right fielder, Dwight Evans, thrilled fans with his consistency and his remarkable arm. And in center was Fred Lynn, a phenomenon. He was twenty-three, a rookie, and he finished second in the league in hitting, drove in one hundred runs, and scored one hundred runs. He played this kamikaze center field—he crashed into walls after fly balls seemingly every other day. He caught most of them. No rookie center fielder since the young Joe DiMaggio had come to dominate baseball the way Lynn did in 1975.

The three young outfielders were so good that the venerable Carl Yastrzemski—the beloved "Yaz"— moved to first base. He had been a symbol in left field, as iconic in Boston as the Wall itself, but he was thirty-five years old, and in 1975 he was more an old warrior than a star. "I'll do whatever I can to help the ball club," he said, and he played all but ten games at first base, and he made the All-Star team for the tenth straight year.

Pitching was a problem, as always in Boston, but Luis Tiant, a cigar-chomping Cuban who claimed to be thirty-four and looked fifteen years older, pitched with verve and gusto and a thousand gyrations. The quirky lefty Bill Lee won seventeen games and the hearts of Boston newspaper writers. Nobody could fill a reporter's notebook like Bill Lee. They called him "Spaceman." "When I get nervous, I yawn a lot," he told those reporters. "By tomorrow, I'll be yawning up a storm."

The Red Sox moved into first place at the end of June and stayed there the rest of the season. Then, surprisingly, they beat the three-time World Champion Oakland A's in three straight games in the playoffs. And the games were stunningly easy. Oakland led only once the whole series, and for only three and a half innings. The Red Sox won even without Rice, who had broken his wrist in the last week of the season when he was hit by a pitch. Rice would not play in the World Series either. This was another reason most people around the nation picked the Reds to breeze through the World Series. It was precisely what the Red Sox wanted.

"Let them underestimate us," growled Carlton Fisk, the team's soul, the tough New England catcher who was born in Bellows Falls, Vermont, grew up in Charlestown, New Hampshire, and went to school at the University of New Hampshire. He could never put into words what it meant to him to play for the Boston Red Sox.

"Let them underestimate us," he said again. "We'll show them again."

Hotel rooms in Boston were scarce. Tickets to the game had sold out in two and a half hours. The Reds stayed at a place called the Statler-Hilton Hotel, and for much of the day leading into the World Series, Reds players tried to come up with the best punch line about the size of the rooms. They went vaudeville. "My room is so small that I have to leave it to change my mind." "My room is so small that the mice checked out." "My room is so small that the bed is in the bathtub." And so on. Pete was the consensus winner. He and a few teammates stepped on the elevator. "Damn," Pete said. "What are all you guys doing in my room?"

They looked good. During the playoff series against Pittsburgh, the Reds had unexpectedly, and to much applause, suspended the rule requiring ties and jackets. "Well, it was getting silly," Bench told reporters. Sparky told the Reds that as long as they wore jackets in public, they did not need ties. It was a relief and an unusual gift of freedom from the Reds' front office. For the World Series, though, order was restored: ties were again mandatory. There were as many stories in the Boston papers about what the Reds wore walking off the plane as there were about what they hit during the season.

"Well, discipline is good," Johnny told the newsmen. "That's the problem with America. Nobody gets any discipline. Kids are desperate for discipline."

Johnny didn't like the reinstatement of the tie rule, but he was in no mood to fight. He felt worse than he had all season. His shoulder still throbbed from the collision months earlier, but now he also had a cold so intense and heavy that he felt like his head was drowning. His marriage was about to end. He was about to play in the World Series, and baseball was no fun at all.

But this was the World Series, this was his stage, his star-spangled rodeo, and he had to perform. The pressure was intense. The Reds had to win this time. There could be no excuses. They were better than the Red Sox, Johnny felt sure of it. If the Machine lost, there would be no hiding the truth.

October 11, 1975

BOSTON
REDS VS. RED SOX
World Series Game 1

The greatest World Series that ever was began on the same day that a new show called *Saturday Night* debuted on NBC. (Later, after the Howard Cosell show *Saturday Night Live* was canceled, they would adjust the name.) *Saturday Night* was a variety show featuring music and stand-up comedy—the show began with comedian George Carlin doing his bit about football and baseball—but mostly there were bizarre skits, the most bizarre of those featuring a performer named

Andy Kaufman. His routine was unlike anything ever seen on television. He stood in front of a record player, stared at the audience, then put the needle on the record. The theme song from the cartoon *Mighty Mouse* began to play. Kaufman stared at the audience silently, and then, when the chorus began, he dramatically lip-synched the words "Here I come to save the day!" Then he stared at the audience for thirty-nine seconds while the song played in the background. When the chorus came up again, he once again dramatically lip-synched: "Here I come to save the day." The skit was bizarre and ridiculous and, quite possibly, brilliant.

Five convicts escaped from a top-security penitentiary in Marion, Illinois, using some sort of mechanical gadget they built in their prison shop course. Singer Neil Sedaka's "Bad Blood"—a song he wrote in honor of Elton John, who revived Sedaka's career—jumped to number one on the charts. In Elyria, Ohio, a seventeen-year-old named Randal Carmen, who had been kept on life support for three weeks while his parents pleaded with the hospital to let him die mercifully, was declared legally dead. In Washington, Democrats and Republicans argued about tax cuts.

In Boston, pitcher Luis Tiant faced the Machine. There was something mystical about Luis Tiant, the ancient El Tiante. He had come from Cuba, and he was of an uncertain age. His face was wrinkled and creased, and his stomach hung over his red belt. He claimed to be thirty-four years old, but Tony Perez said: "All I know is, Tiant was a big national hero when I was a boy growing up in Cuba . . . and now he's one year older than me."

The Tiant name meant something special in Cuba: Luis Tiant Sr., El Tiante's father, had pitched in the Negro Leagues in the years before Jackie Robinson, before men of color could play in the major leagues. Luis Sr. had a hundred different windups: sometimes he threw sidearm, sometimes he hesitated in the middle of his motion, sometimes he stopped and started like a man pitching under a strobe light. Luis Sr. did not throw hard, but he did not have to throw hard:

his pitching was sleight of hand, a rabbit from a hat. It was said that he should have worn a tuxedo to the mound and charged admission. Buck O'Neil, a Negro Leagues hitter, would remember a time when Luis Sr. threw the ball to first base to pick off a runner. The batter was so baffled by the motion that he actually swung at air.

El Tiante, the son, did not need such tricks when he was young. When Luis first pitched for Cleveland in the midsixties, he pitched with power. In 1968, the famed "Year of the Pitcher," Tiant overwhelmed hitters with his fastball. He led the American League in earned run average and shutouts, he struck out more than one batter per inning, and he threw fastballs past bats. Then his arm began to throb, his shoulder hurt, his fastball lost its sting, and in 1971 his career appeared to be over. That was when El Tiante entered the second stage of his career. The son became the father. He began to turn his back to the batter when he pitched. He would pitch from different angles, throw at different speeds, and mix in different spins; he would add in Elvis pelvis thrusts and James Brown slides, and he would talk to hitters while he pitched, talk out loud—he would shout, "Hit it, baby!" while the ball was on its way to the plate. "It looks like Tiant has added another pitch," the Yankees catcher Thurman Munson told the columnist Dick Young that year. "Now, he has about fifty."

The brilliant Roger Angell described several of Tiant's many windups in what would become a classic piece in *The New Yorker*. One Angell called "Call the Osteopath," and this was one where it appeared that Tiant was having a seizure in the middle of his windup. Another he called "the Runaway Taxi," where Tiant seemed to see a taxi rushing at him and, at the last second, violently dived out of the way to escape a certain crash. And perhaps the best one was "the Slipper-Kick," where Tiant abruptly moved like he was kicking off his left shoe.

The Reds players insisted that they would not be mesmerized by Tiant's shell game. "I don't give a shit about that," Pete said. "Hell, his head could fall off while he's pitching, it doesn't mean anything to me. I'm looking at the ball."

"See the ball, hit the ball," Doggie said.

But when the game began, they found themselves under El Tiante's spell. In the first inning, Pete, Joe, and Johnny went down quickly. In the second, Doggie, George, and Davey did the same. They seemed to be hitting the ball hard, but always right at Red Sox defenders. "Come on," Joe screamed at his teammates. "The ball is *right there.*"

Joe did line a single to center in the third, and there was a brief moment of drama. Now it was time for Joe to do some hustling of his own. He took a huge lead off first base, an enormous lead. "Joe wants Tiant to throw to first," Tony Kubek told the national television audience. And Tiant did throw to first—once, and then twice, and on the third throw he almost picked off Joe. "This is a real gunfighters' duel," said his partner Curt Gowdy.

El Tiante's fourth throw to first was called a balk by first-base umpire Nick Colosi, and Joe clapped and happily jogged to second base. The Boston crowd booed. The players on the Red Sox bench screamed so savagely at Colosi that he finally had to point to them as a warning. Tiant himself simply glared at Colosi with hate. Joe felt good. He had gotten into another pitcher's head.

Only he had not. You cannot hustle the hustler. Tiant dueled with Johnny Bench, an interminable thirteen-pitch at-bat with nine foul balls, the last of them a foul pop-up that Carlton Fisk caught near the Red Sox dugout. Then Doggie came to the plate. Everyone on the Reds knew that there was no one in baseball you would rather have at the plate with a man on second base than Tony Perez. But Doggie simply watched strike three zip over the outside corner.

"Nothing," Pete told Fisk the next time he came to the plate, and he said it with wonder in his voice. "The guy's got nothing."

The Red Sox could not score either, though they were having an easier time with Reds starter Don Gullett. In the second, they got two hits and a walk, but failed to score when Dwight Evans was thrown out at the plate by Davey. In the third, Fisk hit a long fly ball to left that would have been a home run on another day; on this day, the ball died in the wind and was caught by George Foster on the warning track. In the sixth, the Red Sox loaded the bases, but then Cecil Cooper grounded into a double play to end the inning. The afternoon was cold and damp, and the game did not have much rhythm.

Then Yaz changed everything. George Foster led off the seventh inning with a single, and Davey followed with a low, sinking line drive that seemed a certain hit. The players in the Reds dugout jumped off the bench. The Reds would have runners on first and second, nobody out . . . only they saw Yaz charging. Yaz was playing left field again; he had moved out there to replace Jim Rice. And even though Carl Yastrzemski had slowed, even though he was no longer the man who, almost single-handedly, carried the "Impossible Dream" Red Sox of 1967 to the pennant, even though he felt a dull pain where his youth used to be, none of that mattered when he played left field at Fenway Park. Yaz was a cop, and left field was his beat. He knew every square foot, he recognized every small hump, and he made sense of every tiny ditch. He rushed in on Davey's ball, and he dived for it, and he dropped his glove underneath the ball just as it was about to hit the ground. It wasn't just a great catch . . . it was a knockout. "He knows how to play left field in this park," Joe would say afterward with grudging appreciation. The Reds did not score the entire game.

And in the bottom of the inning, Luis Tiant—who had not gotten a hit in a major league game since 1972—lashed a single past Pete Rose at third base. The Reds were doomed. Boston scored six runs in the inning, the first by El Tiante himself. He was so surprised by his own good fortune that he actually missed home plate. Tony had the ball at the time, and Davey shouted to him, *"Throw home! He missed the plate!"* But Fenway Park was so loud and chaotic that Doggie did not hear him, and Tiant rushed back and stomped on the plate to make it count.

After the game, the men of the Machine sounded defiant and bitter, like men who had been hustled in Times Square but still could not quite believe it. "It wasn't difficult," Bench griped to reporters who kept asking how hard it was to face Tiant on a day like this.

"That's the weakest five-hitter I've ever seen," Sparky said.

"All he has is a lot of legs and arms," Ken Griffey said.

"I saw him perfect," Pete said. "I wish I could say he was great, but he wasn't. We hit the ball hard all day."

It was the loser's lament. Sparky could not sleep all night. He wondered—he could not help but wonder—if maybe something did happen to the Reds in the World Series, if maybe they did lose a touch of their invincibility, if maybe there was a little something missing. It made him angry to think about it. And it made him sad.

"I was told this was a seven-game series," Sparky told the reporters. "We've been beaten before. The only thing they've won is one game. . . . If they think they're playing a bunch of lambs, they better wait until it's over."

October 12, 1975

BOSTON
REDS VS. RED SOX
World Series Game 2

Johnny Bench sneered. That wasn't like him. He always played baseball with that placid look, a hint of a smile, like he knew something—like he knew that he was better than you, and there was no point in making a big deal about it. But now, ninth inning, he stepped into the box, and he kicked at the dirt and glared at Boston pitcher Bill Lee, and he most definitely sneered. The Reds trailed in the game 2–1. The air was still heavy from the rain. "Here's what I think about Boston," Pete said in the dugout (he was practicing for reporters). "The lobster's good, but the weather's worthless."

The Reds had scored one run in seventeen innings. It was confusing. "We need something good to happen," Pete said to third-base umpire George Maloney, and they did. The Machine simply could not get going. Bill Lee had tied them up all night—Bill Lee and the lousy weather. Rain stopped the game for twenty-seven minutes. The Red Sox scored the go-ahead run after Davey botched a ground ball. "We're playing like a bunch of chumps," Pete said.

For two whole games, the Reds had not managed to hit the Green Monster even one time. And when Johnny sneered, everyone on the Red Sox knew that was precisely what he intended to do— hit a ball over the Green Monster. "I thought he would be trying to pull the ball," Yaz would write in his newspaper column the next day. Everyone thought that. Boston center fielder Fred Lynn took a few steps to his right. And Bill Lee, seeing that sneer, tried to trick Johnny Bench. He threw his first pitch about two inches outside . . . he expected Bench to try to hit it over the Wall, and he would end up coming over the ball and hitting a nice routine ground ball to short.

Only this was the thing: they had all misread the sneer. Johnny knew exactly what everyone was thinking, and he had no intention of trying to hit the ball off the Wall. He waited for the outside pitch, and then he whacked it to right field. The pull hitter went the other way. There was nobody there—right fielder Dwight Evans had shifted so far left that he was not even in the television picture when the ball landed. Bench rounded first, then headed into second base with a double. When he got to the bag, he felt the baseball whack him in the head—Dwight Evans's throw had gotten away and bounced up and hit him. He glared at Evans. Then he turned around, reached into his pocket, and pulled out his batting glove. For reasons all his own, Johnny liked to wear a batting glove when he was on the bases.

He did not smile. He did not clap. He had this look that said, simply, "Okay, now it's time to play like men."

Red Sox manager Darrell Johnson walked out to the mound and called for Dick Drago, Boston's meanest-looking relief pitcher. Drago had a dark mustache and intense eyes, and he was known all around baseball for being one of the loudest and most ruthless name-callers in the game. He was a tough guy from Toledo who would come into games, throw hard and heavy fastballs, and dare you to hit them.

Doggie stepped in, and he could only manage to hit a soft ground ball to short. That did move Johnny to third, though, with only one out. George Foster stepped into the box, and he needed only to hit a reasonably long fly ball to score Johnny and tie the game. Pete and Joe stood on the top step of the dugout, and they screamed at Drago. Then, just as Drago was about to pitch, George did what he loved to do. He held up his hand and stepped out of the batter's box.

"It makes pitchers mad," George had said, and he was right— the move did infuriate many pitchers. But Drago was not the type. He rolled his eyes. They battled, Drago threw his hardest stuff, George fouled off one, then two, then three pitches. "He's really blowing those fastballs," the announcer Joe Garagiola said to the television audience. Drama. The air was so cold, the audience could see Drago's breath. Foster wiggled his black bat. Drago threw another hard fastball. Foster fouled it back again.

"This is great stuff," Garagiola said. And it was great . . . only baseball among the sports could give you this kind of odd tension, the breathless suspense, where nothing much was happening at all. This was Alfred Hitchcock's bomb theory come to life. The British film director James Blue had asked Hitchcock, the great filmmaker, about suspense.

Hitchcock, instead, talked baseball:

He said: "Four people are sitting around a table, talking about baseball, five minutes of it, very dull. Suddenly a bomb goes off. Blows the people to smithereens. What does the audience have? Ten seconds of shock. Now take the same scene. Tell the audience there's a bomb under the table, and it will go off in five minutes. Well, the emotion of the audience is different because you give them the information that in five minutes' time, the bomb will go off."

Hitchcock hated baseball. But nobody ever explained it better. The beauty of baseball was in the suspense of the moment, the suspense of an angry-looking pitcher and loud man from Ohio glaring at a Bible-reading and soft-spoken man from Alabama with a black bat in his hands. Everyone knew Drago would throw the hardest fastball he could throw. Everyone knew Foster would swing as hard as he could swing.

Drago stepped on the rubber and got ready to pitch, and then Foster did it again. He stepped out. This time, Drago looked away in disgust. Only now, he decided to pull off a little trick of his own. When Foster stepped back into the batter's box, Drago set up to pitch, and suddenly, unexpectedly, he shook his head to catcher Carlton Fisk. He shook his head? Why? Catchers signal what pitch they want thrown, of course, but Drago was throwing only one pitch all game—his fastball. It was his best pitch, his only pitch for a moment like this. But now he shook off Fisk. Was he going to try to trick Foster? Was he going to throw a curveball or some sort of sloppy slow stuff and get Foster off balance? No? Well, then, why was he shaking off the signal from Fisk? These are the games between batters and pitchers—one steps out of the box, another shakes off a signal, everyone trying to get in everyone's head.

Then Drago pitched. A fastball, of course. Foster swung hard and hit a high pop-up that was blowing back to the infield. Yaz ran up and kept running and caught the ball just beyond where the shortstop stood. It was not deep enough to score Johnny Bench. Foster had failed. There were two outs. The Reds were almost dead.

Davey Concepcion stepped up, and he crossed himself like he always did. Here it was again: his chance to be a hero. He looked small in the moment. He was listed at six-foot-one, but standing next to the six-foot-two Fisk, he looked like someone's little brother. Everyone stood at Fenway Park, stood and screamed, a wall of sound. Drago threw his fastball, and Davey was overwhelmed. Strike. There seemed no way that Davey could hit that fastball. He would have to swing before Drago even let go of the ball. Drago threw another fastball, which was just high. "That was the hardest one he's thrown all night," announcer Dick Stockton said. The cheers became wails.

Davey tapped the bat on the ground and waited. Drago wound up again, and he threw his hardest fastball yet, only this time Davey's bat flashed. He chopped the ball into the ground, and it bounced up high. Boston's second baseman, Denny Doyle, got a good jump on the ball, he ran hard to the right, he backhanded the ball, and he turned to throw to first base. Only Davey was already on the bag. Johnny Bench had already scored. The game was tied. And Doyle put the ball back in his own glove. Fenway was almost silent.

The run changed the complexion of the game and the Series. Something good had happened. Now Davey Concepcion stole second base (though he came into the bag with such force that he slid right over it; Boston shortstop Rick Burleson should have been able to tag out Davy, but he was too busy arguing with the umpire). Then Ken Griffey was at the plate—he was still hitting seventh in the lineup—and he could not wait for Drago's fastball. Griffey loved fastballs. Curveballs and sliders and knuckleballs still bothered him. But the harder the fastball, the more Ken liked it. He fouled off a couple of Drago's pitches, and then he whacked a ball to the gap in left-center. Davey scored. Griffey eased into second with a double. That was the first time the whole Series that a Reds player had hit a ball that reached the Green Monster.

Rawly Eastwick finished the job in the ninth. Sparky marveled—Eastwick did not look nervous at all. Rawly got Rick Burleson to hit a foul ball that Griffey caught. Pinch hitter Bernie Carbo, a player Sparky had managed and nurtured, lashed a hard line drive to left field, but George Foster was there to catch it. And then Cecil Cooper hit a very high pop-up to shortstop. Sparky breathed out . . . he felt like he had been holding his breath for five innings. Then he looked out on the field, and he could not quite believe what he saw. He saw Davey circling under the ball. And he saw Pete Rose running toward him yelling.

And this is what Pete was yelling: "Catch that ball, Bozo! You better catch it! You're the hero if you catch it!"

Pete was yelling so loud, and he was so close to Davey, and then the wind pushed the ball toward home plate. Davey had to take three steps forward, and Pete had to jump out of the way just to avoid a collision. Davey caught it. He glared for a second at Pete. And the Big Red Machine celebrated. Now, finally, they were going home.

"We have men in this clubhouse," Sparky said. "There are no crybabies here."

October 14, 1975

CINCINNATI
REDS VS. RED SOX
World Series Game 3
Series tied 1–1

Ed Armbrister sat in the Reds clubhouse after the game, and he was surrounded by reporters. He was the hero, the World Series hero, only it wasn't at all what he expected.

"That's destiny, mon," he said.

Destiny involved a simple play, one of the simplest and oldest plays in baseball. It happened in the tenth inning, tie score. The Reds' first batter was Cesar Geronimo; he got a big cheer because he had made a great catch in the tenth on a long fly ball hit by Yaz. "You sit and watch ball games year after year," Curt Gowdy said on TV. "How many times when that player makes a great play in the field does he come in to lead off the inning?" It was a classic baseball question, one that mathematicians tackled later. Their conclusion: it happened about one in nine times.

Geronimo lashed a hard ground ball into center field for a base hit. And Sparky sent Ed Armbrister up to sacrifice-bunt Geronimo to second base. There was no mystery about it. For as long as people had played baseball, they had bunted runners from one base to the next. Armbrister was not especially skilled at this; he had only one sacrifice bunt all season. But Sparky had come to believe that Armbrister was the man to call when he needed small favors. The Boston infielders moved close to the plate. Everyone was ready.

Then it happened, destiny, the play that changed the World Series, the play that would follow Ed Armbrister for the rest of his life.

Armbrister bunted the ball, and it bounced high off the Cincinnati turf. Armbrister took a step toward first, then stopped. He and Fisk collided for an instant. Fisk shoved Armbrister aside, broke free, and threw to second base to get Geronimo. Only his throw sailed high and into center field. Geronimo got up and raced to third, slid in safely. Armbrister ran to second base.

Madness.

"We're going to have an argument," Tony Kubek shouted in the booth. "They may reverse this decision. . . . They are saying the batter interfered with Carlton Fisk in fair territory!"

That is indeed what they were saying—they being the Boston Red Sox. In many ways, the situation was clear. If the umpire ruled interference, then Armbrister would be called out and Geronimo would be sent back to first base. If he did not, then the Reds had runners on second and third with nobody out.

The rules in baseball have always been vague, open to interpretation, much like the U.S. Constitution. The official rule about interference stated: "Offensive interference is an act which interferes with, obstructs, impedes, hinders or confuses any fielder attempting to make a play." In another place in the rulebook, it stated: "It is interference by a batter or runner when he fails to avoid a fielder who is attempting to field a batted ball."

What did that mean? There seemed little doubt that Armbrister did not fail to avoid Fisk. And it seemed equally obvious that he might have interfered with Fisk, might have impeded him, definitely confused him. But home plate umpire Larry Barnett ruled that Armbrister had not intentionally caused the collision. Armbrister had his own right to run to first base. "It was simply a collision," Barnett said. This, of course, did not make the Red Sox happy. But what made this moment unique in World Series history was this: the ruling did not make the people in the television booth happy either.

"[Armbrister] has to give room, regardless, so the catcher can make the play," Kubek shouted. And for the next five minutes or so, Kubek railed on the call. Marty Brennaman, the Reds announcer who was working in the TV booth as well, also thought that Armbrister interfered. Curt Gowdy would only say, "There's going to be controversy for years to come." And he was right.

Red Sox manager Darrell Johnson brought in Roger Moret, a tall, skinny left-hander from Puerto Rico. He walked Pete Rose intentionally. Griffey (back in the number-two spot in the lineup) got ready to face him, but Sparky called him back and sent up a pinch hitter, Merv Rettenmund, who promptly struck out. Then Joe Morgan hit a long fly ball to center, and the Reds won the game.

The Red Sox players were insane with fury.

"Gutless," Dick Drago shouted. "The umpires are gutless. . . . It's terrible to have people who don't give a damn ruining something sixty million people are watching."

"What are we playing, football?" Bernie Carbo asked. "They don't give a damn about the game. They proved that tonight."

"They were lousy," Boston shortstop Rick Burleson screeched.

"The best teams in baseball are in this series, but the best umpires aren't," Yaz said. "They take turns . . . why don't teams take turns? Next year, how about San Diego and the Angels play, no matter where they finish?"

"It was like smashing into a linebacker," Fisk said, perhaps an exaggeration since Armbrister was five-foot-eleven, 150 pounds. But sometimes exaggeration makes the point. "It's a damn shame losing a ball game like that. . . . We lose the damn ball game because the guy is making a joke of umpiring behind the plate."

Even Boston's normally quiet and withdrawn third baseman, Rico Petrocelli, could not hold back: "It was interference, pure and simple. Millions of people saw it. But one man says it isn't. And that's it."

Looking back, the Red Sox complaining seems a bit excessive. If Larry Barnett had called interference, he simply would have called the batter out and told Geronimo to go back to first base. The Reds would have had a man on first base, one out, with Pete Rose, Ken Griffey, and Joe Morgan coming up. They might not have scored. But they might have scored. Even if they did not score, the game would have been tied going into the next inning. But the Red Sox players were so lost in rage that by the end of the night they seemed to believe they had been cheated out of their destiny, cheated out of a victory they had earned. The television broadcast stoked that rage. The Boston newspapers stoked that rage more. And beginning the next day, home plate umpire Larry Barnett began getting death threats.

Back in the Cincinnati dugout, the most respected columnist in America—Red Smith of the *New York Times*—asked Sparky how he saw the play. Sparky paused, and then, with the comic's timing, he said: "To be honest with you, I don't see that well."

Ken Griffey sat in the Reds clubhouse, and he tried to show that smile, tried to let everyone around him know how happy he was that the Reds won. But he was angry. He was confused. He was trying to make sense of the last three days, and he wasn't getting anywhere.

On Sunday, he hit the double that scored Davey, the winning run. In the *Cincinnati Enquirer* on Monday morning, the headline read: "Bench Double Brings Winner." Bench's double? His double had led off the inning. It didn't bring in any runs. And even if you grant that Bench had come around to score, he only scored the tying run. The headline was just wrong. Numerous people called the newspaper and angrily charged that it was driven by racism. They were trying to make a white man, Johnny Bench, the hero of a game that a black man, Ken Griffey, clearly won. Ken did not charge racism. He did not want to say anything about it. He kept to himself.

And then, on this night, with the score tied, with the bases loaded, with a fastball pitcher on the mound—damn, Griffey loved fastballs—Sparky had pulled him for a pinch hitter. Why did he do that? Ken hit .305 for the season. He hit lefties well. Sparky had not pinch-hit for him since July. It made no damn sense at all.

Ken came up with a theory: Sparky did not want him to be the hero. Sparky loved his big hitters—he loved Joe, he loved Pete, he loved Johnny—and maybe that was it. Maybe he called for a pinch hitter, not because he was worried that Ken would fail, but because he was worried that Ken would succeed. Maybe Sparky did not want him to get the Most Valuable Player Award for the World Series. The more Ken thought about it, the more sense it made to him. It all went back to what Sparky had said all the way back in spring training: "Those four are royalty," he said of Johnny, Joe, Pete, and Doggie. "The rest of you are turds."

Ken continued to smile, but he seethed. He wanted to tell someone his theory. He waited for a reporter to come by and ask him how he felt about Sparky sending up a pinch hitter for him in the tenth inning with the bases loaded and glory there to be had. He wasn't going to hide his feelings this time. No, he was going to put it out there for everyone to hear.

No reporter came around.

October 15, 1975

World Series Game 4
Reds lead the Series 2–1

The Armbrister War raged into its second day. The *Boston Globe* found a law scholar and asked him to analyze the interference rule— he ruled that Armbrister did in fact interfere. An anonymous umpire, though, fought back for his brothers in blue: "[Fisk] just made a lousy throw to second base. And he's trying to take it out on Barnett, but it shouldn't happen that way."

Fisk said he tossed and turned until about five in the morning.

"Did you finally get to sleep?" he was asked.

"No," Fisk said. "I finally woke up my wife."

Barnett, it was breathlessly reported, slept very well. He had no regrets about his call that night. He never would regret the call.

"I did not hear a word from Mr. Fisk saying he had been run into by Armbrister when it happened," Barnett said. "And I did not hear Armbrister say a word to me. But all of a sudden when the throw went into center field, then I hear a lot of talk about interference."

He shrugged.

"If I had to do it again, I would do it all over again," he said. "I know I am right."

Ken Griffey did not sleep well. He could not shake off the sting from the night before, and in truth he never would. But crazy things kept happening in that 1975 World Series, and on that Wednesday, Ken Griffey found himself in almost precisely the position he had been denied the night before. This time, Boston led by a run, 5–4, but everything else was the same. Cesar Geronimo led off the inning with a single. Ed Armbrister was sent into the game to sacrifice-bunt, and this time he managed to do so without setting off a riot. Geronimo moved to second base. Then Pete Rose walked. So Ken came up to face Luis Tiant with the game on the line.

El Tiante had not been as sharp this game as he was in the first—he gave up two runs in the first inning, one of those on a double to Griffey, and the Reds had him staggered. But they could not put him away. And for the rest of the night, Tiant bewitched, bothered, bewildered them. "I don't know what the guy gets by with," Pete said, and he shook his head. Mystical.

But even Tiant's mysticism was fading in the ninth inning. He had thrown more than 150 pitches in the game. There was no snap left on his fastballs, no bend on his curve, he had nothing left but guts. Darrell Johnson left him out there to finish the job. Ken dug in—he could see the ball perfectly. He felt certain that he would be the hero. He and Tiant danced—a strike, a couple of pitches low and outside, a foul ball—and then there was a full count. Tiant threw a fat fastball. And Griffey crushed it to center field. "That," he would later say, "was the hardest I had ever hit a baseball."

Fred Lynn raced back on the ball. Nobody since Willie Mays went back on a baseball quite like Fred Lynn. He was fearless and aggressive—the University of Southern California had recruited him as a football player. He saw the ball jump off the bat, and his first reaction was, "I'm going to catch that." That was always his first reaction. Geronimo headed toward third—he intended to score the tying run. But Lynn stretched out his right hand and caught the ball. And then—this was fitting for baseball's new role model—Lynn reached out his left arm to make sure the ball stayed in the glove. It was like coaches always said: catch the ball with two hands.

"Was I nervous?" Lynn would tell reporters afterward. "When I got to the ball, my arm had trouble going up."

Joe Morgan came up next, and Tiant threw a fat fastball to him too, but just as he threw it, Geronimo took off for third base. He was going to steal third base. Everyone on the Reds knew that Morgan hated when one of his teammates tried to steal a base while he was batting. He popped up to Yaz at first, and the Red Sox won the game. There was an instant just after Morgan popped up the ball—and it would forever be caught on video—when Joe turned his head to glare with anger at his teammate Cesar Geronimo.

"Luis," a reporter said, "you had to throw 163 pitches out there tonight."

"I don't care if I throw 3,000," Luis said as he puffed away on a fat cigar. "I throw enough to get those guys, right?"

In the Reds clubhouse, Sparky Anderson was happily chatting away with reporters. This was the beauty of Sparky: you never knew how he would react. He would be angry or thoughtful or sad after victories. And sometimes he was happy after losses. "I don't take anything hard," he said. "It doesn't bother me in any shape or form. To me, baseball is fun. If you look at it as a life-or-death thing, then you're going to have a long struggle."

Cincinnati Enquirer columnist Tom Callahan just stared at Sparky and shook his head. Sparky was not taking losses hard? Right. Tell that to his ulcer. It was funny—after all this time, after writing so many columns about the Reds, Callahan still thought of Sparky as a mystery. Sparky was sensitive and also oblivious, he was loyal and also fickle, he was spiritual and obscene, he was, as the headline on Callahan's column said, voluble and vulnerable.

Callahan never lost his interest in Sparky Anderson. Years later, after he had left Cincinnati and was working for *Time* magazine, Callahan found himself sitting in Sparky's office, and they were talking about Sparky's father. That was a hard subject for Sparky. Major league baseball, at heart, is a game of fathers and sons. And while Sparky admired his father, he never felt close to his father.

"He was saying that his father had never been a gentle man,"

Callahan would remember. "He said, 'My father never played catch with me. That was my grandfather who played catch. My father was a hard man, and we were never close. He was a good man. But he was not gentle.'

"So a few minutes later, the phone rings. And Sparky answers it . . . it's his mother. And she's calling to tell Sparky that his father has died. And now he's talking to his mother, and he's saying, 'Mama, I'm so sorry. He was such a gentle man. Papa was a gentle man.'"

Callahan said it took him a long time to figure out what it meant. But in time he decided that the moment was as close as he would get to understanding Sparky Anderson. He had told Callahan the truth about his father. "But," Callahan would say, "he told his mother the greater truth."

October 16, 1975

CINCINNATI
REDS VS. RED SOX
World Series Game 5
Series tied 2–2

Tony Perez stayed at home. He did not want to see anybody. And he did not want to be seen. And anyway, he did not have much choice: his wife, Pituka, had locked him in the bedroom and told him to watch television and sleep. Doggie did not have one hit, not a single hit, in the whole World Series. He was oh-for-fourteen. He was not quite sure what to do. The day before, he had gone out to break the spell, and everyone around town slapped him on the back and shouted, "You'll get them tonight for sure, Tony!" Only he did not get them. He went hitless again. So now he stayed home.

All of his teammates knew that nothing ever got to Doggie, that he was the Big Dog, impervious to pressure, invulnerable to slumps, the man you wanted at the plate when the game was on the line. Everyone remembered Dave Bristol's famous line: "Sooner or later, if the game lasts long enough, the Big Dog will win it."

That was the man Doggie expected to be. He loved baseball. He loved being around his teammates, loved to start fights with them, loved to coax them into starting fights with each other. He loved being respected, being the Big Dog—it was so much bigger than any of the dreams he had in Cuba. But in the end, he had to hit. He had to drive in runs. He had to come through in the biggest moments. That's what made it work. That's what made him the Big Dog.

He tried to look calm. But Pituka could see through him. She made him drive to the ballpark a different way on that Thursday just to change his luck. "Which way?" he asked her. Pituka said she did not care as long as it was different. He drove down Columbia Parkway in their Oldsmobile Toronado. And Doggie said to her: "I hope I bat fifth tonight. There are no hits for me in the fourth spot." He sounded down.

When Sparky got to the ballpark, Sparky was waiting for him.

"Hey, Doggie, I looked it up," Sparky said.

"You looked up what?"

"You only need a few more at-bats and you're gonna set the World Series record," Sparky said. "Gil Hodges went oh-for-twenty-one in the 1952 World Series. What are you now? Oh-for-seventeen? Eighteen?"

"Fourteen, Sparky," Doggie said, and he tried not to smile.

"Doggie, do yourself a favor and don't get a hit for the rest of the World Series. You know those two little boys of yours, Victor and Eduardo? If you don't get a hit, they can tell their kids someday that Grandpa set a World Series record that nobody ever touched. Whadya say, Doggie? You gonna do it?"

"I don't want that record," Doggie said.

"You don't know what you're saying. Here you are with a chance at the all-time record, and you're turning your back on it?"

Doggie walked back into the clubhouse, and there was Pete, and he said: "So, am I gonna have to carry your sorry ass again today, Big Dog?"

And there was Joe: "Hey, Doggie, I've been telling you all this time. You're nothing but an old Cuban, and you're all washed up. You can't even hit that American League pitching."

And there was Doggie, in the middle of it all, shouting: "I don't want that record. I want some hits." He looked at the lineup card in the dugout. He was hitting fifth. And all of a sudden, he had that feeling. This was going to be a good night. He came up to face Boston's Reggie Cleveland in the second inning. He struck out on three pitches.

The next time Doggie came to the plate, it was the fourth inning and the Reds trailed 1–0, and Johnny Bench had just smashed a line drive down the third-base line that Rico Petrocelli leaped and caught. The Red Sox were making every play. The Reds players were beginning to wonder about destiny.

"I'll tell you what," Pete said to his lifelong friend Don Zimmer, who was coaching third for the Red Sox. "I don't know if we're going to win this thing. But if we do, we'll be beating some battling bastards."

Doggie stepped in, and Cleveland pitched. It was a curveball. And it was not just any curveball—it was a hanging curveball, hanging like a piñata, hanging like a chandelier, hanging like the sorts of pitches that the Big Dog saw in his sleep. If he missed this pitch, well, then maybe it was not meant to be, maybe he was cursed by the fates, or maybe it was simply time to pay back for all the good fortune he'd had in his life.

He did not miss the pitch.

Doggie crushed the ball to left field—you could tell just by the way Cleveland's neck snapped as he tried to follow the ball that it was gone. Doggie ran to first base and clapped his hands happily, his only sign of emotion. Then he jogged easily around the bases while everyone in Riverfront stood for him. After he touched home plate, he jogged straight to the Reds dugout, and they were all waiting for him, all his friends, all those sons of bitches who tortured him. Pete was first, and he slapped Doggie on the butt and grabbed him by the neck and shouted, "You are the Big Dog!" Joe had the biggest smile on his face. Davey hugged him. And Sparky was in the middle of it, and he said: "You blew your chance, Doggie. You blew your chance at setting the all-time record."

"No more talk about the record," Tony said. "No more."

Joe led off the sixth inning with a walk, and then he went to work on Boston's Reggie Cleveland. He took an enormous lead at first base. He taunted Cleveland. The Reds led the game 2–1, and Joe had a feeling. It was time to take over. It was time to get in Reggie Cleveland's head.

Cleveland threw over to first base. Then he threw over there again. And he threw again. And again. A fifth time. A sixth. He threw over to first base a seventh time. It was mesmerizing and boring all at once. The crowd began to boo, but their booing did not seem angry. It was as if they were mocking Cleveland too. Throw over as much as you want, he's *still* going to steal second base. Here it was, finally, that Big Red Machine arrogance that had been missing the whole World Series. Cleveland threw over to first base an eighth time.

Joe loved it. He kept taking a bigger and bigger lead. After Cleveland finally threw a pitch to Johnny—"Finally, he let Johnny in on the action," Curt Gowdy told the TV audience—he threw over to first base four more times. That made twelve total. He threw another pitch, and then threw over to first base five more times. Astonishing. He threw to first base seventeen times in all, surely a World Series record, though, for good reason, nobody keeps up with such things. Then Cleveland threw a pitch to Johnny Bench, who hit a routine ground ball to the second baseman, what looked like a double-play grounder . . . only Red Sox second baseman Denny Doyle wasn't there. He had been so bluffed by Joe Morgan's base-stealing threat that he vacated his spot and moved toward second base. The ball scooted behind Doyle and into right field. Doyle kicked the ground, Morgan ran to third, and Bench ran to second after Dwight Evans made a wild throw.

And Doggie walked up to the plate. The crowd cheered. The hitless stretch was over. He was the Big Dog. He fouled off a pitch that barely reached the seats. He fouled off another pitch. He fouled off a third, and this time it looked like Carlton Fisk would have a chance— Fisk chased madly after the ball, and then he dived into the dugout area where all the photographers snapped pictures. The ball landed just out of his reach.

And then Reggie Cleveland tried to throw another breaking ball, and he left it up again. Hanging. And again, Tony Perez did not miss. He smashed the ball high into the left-field stands. He ran around the bases easily, coolly, the way he had a couple hundred times before. The Reds won. They were one game away from being World Champs.

"Tony Perez was not in a slump," Pete told reporters afterward. "He just didn't get any hits. Big difference. With Doggie, that's a big difference."

October 21, 1975

BOSTON
REDS VS. RED SOX
World Series Game 6
Reds lead the Series 3–2

One of the greatest games in baseball history was delayed by three days because of rain. Three days of rain might have killed the nation's appetite for baseball, but for some strange reason it did precisely the opposite. The rain was like Hitchcock's bomb under the table . . . everyone waited anxiously, nervously, for the bomb to go off.

In Oakland, manager Alvin Dark got himself fired. It was considered impolite to fire a manager during the World Series when everyone's attention was supposed to be focused on the big games, but this was something of an emergency. Dark had gone in front of a congregation at a Pentecostal church and preached that his team's owner, Charlie O. Finley, was going to hell unless he mended his ways. Well, you had to admit, it was a bold move. Finley fired him immediately. When asked for comment, Finley said he had asked his mother and she did not think he would go to hell.

"And," Finley added, "she knows more about those things than Alvin Dark."

Umpire Larry Barnett had his life threatened again, this time by telegram, and it was taken seriously enough that his family was being guarded around the clock. A few columnists made the point that sports in America were being taken too seriously.

The Reds went to work out at Tufts University. They had been offered a chance to work out at Harvard, but Sparky said: "I understand they've grown pretty radical over there . . . and I'm a conservative." The only trouble with Tufts was that nobody knew where it was, and the Reds got lost on the way out there. The team bus stopped for directions, and players in full uniform walked into the gas station—service station, it was called in 1975—and asked for help. "That had to blow the guy's mind," Pete would say. Mind blown or not, the owner's directions did not get them to Tufts. The next time, the bus stopped at a bakery.

When they got to Tufts, Sparky watched the workout, and he sounded happy. "The human mind is a very, very funny thing," he told Red Smith. "If they were sitting around looking at the rain, pretty soon they'd be thinking about the sixth game coming up. Now they're running around, having fun, and not worrying about anything.

"This is a gimmick. And I like gimmicks. Life is a gimmick, for that matter, until the big guy upstairs sends the word."

Sparky Anderson was happy. It even surprised him. Maybe it was because he saw his team, the real Machine, emerge in the last game. Maybe it was because he finally felt that destiny had turned. But, no, it was something else, something personal. Sparky sat down with Dave Kindred, the young newspaper columnist from Louisville, and opened up. He told Kindred all about the fight he had been having with his son Lee.

"There was no way I could win," Sparky said. He told Dave that the fight had been over the length of Lee's hair. He talked about how it had broken up his family, and how his wife had asked him if he would stand by his son if he committed murder. "Of course I would," Sparky had said. And then he thought about it, and it all made sense to him.

Sparky said: "When we had argued there in the garage [a year earlier], I told him, 'Someday you'll respect me as your father.' And he said: 'I already do respect you.' I didn't understand how he could say that and still have the long hair.

"I was being the child, and Lee was being the man. I wasn't man enough to father my own son."

Dave Kindred realized something: this was not Sparky Anderson talking. No, there was no show here. There was nothing behind his words. He was not looking to motivate, not looking to teach, not looking to entertain. This was George Anderson, who had scrapped for everything his whole life, who had made the major leagues though he could not hit, who had managed games with such fury that he drove himself out of the game, who had sold cars for Milt Blish when baseball seemed lost, who had come back to manage the best damned team that had ever been put together.

"I always hid my feelings before," Sparky said. "But now . . . we're together. That's all he wanted. Affection."

And what George Anderson did not say, could not say, not in the middle of the World Series, was this: that was all he wanted too.

By the time the rain finally subsided and they played Game 6, anticipation was frenzied. Scalpers—if you could find any around Fenway Park—were asking for $60 and $70 dollars per ticket, about ten times street value. More people around the country huddled around their televisions than had ever watched a baseball game. It was delicious. Here were the Red Sox, destiny's punch line, a team that had not won a World Series since 1918, when World War I was raging and a young pitcher and outfielder named Babe Ruth hit eleven of the team's fifteen home runs. For almost sixty years after that, the Red Sox came to represent something heroic and doomed: brilliant possibilities and inevitable disappointment. The Red Sox won the pennant in '46, after Ted Williams came home from war, but they lost to the St. Louis Cardinals in a heart-wrenching seventh game of the World Series. In '48, the Red Sox tied Cleveland for the pennant and then lost to the Indians in a one-game playoff. In '49, they lost the last two games of the year to the ever-present Yankees and lost the pennant with it. In '67, carried by Yaz and a sense of providence, they won the pennant again. And they lost to the Cardinals one more time in a heart-wrenching seventh game of the World Series. Yale professor and Red Sox fan A. Bartlett Giamatti—who would, late in his life, have his own sad waltz with Pete Rose—summed up the cursed voyage of Red Sox fans with his eleven-word summation of baseball: "It breaks your heart. It is designed to break your heart."

And here were the Cincinnati Reds, remarkable and coarse and emotional and family and Machine, a team that spoke for the heartland. Here were the Reds, baseball's first professional team, the best team in baseball for five years running, but still uncrowned, still uncertain of where they belonged.

In the bottom of the inning, Gary Nolan tried to sneak a fastball past Fred Lynn and failed: Lynn crushed a long, three-run homer to center field. And that was how it began, this four-hour-one-minute game that would leave everyone spent, would get players babbling, and would set off church bells. The Red Sox led 3–0.

Luis Tiant started for the Red Sox, and for a while he was as elusive as ever. In the second inning, he struck out Doggie. In the third, he struck out Geronimo, and in the fourth he struck out Bench again. Johnny was in agony. His shoulder hurt, he had an awful cold, and he was ready to end his marriage and become an eligible bachelor again. Vickie was already telling people about their wedding night: she said that after the guests had been fed and the dancing had been done, Johnny had slipped away to play a new video game called "Pong" with his friends. When she later told this to Tom Callahan, a mistake was made by editors, and it was reported that Johnny Bench had played Ping-Pong with friends on his wedding night.

Sparky was working frantically, Captain Hook on five cups of coffee. He pulled Nolan for a pinch hitter in the third. He pulled Freddie Norman after he had faced only five batters. He pulled Jack Billingham for a pinch hitter in the fifth. All of that inner peace Sparky was feeling the previous couple of days was gone now. The Reds had to get to Tiant. They had to figure out a way to beat that old man.

Sparky's pinch hitter in the fifth inning—the ever-present Ed Armbrister—walked. Pete singled to center. Then Ken Griffey, once more in position to do something heroic, hit a triple off Tiant to score two runs. With two outs in the inning, Johnny Bench—even in pain— rapped a single to left field, scoring Griffey and tying up the game.

"That son of a bitch has been doing it with mirrors," Pete shouted in the dugout as he looked out at Tiant. "He should be sawing ladies in half. Are we going to get to this guy already?"

They were ready. Seventh inning, Ken Griffey singled, Joe Morgan singled. Tiant looked like he might wriggle free one more time after he got Johnny to hit a deep but playable fly ball and he got Doggie to do the same. But there was no more magic. George Foster crushed a double to center, and Ken and Joe scored. El Tiante had run out of time. He started the eighth inning, and Cesar Geronimo blasted a long home run to right field. And then Darrell Johnson came out to the mound and took out Boston's hero. The applause for Luis Tiant was deafening, but it wasn't just for Tiant. It was also for their season, another beautiful failure. The Reds led 6–3. Marty Brennaman began to make his way down to the Reds clubhouse; the baseball writers had already chosen reliever Rawly Eastwick as the World Series MVP. And sure enough, in the eighth inning, Eastwick entered the game to put away the Red Sox once and for all.

Sparky loved Bernie Carbo. Back in 1968, in the mountains of Asheville, North Carolina, he made Bernie his personal project. Carbo had loads of talent. He had been the Reds' first pick in the 1965 draft—the Reds took Carbo before they took Johnny Bench that year—but he was goofy and he didn't take the game seriously. Sparky had been selling cars; he knew how precious baseball talent was, and he decided that he would not let Bernie Carbo waste away his career. He would get Bernie at ten o'clock every morning to work out. He would send two coaches out to the field after every game to work him out again. Sparky intended to leave Bernie no time to party or be a fool.

Whenever Bernie complained, Sparky would ask him: "What did you hit last year?"

Carbo would say, "I hit .201."

And Sparky would say again, "That's right. There ain't no place in baseball for .201 hitters, take it from me. Now get your ass out there and work."

It was exactly what Carbo needed. He raised his average eighty points in Asheville, and he mashed twenty home runs. The next year, he hit .359 in Triple A. Sparky had worked his magic. They were reunited in Cincinnati in '70. Sparky the rookie manager led the Reds to the World Series. Bernie the rookie outfielder hit .310 with twenty-one homers and was named the *Sporting News* Rookie of the Year.

Then Bernie started goofing off again, or at least that's how Sparky saw it. Sparky didn't have the time or the energy to save Bernie Carbo's career again. The Reds traded him to St. Louis. Sparky said: "I never loved a player more than I loved Bernie Carbo."

And so it was Bernie Carbo standing at the plate with two outs in the eighth inning. He was the tying run for Boston—Fred Lynn and Rico Petrocelli were on base. The air was cool but light—the rain had finally gone—and the crowd was pleased, and Sparky knew that this was the moment. He worked some quick calculations in his head. Carbo was a left-handed hitter. If Sparky brought in his own left-handed reliever, Will McEnaney, then Darrell Johnson would replace Carbo with a righty, Juan Beniquez. Sparky had to make a choice: should he have Rawly pitch to Bernie Carbo or have Will pitch to Juan Beniquez?

A manager has to make these sorts of decisions all the time, and they are based on so many things, seen and unseen—statistics, emotion, gut feelings. Sparky looked out at the field, and he saw the Wall, that great hulking thing out in left field. And he decided. He would let Rawly face Bernie for the World Series. He did not want a right-handed hitter at the plate, someone who would pull-hit a pop-up over that damned wall.

And it looked like he had made the right call. Rawly quickly got two strikes on Bernie. Sparky stood up suddenly and moved toward the top step. He had this idea: he would bring in Will McEnaney *now*, with two strikes, because with two strikes there was no way that Darrell Johnson would bring in Beniquez to hit. Yes. It was brilliant. He would bring in McEnaney to get the final strike. And Bernie could not hit left-handed pitching. Sparky took a step toward the mound. He was ready to make the move.

Only then, something stopped Captain Hook. He thought many times about it for the rest of his life . . . he never did figure out what stopped him. He stayed in the dugout and let Rawly pitch to Bernie Carbo with the stadium shaking, with the nation watching, with the Reds four outs away from the championship. Rawly threw a fastball, and it was a beauty, Carbo had no chance, strike three, only somehow, some way, Carbo fouled it off with what Johnny would call "the weakest swing you ever saw."

Next pitch, Rawly threw a high, straight, and fat fastball. Bernie Carbo crushed it to deep center field. It was gone. The Red Sox scored three. The score was tied. Fenway Park never sounded louder, at least to that moment in time. There was another homer to come.

"Pete!" Bernie yelled as he rounded third base. "Don't you wish you were that strong?"

What followed Bernie Carbo's homer was Hollywood, that's all. It was baseball with special effects. Remarkable play followed remarkable play. Heroes escaped the jaws of death. All of that. In the bottom of the ninth, the Red Sox loaded the bases with nobody out, and then Fred Lynn hit a fly ball down the left-field line. It was drifting foul, and George Foster considered dropping it on purpose because he was not sure if he could prevent Denny Doyle, the man on third, from tagging up and scoring. Foster caught it anyway, and Doyle took off because he thought third-base coach Don Zimmer was yelling "Go! Go! Go!" Zimmer was in fact yelling "No! No! No!" Foster's throw wasn't perfect, but it was good enough. Doyle was tagged out.

In the top of the tenth inning, Davey singled and stole second base. But Dick Drago, looking angrier than ever, struck out Geronimo and overpowered pinch hitter Dan Driessen.

In the bottom of the tenth, the Reds sent their rookie pitcher Pat Darcy to the mound . . . Sparky really had nobody else left. Darcy had pitched well for the Reds all year long, but Sparky was never sure about the kid. On this night, Darcy had his good stuff; he got the Red Sox in order.

"I don't believe it," Bench said to Carbo.

"John," Carbo replied, "I don't believe it either."

In the eleventh, Pete Rose led off, and he turned to Carlton Fisk and said: "Wow, this is some kind of game, isn't it? We'll be telling our grandkids about this game." And Fisk, in spite of himself, nodded. Then Dick Drago hit Rose with a pitch.

"This is the greatest game I ever played in," Pete told Yaz at first base. And Yaz, in spite of himself, nodded too.

There would be two more moments in this breathless game that would stay fresh in people's memories for decades. The first of those came in the eleventh inning. Ken Griffey was on first base. Joe Morgan smashed a long fly ball to deep right field. It looked like a double for sure, maybe even a home run, and Ken began running hard around the bases—he was going to score. Joe ran hard to first—he had ideas of stretching this into a triple—only then he saw something that really disturbed him. He saw Boston's right fielder Dwight Evans running back on the ball and running hard.

And Joe thought: *Where does he think he's going?*

Evans thought he might catch the ball. He knew it was risky to even try—if he dived for the ball and did not catch it, then Griffey would score from first base and Morgan would probably have a triple—but in the moment, in that game, with improbable things happening every minute, he ran back, and he jumped up, and he simply threw his arm up in a desperate hope that the ball would hit his glove. The ball did hit his glove. Sparky Anderson would say it was the greatest catch he ever saw.

Then Evans whirled and threw the ball to first base. The throw was not on target, but it did not matter—Griffey had no chance to get back. He had gone full speed after the ball was hit—he was almost at third base when Evans caught it. Double play. There was simply no comprehending the noise in Fenway Park.

And then in the twelfth inning, at 12:34 A.M. Boston time (and 12:33 A.M. New York time, according to the *New York Times*), Carlton Fisk led off to face Pat Darcy. Years later, people would assume that Darcy was nervous. A movie would come out—*Good Will Hunting*—and a main character played by Robin Williams talks about the emotion of the night. The movie would use footage that made Darcy look nervous. Darcy hated the movie.

"I was not nervous," Darcy would say. He had already pitched two scoreless innings under intense pressure. He was not nervous . . . he was tired. Darcy had put so much into those first two innings that his fastball had lost a bit of its speed. As he warmed up, he could tell that he did not have his best stuff. And he was not the only one: Johnny Bench could tell too. "I knew we would not get out of that inning," he would say.

Fisk stepped in, and he crushed a high fly ball down the left-field line. At first, it seemed like the ball might hook foul. "I knew it was not going foul," Pete Rose would say. "He hit it too hard."

Fisk was not so sure. He watched it all the way. And when it did stay fair, when the Red Sox had won, he leaped for joy, then ran around the bases as Red Sox players raced out of the dugout onto the field like children on the last day of school. Fans ran on the field, and Fisk had to elbow his way through them. He leaped and landed on home plate with both feet and was mobbed by his teammates. In the Cincinnati dugout, Sparky Anderson stared out into space, thinking only of that moment he had to finish off Bernie Carbo. In Charlestown, New

Hampshire, Carlton Fisk's hometown, David Conant ran out and rang the church bells. "My wife used to change his diapers!" Conant told the newspapers. In the press box, Boston columnist Ray Fitzgerald wrote: "Call it off. Call the seventh game off. Let the World Series stand this way, three games for the Cincinnati Reds, and three for the Boston Red Sox."

It was, simply, the most famous home run in baseball history. There have been so many others—Bobby Thomson's shot heard round the world that won the Giants the pennant, Babe Ruth's called shot against the Chicago Cubs in the 1932 World Series, Henry Aaron's 715th home run that moved him past Babe Ruth, Ted Williams's home run in his final at-bat, Bill Mazeroski's home run that stunned the Yankees in '60. There have been so many. But this one ended the greatest game. It was hit over the most famous wall. And it provided the most famous television shot in baseball history. Lou Gerard was NBC's cameraman inside the left-field scoreboard, and just before Fisk came to the plate, he noticed that there was a rat near him and it was getting closer, and he was not feeling too good about things. When Fisk hit the ball, he was so frazzled that he could not pick up the ball, and so he trained his camera on Fisk. What he got was Fisk dancing up the first-base line and waving at the ball—"Stay fair! Stay fair!" And the ball did stay fair. And Fisk leaped up in the air. And this was what made the Fisk home run even more powerful than Thomson's home run or Mazeroski's. For perhaps the first time on television, the game seemed to jump through the TV screen. The emotion was alive.

"If this ain't the number-one pastime, I don't know what is," Pete babbled to reporters after the game. "My God, you couldn't have more exciting things than that. It has to be the greatest World Series game in history. My son and I will be talking about this one for a long time to come."

October 22, 1975

World Series Game 7
Series tied 3–3

Losers. Pete Rose stomped the dirt off his cleats, marched through the dugout, a crazed look on his face. He stopped in front of each man, glared, his face a mask of rage, an angry drill sergeant, a harsh father, an unforgiving judge. In the moment, Rose hated every last one of these sons of bitches. He knew that, in the moment, they hated him too. But they did not hate him enough. They could not hate him enough. They could not hate him with the white-hot disgust that burned inside him right now. The Cincinnati Reds were going to lose. He could not believe it. Impossible.

All year, Pete had felt sure of the ending. They all felt sure of the ending. Yes, there would be some drama. There would be some hard moments. That was baseball. That was life. But in the end, Pete, Joe, Johnny, Doggie, Sparky, Ken, George, Jack and Gary, Rawly and Will, all of them, they all believed that the Big Red Machine would prevail. They believed it. And now they trailed the Red Sox 3–0, and it was the bottom of the sixth inning, and Fenway Park was alive with something that sounded out of place in Boston—a hopeful cheer, a cocky cheer even, the feeling in New England that it was finally their time, finally the Red Sox would win.

Sparky was sweating through his uniform. He had not slept. He blamed himself for the loss in Game 6, and now he blamed himself again. How could he lose with this team? How? He thought about the long walk, the one he had made after the Reds lost the World Series in 1970, and the one he made again after they lost the World Series in 1972. When a manager loses, he has to do the right thing and walk to the other side, congratulate the victors. That walk hurt more than anything else. Sparky started to think that he would have to make that walk again. Sparky did not know if he had the strength.

"What are you so worried about?"

Sparky looked up. It was Doggie, and he had that smile on his face.

"What do you mean, Doggie?" Sparky said. "We're losing 3–0."

"Ah," Doggie said. "Don't worry. I hit a home run."

And Sparky came alive. Doggie was right. This wasn't any normal baseball team. This was the Machine. Sparky got up, and *he* started pacing the dugout too, just like Pete, and he was saying: "Look, fellas, we got some outs left. I don't want anyone to panic. . . . Somebody get on base, and Bench, Morgan, or Perez will hit a home run."

Doggie went up in the sixth inning with Johnny on first base after Pete had, typically, barreled into second base and forced Denny Doyle to make a bad throw on what looked like a sure double play. Doggie went up to the plate looking for Boston starter Bill Lee to throw him that slow curve just one more time. Lee had gotten a strike on Doggie with that curve back in the second. Doggie wanted just one more look at it.

Fisk did not call for that curve—he knew better. But Bill Lee threw it anyway. Fred Lynn was standing out in center field, and he saw that curveball floating, and he saw the look in Tony Perez's eyes. He thought: *Oh, oh.* Perez started his swing, then pulled back and started it again.

Up in the Fenway Park press box, the dean of Cincinnati sports-writers, Si Burick, watched the pitch come in. Si had been writing for the *Dayton Daily News* for fifty years. He was the son of a rabbi, and he had started writing about sports in the paper when he was sixteen— four years before the stock market crashed. Si saw the pitch, and he watched Tony double-clutch, and before Tony even swung the bat, he whispered two words that he thought nobody else could hear.

"Home run."

And it was a home run, a long home run that sailed over the Green Monster, into the black of night, and nobody ever saw it land.

After Doggie hit his home run, the Reds still trailed by a run, but the Machine arrogance had returned. It's a sports cliché for a player to say, "We knew we were going to win." But it is the sports cliché that every member of the Big Red Machine would repeat in the months and years after Game 7. The long season of triumph and failure, jokes and hurt feelings, arrogance and charity, it all had to end with glory. They were the Machine.

"It's not something that most people can understand," Pete Rose would say. "But we were too good to lose that World Series. The Red Sox were a good damned baseball team. But we could not lose that World Series. If the Red Sox had scored ten runs, we would have scored eleven. We could not lose."

The final details lacked the drama of Doggie's home run or Carlton Fisk's home run or Joe Morgan's clubhouse rant or Sparky Anderson's bullpen genius. In the seventh inning, Ken Griffey walked, stole second base (yes, he was hitting seventh in the lineup again, where he could steal bases without upsetting Joe Morgan), and scored on Pete's single. And Pete could sense a shift in the crowd then. To his ears, they no longer sounded hopeful.

Then, ninth inning, with the scored tied, Griffey walked again. He moved to second base on a bunt. Rookie left-handed pitcher Jim Burton walked Pete with two outs. And Joe Morgan came to the plate. Joe would always remember how cold it felt, that New England chill. He would always remember how aware he was of the situation, how he knew that this was the childhood dream, the one he had talked about with his father time and again: seventh game of the World Series, two outs, winning run on second base. Joe's father would ask: are you good enough?

With the count two and two, Joe chased after a nasty slider. He connected with the ball, but he did not hit it well . . . vibrations shook through his hands. He heard a hollow sound. The ball blooped toward center field. Joe did not know if the ball would land; the Red Sox had Fred Lynn playing center.

But Fred Lynn was playing deeper than he normally would. He had no choice; the Fenway outfield was mud, and he simply could not take the chance of a ball getting hit over his head. Lynn raced forward. He would always believe, for the rest of his life, that if the outfield had been dry, he would have caught Morgan's ball. But he did not catch it. The ball dropped for a soft single. Ken Griffey scored the run. The Reds led the game.

In the ninth, Will McEnaney—that quirky lefty—got Juan Beniquez to fly to right field, and Bob Montgomery to ground out to shortstop. And finally, he faced the great Yaz. Of course, Yaz was one of McEnaney's heroes—Yaz was everybody's hero. McEnaney threw his best fastball, and Yaz hit a high and lazy fly ball to Cesar Geronimo in center field. "I knew right as soon as he hit it," McEnaney would say years later, "that Geronimo would get it and we had won. There wasn't a place Yaz could hit it out there that Geronimo would not chase it down."

Geronimo did catch it. And then jumped up and down in joy. Marty Brennaman shouted, "This one belongs to the Reds." Johnny Bench raced to the mound, and Will McEnaney jumped into his arms—a perfect shot for the cover of *Sports Illustrated*. Pete ran to Joe, and they hugged for a long time. The whole team huddled together in the Fenway chill. All of them except Sparky. He walked back into the clubhouse. He did not want to be on the field—that was for the players. He wanted his moment alone. There were tears in his eyes. The Reds were what he had always hoped. Winners.

Joe Morgan said, "I promised myself I wasn't going to do this." And then he started to cry. Joe stepped away from the lectern, stood silently for a few moments, and then began again. "I shouldn't be crying," he said. "This is not supposed to be a sad occasion."

There were many different people in the retirement home. There were baseball people, and family members, and a few old friends. Bob Howsam had died. Joe was right, no one wanted this to be a sad day. Howsam lived to be eighty-nine years old. He had done everything he wanted in his life. He had owned a baseball team and a football team, he had built a stadium, he had raised a family. Buck O'Neil, the great Negro Leagues player, always said that funerals were for people who died too young. Everyone else deserved a celebration.

But Joe said he was not crying for Bob Howsam. He was crying because the man was gone. And his time was gone. And baseball—the kind of baseball Bob Howsam stood for—was gone too. Joe had stayed around baseball. He won two Most Valuable Player Awards with the Reds. He played for another decade or so. He became a famous baseball announcer. And he believed something got lost, something that we will never get back.

"I remember standing with Bob Howsam after we won the World Series in 1975," Joe was saying. "And we were kings of the world."

It is true, there was no drama for the Reds in 1975, no story line. Geronimo caught the final pop-up, and Will McEnaney jumped into Johnny Bench's arms. Almost immediately after the season ended, Johnny and Vickie divorced. She would tell Tom Callahan that his exact words to her after that season were: "Now I'm through with two things I hate: baseball and you."

Joe got the Most Valuable Player Award, and Pete was named *Sports Illustrated*'s Sportsman of the Year, and Sparky spent the off-season talking to clubs and groups. Doggie went home to Puerto Rico as a hero—nobody was talking about trading him.

In 1976, the Reds just won boldly and decisively. They toyed with the Dodgers for the first two months and then, in early June, moved into first place for good. They led the National League in every single offensive category in 1976—every single one. They scored the most runs, got the most hits, cracked the most doubles, triples, and home runs, stole the most bases. It was a rout. They swept the Philadelphia Phillies in the playoffs, clinching the final game with a three-run rally in the ninth. George homered. Johnny homered. And Ken Griffey, who always found a quiet way to be the hero, drove in the game-winning run.

The Reds then swept the Yankees four straight in the World Series. Nobody even seemed willing to argue the point anymore. The Big Red Machine, the team that Bob Howsam built, was as good a team as had ever been put together. And they might have been a little bit better.

Joe said he was standing with Howsam in the hotel after the Reds had put away the Yankees in the Series, and he saw tears building in the old man's eyes. "Then he turned to me," Joe said, "and he said, 'Joe, this is it. There will never be another team like this. Ever again.'"

Joe began to cry again. Things did change after 1976. Players won the right to become free agents, so players did not stay in the same place as much. Players started earning larger salaries, which made owners reluctant to hold on to stars. The Machine broke up. They traded away Doggie and Will McEnaney before the 1977 season. Howsam and Sparky finally gave Danny Driessen a chance to play first base. He hit well, but something was lost.

Sparky was fired in 1978—Johnny Bench himself told reporters that he thought Sparky had lost the team and he no longer had the fire he'd once had. Dick Wagner flew out to California to fire Sparky personally. Then Sparky saw something he never expected: he saw Dick Wagner cry. Sparky went to Detroit the next year, and he won another World Series there. He went on to the Hall of Fame.

Pete Rose left Cincinnati after the 1978 season too; he always believed the Reds did not want to pay him fairly after he got divorced from Karolyn. He would come back to Cincinnati in 1984 to play and manage. In 1985, he broke Ty Cobb's all-time hit record. In 1989, he was suspended for life for gambling on baseball games.

Johnny stuck around in Cincinnati to the bitter end. He was only thirty-five when it became clear to him that he could no longer play well enough to go on. He hurt and ached all over. He and Carl Yastrzemski retired the same year, 1983. And they went into the Hall of Fame together six years later.

Joe himself left after the 1979 season. He signed with his old team in Houston, of all places. He was released a year later, signed again, traded, released, and signed one more time. He had a hard time letting go of baseball, though to the end he was able to do the little things that great players do. To the end, he was able to mess with pitchers' minds.

"I look back now," Joe said, "and I think Bob was exactly right. I don't think there will ever be a team like us. We cared about each other. We still care about each other."

He looked around the room. He was the only member of the Big Red Machine there.

November 2008

The eight men—the Great Eight, they call them in Cincinnati—sat around two tables in a sports art gallery. They were not sitting in any particular order. Pete Rose was on the end. Joe Morgan was on his right, Johnny Bench on Morgan's right, and Tony Perez on Bench's right. At the other table, George Foster sat next to Ken Griffey, who sat next to Cesar Geronimo, who sat next to Davey Concepcion. They were there to talk about the old days and eat some food. The ticket price was $2,500.

There were no pitchers there, which was typical. No one ever gave the pitchers of the Machine much credit. Sometimes the pitchers felt slighted. "You would think that we couldn't pitch at all," Gary Nolan would say.

"We had a damned good pitching staff," Jack Billingham would say.

"It's all a bunch of horseshit," Will McEnaney would say.

Still, they all knew that this was how it was—that when people thought of the Machine, they thought of these eight men, the greatest baseball team ever put on the field.

"Okay," Marty Brennaman said. He was the master of ceremonies. "Who was the one guy who wound everybody up, the one guy who started the most trouble?"

Seven Reds all looked and pointed at Tony Perez. He had a look of mock horror on his face. "Me?" he asked. "I don't do nothing."

They all laughed, and drank wine, and talked about the old days. They remembered how Sparky used to pull his pitchers. They remembered how much Davey wanted to be a star. They remembered how quiet George used to be. George, in his later years, had found his voice. He had started a petition to get himself on the television show *Dancing with the Stars*.

"Can you even dance?" Johnny asked him.

"All black guys can dance," George said.

They remembered certain games, certain stadiums, the good moments. Johnny remembered how they were color-blind—"I didn't see black or Hispanic or any of that, I just saw teammates," he said—and Davey Concepcion remembered how they all kidded him, and Ken Griffey mostly stayed quiet and in the background. Joe did most of the talking; he always did. He talked about how they were family—they bickered and they fought and they didn't like each other and they loved each other.

"What is your best memory?" someone asked Joe, and Joe looked around the room at the Big Red Machine. For a moment, he seemed at a loss for words.

Then he said: "All of it."

Pete Rose sits in the Field of Dreams, a sports store in the Caesars Palace Shops in Las Vegas. He sits behind a card table and a velvet rope and two young men who scream like circus barkers: "Come see Pete Rose! Come see the Hit King!" Pete Rose calls himself the Hit King, signs his baseballs that way too, because he cracked 4,256 hits in his long career. No one ever got more.

Pete is guarded by a young woman, Sarah, who, he rarely fails to point out, has a great ass. She does not seem to mind being reminded about her ass, or anyway, she has grown used to it. There are various job-related quirks when it comes to working with Pete Rose. Appreciating ass compliments seems to be one of them.

"So this woman, she sits down right here, right next to me," Pete is saying, and he points at the spot next to him as if it were a historical landmark. "And she has really big breasts, you know? I mean, really, she has big breasts. And she's like leaning over the table, like, um, you know . . ."

Pete realizes that at this point in his presentation he needs a stand-in to give the story a visual. He calls over to Sarah and asks her to play the woman with the big breasts. She nods. You get the sense that this is a recurring role for her. She sits next to Pete, leans far over the table.

"So," Pete says, "she's really showing off her breasts, you know, like I didn't notice them. And then I say to her, 'Where are you from?'"

At this point, he pauses and begins the little demonstration.

"So, where you from?" Pete asks Sarah, who plays the large-breasted woman.

"Titsburgh!" she says triumphantly.

"Titsburgh?" Pete asks. "Is that in Tennsylvania?"

And then Pete Rose laughs. He does not laugh casually, no, he laughs hard, hard enough that he can hardly breathe, hard enough that if he were drinking, liquid would spew out of his nose. He laughs like this is the single funniest thing he has ever heard, and he is hearing it now for the first time.

Pete Rose is sixty-seven years old and defiantly not retired. He sits here on a chair at the Field of Dreams four times a week, six hours a day, and he listens to people praise him and ask him the same questions and tell him that he got screwed by the people who run baseball. Pete was banned from the game in 1989 when an investigation determined that, while managing the Cincinnati Reds, he gambled on baseball games. Gambling is the cardinal sin of baseball; there is a sign in every clubhouse in the major leagues that warns against it. For almost twenty years, Pete adamantly denied that he bet on baseball. Then he wrote a book in which he admitted that, in fact, he did bet on baseball, he even bet on his own Cincinnati Reds. But, he aggressively pointed out, he always bet on his Reds to win. To him, this makes all the difference. He was a competitor.

Every day Rose sits on this chair, and he signs the baseballs and photographs and jerseys and posters and homemade paintings and baseball cards that people bring to him. "One woman, she brought me a Babe Ruth card," Pete is saying. "She couldn't see too well. I said to her, 'This is a Babe Ruth card.' She said, 'Isn't that you?'"

"What did you do?"

"I signed it," Pete says. He will sign anything. He has been known to sign the Dowd Report—the 225-page report prepared by special counsel John M. Dowd that led to Pete getting banned from baseball. He has been known to sign the police mug shot taken after he was arrested and then jailed for tax evasion. Pete sits in this spot six hours a day, four days a week, and he waits for Las Vegas tourists to come in. People ask him if he's sad. He says, "Hell, no, I'm not sad. I get paid a lot of money." He will not say how much.

"I get paid seven figures," he says. He will not be more specific.

"It isn't just barely seven figures either. I mean, I get paid a shit-load of money," he says.

"I got no problem with Johnny Bench," Pete is saying now. While he talks, Sarah walks over to the computer and starts working on something. "The only thing is, Johnny is moody. He's goddamned moody. You never know what you're going to get. Like with me, I'm the same all the time. But Johnny's just moody.

"The thing with Johnny is he never could accept the fact that I'm from Cincinnati. That's why Pete Rose Way is there, you know? I never got mad at him because in Binger, Oklahoma, there's a Johnny Bench High School. Cincinnati's my hometown, that's all. He never could accept that.

"It's not important to be the best player ever with the Reds, right? I mean, we were all great players. Johnny was one helluva player. Joe was a helluva player. Tony was a helluva player. I was a helluva player. Davey, George, we were all great players. But Johnny thinks it matters. I mean, I get along with him all right. He said that stuff about me after I got suspended, stuff about me not respecting the game and what have you. I mean, that was bullshit, because nobody respected the game more than me. Johnny Bench didn't respect the game more than I did. But we get along all right."

Just as he says those last words, Sarah walks over. She has printed out a photograph: it is of Pete and Johnny from a few months before, and they have their arms around each other's shoulders, both of them smiling deep.

"See," Pete says, right on cue, "we get along. We just took that picture. I like Johnny all right. We've been through a lot together, you know? We get along."

Sarah walks away smiling. "Am I right?" Pete asks as he watches her. "Doesn't she have a great ass?"

"I had a way of making guys better," Pete says. "Maybe that's because of the way I was brought up in the game. They all treated me like shit when I was a rookie. All of them. Except the black players. Frank Robinson. Vada Pinson. Those were the only guys who treated me like I was a man. The rest of them would get on me. They would rip me for running to first base on walks. Hell, I started running to first on walks when I was nine, and I'll do it when I'm ninety. That's how my dad believed the game should be played. But they treated me like a dog. And I said I would never let that happen to a young player again."

I tell Pete that, almost to a man, every player on the 1975 Reds had some story about Pete helping them, inviting them to his house for dinner, picking up their check at a restaurant, helping them find a place to live. Pete does not smile. He only nods.

"Yeah, that was the disappointing thing that happened when I had my problem," Pete says. "It wasn't just players. It was reporters too. I helped them. And when I had my deal, they all turned on me. That was disappointing. No one has any recall of anything good. That's the problem with fucking society. Once they judge you guilty, you're guilty for life."

His mood turns dark now. When Pete gets this way, he cannot

hear, and he cannot see. He talks, but he is not talking to anyone specifically. He is only talking.

"I'm the biggest winner in the history of sports," he says. "Think about that. It's safe to say baseball players play more games than any other sport. And I'm the all-time leader in games won. That has got to mean something, doesn't it? That has got to mean something.

"That's why it's so strange what I did. When I was wrong. I respected the game. I respected the game more than anybody. I lived for the game. It was all I thought about, it was all I dreamed about, it was everything to me. And maybe that was my problem. Maybe the reason I did what I did is I am what I am. When I was finished as a ballplayer, I needed more. You know, I played every game in 1975. Every single game. Sparky must have come up to me fifty times that year and asked me to sit down. We won that year by, what, twenty games, right? He wanted me to sit down. He didn't understand . . . I couldn't sit down. I needed every fucking game. I needed every fucking at-bat. That's who I was, and when I didn't have that anymore . . . well, I was wrong. I had a standard bet, two thousand dollars every day on the Reds to win. No one knew about it. And I was wrong. I was wrong. And I paid dearly for it.

"But you know what? I don't think I had anything to do with the integrity of the game. That's horseshit. Because I never directly had any impact on the outcome of the game. The guys today, with the steroids, they're cheating. They're cheating the game. They're cheating Babe Ruth, they're cheating Ty Cobb, they're cheating fucking Tris Speaker, Cy Young. I didn't do that. And the sad thing, the really sad thing, is Jose Canseco came out and said how many times he took steroids, he cheated, but if somebody wanted to give him a job in baseball tomorrow, he could take it. And I can't. I'm banned. And who put more into the game of baseball than me? I'll tell you who. Nobody. That's who. Nobody. I've been suspended for nineteen years. Nineteen fucking years. You kill somebody, you're not suspended that long. . . ."

While he talks, one of the store employees walks over and chirps: "Hey, Pete, we need an apology ball. We just sold the last one."

An apology ball. What the hell is an apology ball? Pete Rose grabs the ball, and he grabs a pen, and he carefully writes on the baseball: "I'm sorry I bet on baseball. Pete Rose." If someone buys the apology ball, Pete will personalize it. A personal apology ball. Now, though, he slams it down on the table.

"I'm in jail," he says softly.

Pete shakes his head. "I'd like to sit here and tell you that we had the greatest team in baseball history," he says. "I wish I could tell you that. I mean, I didn't see the '27 Yankees. I didn't see those Brooklyn Dodgers teams.

"But I'm gonna tell you right now that I seriously believe we had the most entertaining team in the history of baseball, and that's not even close. We had everything. We had Johnny and Doggie and George hitting home runs. We had Joe and Davey and Ken stealing bases. We had me playing my butt off every single night. We had Cesar playing center field, and I never saw anyone play it better. We had everything. We had white stars, we had black stars, we had Spanish stars. We had speed, we had Gold Glovers, we had power, we had daring base running, and we had a flamboyant manager. We had everything you need. And we had a good bullpen.

"You can always argue. You can argue the '27 Yankees or '61 Yankees or the Brooklyn Dodgers. Let me tell you this: any team that's got four Hall of Famers and a couple of others on the verge has gotta be one of the best teams in baseball history."

The Machine actually had three players in the Baseball Hall of Fame—Joe Morgan, Johnny Bench, and Tony Perez. There is a fourth Red if you count the manager, Sparky Anderson. But Pete does not mean Sparky. He means himself. Pete is not in the Hall of Fame and likely never will be in the Hall of Fame. Two years after he was banned from the game, he was taken off the Hall of Fame ballot. Every year, a handful of writers put Pete down as a write-in candidate, but those votes are not counted. If he ever managed to get on the ballot (an unlikely scenario), he would not get nearly enough votes. It takes 75 percent of the votes to get in the Hall of Fame. Pete Rose does not have 75 percent support. None of that matters. Pete views himself as a Hall of Famer.

"You know who shocks the hell out of me?" Pete asks suddenly. "George Foster. You know, when he was playing, that guy wouldn't say shit if he had a mouthful. We used to call him 'Gabby' because he never said anything. Now the guy won't shut up. He's really changed.

"Johnny hasn't changed. He's the same moody guy he was. . . . Davey, he's still the same. Ol' Bozo. We used to give him hell. . . . Doggie's the same. I first met Tony when we were together in Geneva, New York, back in 1960. I was two days out of high school, and he was two months out of Cuba. There's a closeness there with Tony. I spoke to him a week ago for a half-hour. And you know what? I have no fucking idea what he said.

"Geronimo? He was another quiet one. Chief didn't say a word. . . . Griffey would talk a little bit, I always liked Ken. He was a damn good player. He could really run. I'll tell you a story, Griffey did something one time. He was battling for the batting title with Bill Madlock, I guess it was 1976. And he had a couple-point lead the last day. He asked Bench what he should do, and Bench told him to sit out the last game. Now, why take Bench's fucking word? Bench never went through anything like that. What did he know about batting titles? I'd won them. I'd have told him to play the last day, get two hits, and put the fucking title away. But he asked Bench, and Bench told him to sit, and Madlock caught him on the last day. That's what you get asking Bench about winning a batting title.

"But, hey, I liked everybody. I liked our coaches. I loved Big Klu, Ted Kluszewski. I loved that man. He had those big arms. You know, he would walk over to you, and he would hold out his arm, and he'd say, 'You know what that is? That's a Polish-joke stopper.' He was one helluva man. Sparky was too. I learned a lot from Sparky. I liked everybody. I liked our pitchers. I used to take McEnaney out to eat sometimes. He was fucking crazy. It was a good group. We really enjoyed playing together. We wouldn't have been as good if we didn't like each other, you know?" He shrugs. "You know what?" he says. "I don't even know who the fuck our extra men were."

"You know what I get a kick out of?" Pete Rose was asking. "I get a kick out of people saying they are going to break my record. Guess what. Nobody's breaking that record. The first three thousand hits are easy. Baseball's an easy game to play when you're 100 percent. But try getting those hits when you're old, when your bat's slow, when your back hurts. Hell, it was easy in '75. I was young. We were all young."

A steady trickle of people have been wandering up for autographs, but all in all it has been a slow day in Vegas for the Hit King. Some days, the crowds line up to get a peek at Rose, to say a few words to him, to pay Pete to scribble his name. And why not? As Pete says, he's the best deal in Vegas. For the price of your ticket, you get to meet the Hit King, talk to him, get a picture with him, ask him who was the toughest pitcher he ever faced and what was he thinking at first base after he got the hit that broke Ty Cobb's record and . . . well, what the hell, they all ask the same questions. But the point is, he answers the questions. He puts his arm around strangers. And he asks: Does Bette Midler come out and take a photo with everybody? You can pay a hundred bucks to hear Celine Dion sing, but will she come out and shake your hand?

"Well, will she?" Pete asks.

No. Pete rests his case. The Hit King wins again.

Yes, on those busy days, Pete gives all those people a thrill, something to hold, a brush with greatness. And what he won't tell you, what he can't bear to say, is that he needs those days too. Because it's on those days, when he's in demand, when there's action going, when he can hear the slots bells ringing, when the people are shouting, "You're the greatest, Pete" . . . maybe he feels invincible again. And maybe he feels like a Hall of Famer. The quiet days are harder. This is a quiet day.

"We live in a fucked-up world," Pete says suddenly. "*USA Today* had that survey of the top ten sports disasters or whatever the hell they called it. And you know who won? Mine. Mine was ahead of O. J. Simpson. How the fuck is that possible? Ahead of Rae Carruth. Those guys fucking killed people. How is betting on your own team to win a bigger story than that? What the fuck are they talking about?"

I try to get him back to talking about the '75 Reds. He seems happiest talking about the Machine. But first this mood has to pass. He rants for a while longer about how he was wrong but he wasn't this wrong, he deserved punishment but it's too much, how quickly people forget. Finally he is exhausted. A woman walks up and asks him who was the toughest pitcher he ever faced.

"Bob Gibson," he says automatically, and he signs her baseball.

He pulls out his money clip and looks at it closely. "Joe gave me this," he says. "I went and spoke for him out in Oakland a couple of months ago. He didn't invite Bench. He didn't invite Perez. He invited me. So I went. He gave me this money clip. It's a nice one too. It's nice. Gold."

He runs his fingers over the money clip, which is clipped around several $100 bills. Joe was his closest friend on the Machine. They ripped each other and hugged each other and pushed each other. "Joe will tell you that I made him a better baseball player," he says, and it's true, Joe does say that. But Joe also ended up living the life after baseball that Pete felt sure would be his. Joe is in the Hall of Fame. Joe is nationally famous as an announcer. Joe is one of the most respected men in the game. It's different for Pete.

"I was talking to Joe just the other day," he says. "We talk a lot. But we don't talk about old times. We talk about stuff that's going on today. No point in talking about old times all the time. We lived them. They were good. But we can't live them again."

I ask Pete Rose if there is a single memory, a single moment from that 1975 season, that he thinks about more than others. Pete says he remembers all of it. He remembers the slow start. He remembers when Sparky asked him to go to third base. He remembers the hot streak that seemed to last all summer. He remembers destroying the Pirates in three straight. He remembers Game 3 of the World Series, when Fisk and Armbrister collided. He remembers Game 6, when he was hopping from man to man and shouting, "Isn't this the greatest game you ever played in? You'll be telling your grandkids that you played in this game." He remembers Game 7 and the way he paced in the dugout and shouted at his teammates, not to inspire them but to inspire himself. He remembers it all. He remembers exactly how many hits he got that year.

"You know what makes me feel good?" he says. "How many kids come up and ask for my autograph. They're saying, 'There's Pete Rose, he's the best hitter ever, he's the best player ever.' I always tell them, I'm not. That's Babe Ruth. He's the best player ever. Me? I'm one of the most consistent players ever. I think I consistently hit the ball harder than just about anybody. I hit the ball hard."

He pulls out the money clip and looks at it.

"Joe Morgan gave this to me," he says again, like he forgot saying it the first time. "It's pretty special, you know? Joe still likes me. I really think Joe still likes me."

AFTERWORD

The Big Red Machine towered over my childhood. That is at the heart of why I wrote this book. I grew up in Cleveland, and I was eight years old in 1975. Sometimes, it seems to me, we all just want baseball to forever feel like it does when we are eight years old. The good players seem great. The great players seem legendary. And the legendary players are like flashes of light.

Well, there were legendary players in Cincinnati. Rose. Bench. Morgan. Perez. At the time, the Cleveland Indians were a ragtag bunch playing in blood-red uniforms in a cavernous old stadium that always seemed to have more birds than fans. Those Indians were my team, and they would have been the subject of this book . . . if I thought anyone else wanted to read a book about the 1975 Cleveland Indians.

The Reds played a four-hour drive away, and they were perfection. They took the field with their hair cut short, with their shoes polished black, with their uniforms pristine white and worn just so. They could beat you, in the words of Joe Morgan, any way that you could be beaten. They were too brilliant to love, and too unassailable to hate. But being a good Clevelander, I tried to hate them anyway.

The last thing anyone wants is another book claiming another team was the greatest ever. The shelves are filled with the greatest—the greatest match, the greatest game, the greatest player, the greatest team, the greatest sports book, and so on. I do believe the 1975 Cincinnati Reds (and the '76 Reds that followed) were the greatest team in baseball history. I don't believe any other team—not the 1927 Yankees, not the "Boys of Summer" Dodgers, not the Casey Stengel Yankees, not the Oakland A's of the early 1970s or Derek Jeter's Yankees of the late 1990s—could match those Reds for power, speed, defense, star power, innovation, and personality. We can sword-fight with statistics and logic forever and never come up with a correct answer. I believe the Reds were the best.

But that is not what drew me to the book. No, it was the chance to write about baseball from my childhood. It was a chance to relay the brilliance of Joe Morgan the baseball player to those who missed his singular career and know him only as the baseball announcer. It was a chance to write about Johnny Bench's brilliance, and George Foster's power, and Ken Griffey's breathtaking speed, and the grace of Cesar Geronimo. It was a chance to write about a year in America that, in memory, feels as faded and distant as the crackling color footage of the 1975 World Series.

It was a chance to catch up again with the ol' genius Sparky Anderson.

And mostly, for me, it was a chance (I hope) to resurrect a little bit of the Pete Rose as I remembered him from 1975. The story of Pete Rose's fall has been written and rewritten so many times that I sometimes think America has forgotten the one-of-a-kind player who refused to sit out a single game during the 1975 season even though the Reds won the division championship by twenty games. I sometimes think that we lost the player who was so driven that he would get to the ballpark first, leave the ballpark last, and then go to the car in his driveway so he could listen to West Coast games. Nobody ever loved baseball more. Nobody ever gave baseball more. It doesn't pardon Pete his sins, not at all, but it seems to me the man thrilled too many people and played too hard to be remembered only as the man who gambled on his team, was thrown into jail for tax evasion, and now spends his days signing autographs at a memorabilia shop at Caesars Palace in Las Vegas.

Pete Rose was my inspiration for this book, but so were Bench and Morgan and Ken Griffey and Gary Nolan and Jack Billingham and all the rest of them. There's an old saying in sports: talent wins. And it does. But there is something beautiful about a team coming together.

I have to share one more story with you because it so perfectly describes this book for me. I was driving back home from Cincinnati one evening, and I was pulled over for speeding in Indiana. The highway patrolman walked to the window, asked for my driver's license, and then noticed I had a stack of books in the car about the Reds.

"You a Reds fan?" he asked.

"Sort of," I said. "I'm writing a book about the 1975 Cincinnati Reds."

And suddenly, without hesitation, he said: "Tony Perez, Joe Morgan, Dave Concepcion, Pete Rose, George Foster, Ken Griffey, Johnny Bench, and, uh, Cesar Geronimo."

And he let me go.

ACKNOWLEDGMENTS

One of my family's favorite activities every year is yelling at the television when Academy Award acceptance speeches go on too long. This doesn't necessarily speak well of us, but we never seem to tire of mocking people on the big stage looking petrified that, in what may be the grandest moment of their lives, they will forget to thank somebody.

And so it's fitting, I suppose, that here I am feeling entirely certain that I am going to forget someone who was critical to me writing this book. I apologize to those people in advance. I'll send you something in the mail, I promise.

I want to begin by thanking Pete Rose. Not only was he the stimulus for this book, but he was also extremely generous with his time and memories. Everyone has at least one opinion about Pete Rose, and I have several, but he has always been extremely kind to me, and this book is in large part a result of that kindness.

I want to thank the many people who were willing to take the time to talk to me for this book. These include: Buddy Bell, Johnny Bench, Jack Billingham, Pedro Borbon, Marty Brennaman, Tom Callahan, Dave Concepcion, Pat Darcy, Paul Daugherty, Frank Deford, Dan

Driessen, Rawly Eastwick, John Erardi, Jim Ferguson, George Foster, Cesar Geronimo, Ken Griffey, Ernie Harwell, Robert Howsam, Bill James, Ferguson Jenkins, Randy Jones, Pat Jordan, Reuven J. Katz, Dave Kindred, Jim Lonborg, Fred Lynn, Mike Marshall, Hal McCoy, Will McEnaney, Joe Morgan, Gary Nolan, Steve Palermo, Tony Perez, Bill Plummer, Greg Rhodes, Jeff Ruby, Bob Ryan, Mark Sackler, George Scherger, Diego Segui, Art Stewart, Brent Strom, Tim Sullivan, and Frank White. I also relied on earlier interviews I had with Sparky Anderson, Johnny Bench, George Brett, Steve Garvey, Hal McRae, Joe Morgan, Pete Rose, and Marge Schott.

I must thank research assistant Minda Haas for her hard work in re-creating 1975 through magazine articles and for almost getting an interview with George Clooney—we're hoping he's still available to play in the movie. Josh Katzowitz spent countless hours in the library scanning microfilm, and I thank him for that, and my weak stomach also thanks him. Greg Gajus was helpful on many fronts.

There is no way I can thank my friends enough for pushing and pulling me through. I want to thank Scott Raab for his inspiration, Michael Rosenberg for his late-night instant-message pep talks, Adrian Wojnarowski, Alex Belth, Seth Mnookin, Mechelle Voepel, Jim Banks, Bob Dutton, Richard Bush, Dinn Mann, Ian O'Connor, Brian Hay, Tommy Tomlinson, and Bill James for always seeming so convinced that the book would actually get done. I always have special thanks for my brother-in-arms Mike Vaccaro. And I need to throw an extra thank-you to Michael Rosenberg for also taking the time to mark up the manuscript with red ink.

I thank my editor, David Highfill, and his assistant, Gabe Robinson, for working so hard on this project. This is my second book with David, and both have been great experiences. I have to thank my fabulous agent, Sloan Harris, even though I will admit that it is precisely when actors start thanking agents at the Oscars that my family gets particularly unruly. I thank Nate Gordon at *Sports Illustrated* for helping me track down photographs, and by "helping me" I really mean tracking down photographs by himself.

There is no way I could have done this book without the support of my editors at the *Kansas City Star*, Holly Lawton and Mike Fannin, who are also two of my best friends. I also got great support from my editor at *Sports Illustrated*, Christian Stone, even though as a young boy he undoubtedly wanted the Red Sox to win that World Series.

Finally, we come to family. My parents, Steven and Frances Posnanski, came to America in 1964 and hoped their oldest son would be a doctor, maybe a lawyer, at least an accountant. They got a sportswriter, and while they don't get free medical advice or their taxes done, they do seem fairly proud to have books with their last name in their library. While I was writing this book, my youngest brother, Tony, lost more than two hundred pounds, so he achieved more during the time frame. My other brother, David, will no doubt remember baseball games we played in the backyard while growing up in Cleveland. Because I was the Cleveland Indians. He had to be the Cincinnati Reds.

I dedicate this book to my two beautiful daughters, Elizabeth and Katie, who do not know or care about baseball or the Cincinnati Reds but were always there with hugs and helpful suggestions such as "Are you finished with your book yet?"

And, last, most, I thank my beautiful wife, Margo, for putting up with the crazy life of a sportswriter, the hectic life of a blogger, and the feverish life of an author, all at the same time. In addition to her infinite patience, her editing talents, and her rare talent to panic when I'm on a tight deadline, she is much more artistic than I am. She was instrumental in getting the photographs for this book. She claimed it was a pain, but I'm quite certain that she enjoyed every minute of it.

A NOTE ON SOURCES

A baseball writer in 2009 has so many advantages over writers of the past because of extraordinary baseball websites such as BaseballReference.com and Retrosheet.org. I spent countless hours on those two sites looking up box scores, statistics, and dates. It is not an exaggeration to say that this book, as presented, would have been impossible to do without the tireless work of Sean Forman, David Smith, and countless others who make those remarkable baseball websites possible.

The information gathered here came in large part from extensive interviews with the members of the 1975 Reds and various other players and observers. A complete list of people interviewed is in the acknowledgments.

The day-to-day information was mostly harvested from 1975 daily newspapers, particularly the *Cincinnati Enquirer* and the *Cincinnati Post*. Additional information was found in the *Los Angeles Times* and the *New York Times*, along with Associated Press and United Press International wire service reports printed in various papers across the country. I had the honor of working for the *Cincinnati Post*, which printed its final edition on December 31, 2007; Cincinnati and the country are poorer for losing the *Post*.

Among magazines, *Time* and *Newsweek* helped me get a better feel for the time and place, as did *The New Yorker*, and *Playboy*'s interviews with Pete Rose and Sparky Anderson were both beneficial. *Sports Illustrated* was an invaluable reference, particularly Frank Deford's wonderful story "Watch on the Ohio" (September 29, 1975).

A more complete list of the books used is in the bibliography, but the most crucial to me include Bob Hertzel's *The Big Red Machine* (Prentice Hall, 1976), Ritter Collett's *Men of the Machine* (Landfall Press, 1977), Hub Walker's *Cincinnati and the Big Red Machine* (Indiana University Press, 1988), and especially *Big Red Dynasty* (Road West, 1997) by Greg Rhodes and John Erardi. Greg and John were kind and unceasingly accommodating to me during the writing process.

There is no shortage of books about Pete Rose, but the diary he wrote with Bob Hertzel called *Charlie Hustle* (Prentice Hall, 1975) was particularly useful in trying to find the young Pete Rose, before his world went mad. Johnny Bench's autobiography (with William Brashler; Harper & Row, 1979) was unusually blunt and informative, and one of the real pleasures of my obsessive Reds readings was *Joe Morgan: My Life in Baseball*, which I found to be as interesting and complicated as Morgan himself. One of my regrets was that, for one reason or another, I failed to connect with Sparky Anderson, but I have spoken with him on a number of occasions through the years and heard his voice come through clearly in *The Main Spark* (Doubleday, 1978) and *Sparky!* (Prentice Hall, 1990).

I also did not get the chance to speak with the architect of the Machine, Bob Howsam, before he passed away in February 2008, just as the project was beginning. But his unpublished book *My Life in Sports*, written with Bob Jones, was indispensable. I want to thank the Howsam family for their kindness and Greg Gajus for finding me a copy of the book.

Cincinnati was blessed in 1975 with some of the best newspaper sportswriting in the country. The columns of the *Cincinnati Enquirer*'s Tom Callahan were priceless, as were his Reds memories in *The Bases Were Loaded (and So Was I*; Crown, 2004). And I'm proud to call J. G. Taylor Spink Award–winning sportswriter Hal McCoy of the *Dayton Daily News* a friend of mine. His season wrap-up, *The Relentless Reds* (PressCo, 1976), was filled with wonderful stories and details.

The Baseball Hall of Fame, the Cincinnati Public Library, and the Cincinnati Reds Hall of Fame were all exceedingly attentive, and they went out of their way to help.

BIBLIOGRAPHY

Alfred Hitchcock by Alfred Hitchcock and Sidney Gottlieb, University Press of Mississippi, 2003.

Baseball My Way by Joe Morgan, Atheneum, 1976.

Baseball's Great Dynasties: The Reds by Peter C. Bjarkman, Gallery Books, 1991.

The Bases Were Loaded (and So Was I) by Tom Callahan, Crown, 2004.

The Best Sports Writing of Pat Jordan by Pat Jordan and Alex Belth, Persea, 2008.

Beyond the Sixth Game: What's Happened to Baseball Since the Greatest Game in World Series History by Peter Gammons, Houghton Mifflin, 1985.

Big Red Dynasty: How Bob Howsam and Sparky Anderson Built the Big Red Machine by Greg Rhodes and John Erardi, Road West, 1998.

The Big Red Machine by Bob Hertzel, Prentice Hall, 1976.

Black and Blue: Sandy Koufax, the Robinson Boys, and the World Series That Stunned America by Tom Adelman, Back Bay Books, 2006.

Blockbuster by Tom Shone, Scribner, 1975.

Born to Run: The Bruce Springsteen Story by Dave Marsh, Thunder's Mouth Press, 1996.

Byline: Si Burick, a Half-Century in the Press Box by Si Burick, Dayton Daily News, 1982.

Catch Every Ball: How to Handle Life's Pitches by Johnny Bench, Orange Frazier Press, 2008.

Catch You Later: The Autobiography of Johnny Bench by Johnny Bench and William Brashler, HarperCollins, 1979.

Charlie Hustle by Pete Rose and Bob Hertzel, Prentice Hall, 1975.

Cincinnati and the Big Red Machine by Robert Harris Walker, Indiana University Press, 1998.

Cincinnati: From River City to Highway Metropolis by David Stradling, Arcadia, 2003.

The Cincinnati Reds by Lee Allen, Kent State University Press, 2006.

The Cincinnati Reds: A Pictorial History of Professional Baseball's Oldest Team by Ritter Collett, Jordan-Powers Corp., 1976.

Cincinnati Seasons: My 34 Years with the Reds by Earl Lawson, Diamond Communications, 1987.

Collision at Home Plate: The Lives of Pete Rose and Bart Giamatti by James Reston, Bison Books, 1997.

Dear Pete: The Life of Pete Rose by Helen Fabbri and Larry D. Names, Laranmark, 1986.

Echoes of Cincinnati Reds Baseball: The Greatest Stories Ever Told by Mark Stallard and Jim O'Toole, Triumph Books, 2007.

The 50 Greatest Red Sox Games by Cecilia Tan and Bill Nowlin, John Wiley & Sons, 2006.

4 Hispanic Heroes of the U.S.A. by Warren H. Wheelock and J. O. Maynes Jr., EMC Corp., 1976.

The George Foster Story by Malka Drucker with George Foster, Holiday House, 1980.

Hustle: The Myth, Life, and Lies of Pete Rose by Michael Sokolove, Simon & Schuster, 1990.

Joe Morgan: A Life in Baseball by Joe Morgan and David Falkner, W. W. Norton, 1993.

Johnny Bench Catching and Power Hitting by Johnny Bench, Viking Press, 1975.

The Last Real Season by Mike Shropshire, Grand Central, 2008.

The Long Ball: The Summer of '75—Spaceman, Catfish, Charlie Hustle, and the Greatest World Series Ever Played by Tom Adelman, Back Bay Books, 2003.

The Main Spark by Sparky Anderson and Si Burick, Doubleday, 1978.

The Mayor of Castro Street: The Life and Times of Harvey Milk by Randy Shilts, St. Martin's/Griffin, 2008.

Men of the Machine: An Inside Look at Baseball's Team of the '70s by Ritter Collett, Landfall Press, 1977.

My Bat Boy Days: Lessons I Learned from the Boys of Summer by Steve Garvey, Ken Gurnick, and Candace Garvey, Scribner, 2008.

My Life in Sports by Robert Lee Howsam and Bob Jones, unpublished, 1999.

My Prison Without Bars by Pete Rose and Rick Hill, Rodale, 2004.

The New Bill James Historical Abstract by Bill James, Free Press, 2003.

The Neyer/James Guide to Pitchers: An Historical Compendium of Pitching, Pitchers, and Pitches by Bill James and Rob Neyer, Fireside, 2004.

Pete Rose (Mr. .300) by Keith Brandt, Putnam Sports Shelf, 1977.

Pete Rose: My Life in Baseball by Pete Rose, Doubleday, 1979.

Pete Rose: My Story by Roger Kahn and Pete Rose, Macmillan, 1989.

The Pete Rose Story by Pete Rose, World, 1970.

Redleg Journal by Greg Rhodes and John Snyder, Road West, 2000.

The Relentless Reds by Hal McCoy, PressCo, 1976.

The Royal Reds: Baseball's New Dynasty by Hal McCoy, PressCo, 1977.

'75: The Red Sox Team That Saved Baseball, edited by Bill Nowlin and Cecilia Tan, Rounder Books, 2005.

Sparky! by Sparky Anderson and Dan Ewald, Prentice Hall, 1990.

Sports Hero: Pete Rose by Marshall Burchard, Putnam's, 1976.

Summer of '49 by David Halberstam, Harper Perennial, 2006.

INDEX

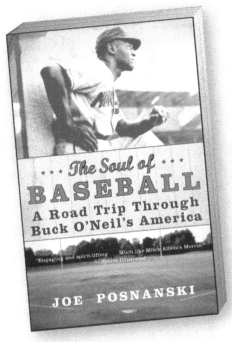

Johnny Bench, who won ten straight Gold Gloves for defensive excellence, going back for a foul ball. "Don't ever embarrass anyone by comparing him to Johnny Bench," Reds manager Sparky Anderson once said.

National Baseball Hall of Fame Library, Cooperstown, New York

From left to right: Pete Rose, Joe Morgan, and Johnny Bench strike a pose behind the batting cage before a game.

Focus on Sport/Getty Images

Johnny Bench gets ready to put a tag on Philadelphia's Ollie Brown during a regular-season game. *Rusty Kennedy/AP Images*

Pete Rose and Joe Morgan, as usual, clowning around before a game. "Pete helped make me the player that I am," Morgan said.

Bettmann/Corbis

Dave Concepcion goes high for a throw while Houston's Cesar Cedeno steals second. Concepcion won a Gold Glove in 1975 as the best defensive shortstop in the National League.

Bettmann/Corbis

Ken Griffey gets back to first base during the 1975 World Series. Griffey stole 16 bases in 1975, but felt like he could have stolen many more if he'd been given a real green light to run.   *Bettmann/Corbis*

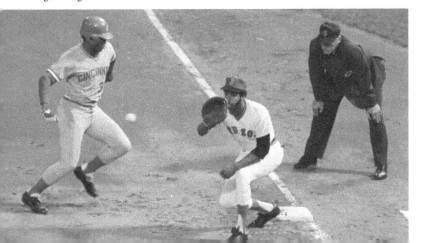

Reds pitcher Gary Nolan came back from almost two years of inactivity and led the Reds with fifteen victories in '75.

National Baseball Hall of Fame Library, Cooperstown, New York

Joe Morgan, who spent hours studying pitchers' moves so he could become one of the league's best base stealers, takes second base against the Dodgers.

National Baseball Hall of Fame Library, Cooperstown, New York

Outfielder George Foster did not say much, but he was lethal when he swung his black bat.

National Baseball Hall of Fame Library, Cooperstown, New York

Don Gullett was one of the best pitchers in baseball, but it was his injury that inspired Sparky Anderson to come up with a new way to use a bullpen.

National Baseball Hall of Fame Library, Cooperstown, New York

Pete Rose happily accepts the American Motors car he won for being MVP of the 1975 World Series.

Bettmann/Corbis

Johnny Bench shows off his unique ability to hold seven baseballs in one hand, while his new bride Vickie cheers him on.

Bettmann/Corbis

Boston icon Luis Tiant pitches to Tony Perez during the 1975 World Series.

Heinz Kluetmeier/Sports Illustrated/Getty Images

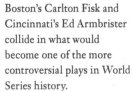

Boston's Carlton Fisk and Cincinnati's Ed Armbrister collide in what would become one of the more controversial plays in World Series history.

Heinz Kluetmeier/Sports Illustrated/Getty Images

Tony Perez hits the Game 7 home run that turned around that contest and the whole 1975 World Series.   *AP Images*

The *Sports Illustrated* cover shot of reliever Will McEnaney jumping into the arms of Johnny Bench after Game 7 of the 1975 World Series.

John Iacono/Sports Illustrated/Getty Images

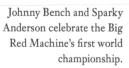

Johnny Bench and Sparky Anderson celebrate the Big Red Machine's first world championship.

AP Images

Sparky Anderson leads the party, with Johnny Bench hugging Rawly Eastwick in the foreground.

Heinz Kluetmeier/Sports Illustrated/Getty Images

Printed in the USA
CPSIA information can be obtained
at www.ICGtesting.com
LVHW030300220724
786067LV00008B/72